# SUBJUGATED

# SUBJUGATED
## Humanity Unraveled

WHY ARE WE SO CONFLICTED?
IS POLITICS GENETIC COMBAT?

J. A. PATRINA

ISBN: 979-8-9889094-2-2 [Paperback Edition]

*Self-published by*
*LittleHouse Publishing*

Joe Patrina is a singer/songwriter,
researcher, book author and technology
entrepreneur from Connecticut.

Please visit: *JoePatrina.com*

# THE SUBJUGATED COLLECTION

In Three (3) Volumes

After years of digging for insights buried within historical texts, many urged me to summarize findings into "a more likely explanation" of humankind's origins ... primitive humans upgraded to homo sapiens via alien genetics. Findings are organized across three (3) volumes.

## VOLUME I – *RESEARCH*

### *"A More Likely Explanation"*

... offering fresh views of ancient writings, seeing them as "sincere accounts" of what Homo Sapiens actually witnessed during the 4,000 B.C. to 1,000 B.C. expanse of the early Homo Sapient race.

## VOLUME II – *THE PRIMATES & ALIENS SERIES*

### *"Humanity Re-imagined"*

... a five-season, 38 episode series that reenacts the formative years of the Homo Sapient species within the primate/alien context – covering Sumerian, Hebrew, Egyptian, Indian, Chinese, Greek and American episodes.

## VOLUME III – *GENETICS DRIVES POLITICAL PREFERENCE*

### *"Primate/Alien Conflict Now"*

... applies the theory that one's genetic pull is either more Primate or more Alien, and that *this pull alone* determines one's political preference for socialism versus libertarianism, logic superfluous.

# ABOUT THIS THREE VOLUME COMPENDIUM

SUBJUGATED volumes I, II & III, proposes that 6,000 years ago outsiders altered primitive Humans to craft a new Homo Sapient species. "Homo", refers to the *genus* of *primates* of which modern humans are the *present-day* representatives; "Sapiens" means with wisdom. In by-passing natural formulations, these engineered Homo Sapiens were afforded an advanced intellect, but with unbalanced emotional properties

The original non-sapient Humans, who for over a hundred thousand years remained hunter/gatherers, had only achieved control over fire, camp dogs, pottery, stone tools, cave art and a bit of language. They may have had a degree of self-consciousness, but they lacked Homo Sapient imagination, the ability to discover new concepts, test them and build upon them.

Besides discovery, the newly formulated Homo Sapiens were also provided with a moral/philosophical/religious gyroscope that partially tempered behavior. This modulating dimension did not come from evolutionary cellular mutations, but from a fully-assembled genetic infusion.

Darwin mused that his natural selection proposition – describing how species adapt to biospheres – did not explain the starting place behind the intellectual/moral capabilities of the Homo Sapient species.

Likely, these capabilities came from an intervention that added new traits to the primate gene pool, and SUBJUGATED explains this intervention as an alien initiative to bring the then primitive humans up to teachable levels. Based upon the earliest writings of humankind, presented herein, a genetic upgrade for this purpose took place just 6,000 years ago.

In pursuing the upgrade, our alien friends were not at all concerned with the unintended consequences of placing our base primate instincts in conflict with the proliferating intellectual progressions coming out of the alien side. The by-product of this biological collision? Rather than kindness and cooperation amongst specie members – as found with Zebra communes, Buffalo herds, Fish schools, Geese squadrons, Wolf packs, Monkey troops, etc. – our alien-implanted capabilities led to justified cruelty, selfishness, revenge, warfare, deceit, manipulation and many other affronts against others.

This behavior was further fueled by our diversity of thinking, not found in other species.

Natural animals adhere to *uniform* societal mores based upon species-specific, instinct-driven genetic code (Wildebeest migrate at a certain time of year, male lions eat first, etc.). But once imagination, ideas and know-how were introduced, the new Homo Sapiens conceptualized different views of reality, and accordingly, individuals pined for *diverse* behavioral mores that suited their views.

For protection, Homo Sapiens then formed political alliances to ally themselves with others of similar orientations. SUBJUGATED proposes that two high-level survival orientations coagulated in Homo Sapiens:

> *Pyramid of Control* – Here, one seeks "survival of the fittest" protection against humankind's more ambitious players. To pursue this, one supports an elite-managed, obedience-based *Socialist (Autocratic)* society. In exchange for protection, law becomes a behavior cudgel, with liberty and property subordinated altogether (e.g. China) or via taxation (everywhere else) and,

*Elective Cooperation* – One seeks flexibility in navigating "survival of the fittest" challenges using "do it yourself" grit and wit, operating within a self-managed, self-determined *Libertarian (Laisse Fair)* society. Here, law follows "Due Process", and property rights stand inalienable, free from taxation and code encumbrance.

But more significantly, one's political destiny is not random, but an inherited trait stemming from the primate/alien genes of the species. Genetically, one is either pulled more by one's *primate* roots, seeking stricter troop-directed behavior mores, or one follows alien lines, seeking individual flexibility in carving out personal life frameworks.

Mixed gene compromises also manifest, but in all cases political choice is genetically pre-determined, facts and logic superfluous.

Overall, divergent views, divergent solutions and manufactured genetics that skipped "natural selection's filters", left conflicts within what we call the "human condition". These include our mental illnesses, our mis-treatment of nature, our intellectual dogmas, our religious intolerance, and our unsolvable political polarizations.

SUBJUGATED juxtaposes the dynamics of this troubled "human condition" against the writings of ancient civilizations from 4,000 B.C. to 1,200 B.C. – when our alien overlords lived with and then finally left us … *Yes! Zeus was real; they all were!* And it unpacks how Homo Sapient conflict coalesced in the modern era from A.D. 1600 to the present day, describing its acute impact on United States' history, defined by perpetual libertarian/socialist tugs-of-war.

Along with many other interrelated historical events, SUBJUGATED ponders the flood demise of the original Primitive Humans, how the new volatile Homo Sapient species might behave in the coming artificial intelligence era, and whether our alien "friends" are revisiting us again. Everything is on the table.

Welcome to SUBJUGATED, in three volumes – complete.

After 70 years of broad study, business and historical travel, plus technology innovation, song writing emersion and most of all …

contemplation, SUJUGATED presents my findings of who we really are. Over the years, SUBJUGATED became a three book series, and these have now been combined into this single, complete publication. I trust you find the conclusions less about guesswork, and more about what was uncovered.

The longshot hope is that if we understand ourselves we might somehow get along, or at least co-exist. The alien-libertarians simply want to be left alone. But a *compulsion* to divert, subjugate, tax, silence and cancel anyone daring to live outside the pyramid, seems an immutable baked-in trait held by the primate-socialists.

At least now, I understand it.

*Joe Patrina*

SEPTEMBER, 2023

# SUBJUGATED
## VOLUME I

*Research*

From ADAM & EVE

To

Artificial Intelligence

*"A More Likely Explanation"*

# THE REVELATION

*Apparently, we wandered the earth for 100,000 years and then suddenly began building cities around 2,200 B.C.*

*Who are we? ... Really!*

By taking ancient writing at face value, we find "dull" Human primates upgraded around 4,000 B.C. to become Homo Sapiens. But how, and why?

What happened, before and after the flood, around 2,400 B.C. ?

What genetic traits still stand buried in us from those times?

Are we a balanced, natural species, or are we unbalanced, conflicted both amongst ourselves and with our environment?

Why do today's left and right not fathom the thoughts of the other?

Sumerian, Hebrew, Egyptian, Greek, Indus Valley, Yellow River, Mayan and American Indian voices still speak through their writings.

Shouldn't we be listening?

Drawing from the earliest accounts of humankind, *Subjugated* suggests the true origins of Homo Sapiens as voiced by ancient writers who actually witnessed Homo Sapient subjugation by their Alien overlords.

By becoming clear eyed as to how outsiders transitioned simple Human primates into advanced Homo Sapiens, we next learn how this experiment played out once Homo Sapiens strove for freedom.

From 200,000 to 4,000 B.C., primitive humans wandered, a primate species that never progressed, troop based, chief dominated, with no tolerance for individuals – dependent upon nature.

In 4,000 B.C., Aliens arrive looking to exploit resources, at heart adventurers, espousing self-reliance, risk taking, social mobility and technology – masters of nature.

Genetically, the two mix to make "us", the Homo Sapiens, a new breed of teachable workers.

But the hybrid human runs volatile, prone to emotional imbalance, violence, acting aggressively against nature, and perpetually conflicted by unreconcilable primate and alien traits.

God and evolution have nothing to do with it.

Over time, inter-alien warfare ends the Alien rein on Earth..

Once on our own, genetic conflict fuels our political battle between primate cravings for managed societies and alien impulses for liberty.

That is until now, when we are about to face the impact of artificial intelligence on an already flawed species.

What are we to do with ourselves?

# "A MORE LIKELY EXPLANATION"

Welcome to SUBJUGATED I, Humanity Unraveled – From Adam & Eve to Artificial Intelligence. Please continue to read books II & III, which carry the findings further, both historically and into present times.

Proof of historical events becomes daunting the further back in time one goes. The early Homo Sapient writings that are relied upon here in *Subjugated* – Sumerian, Hebrew, Indian, Chinese, Greek, Mayan, Cherokee writings, etc. – have the additional problem of ancient writers being limited by the knowledge shortcomings of their era, easily misinterpreting what they saw.

Nevertheless, the words of the ancients represent sincere accounts of the past which we can then upgrade by applying today's improved level of scientific and historical awareness. This upgrade process yields a still imperfect, yet "more likely explanation" of Homo Sapient origins than do prior interpretations.

And so, inviting you to keep an open mind, welcome to SUBJUGATED I, covering the original source research into ancient times.

# BEFORE WE GET STARTED ...

Please consider these:

*In the end, more than freedom, they wanted security. They wanted a comfortable life, and they lost it all—security, comfort, and freedom. When the Athenians finally wanted not to give to society but for society to give to them, when the freedom they wished for most was freedom from responsibility, then Athens ceased to be free and was never free again.*

—EDWARD GIBBON—


*The policy of American government is to leave its citizens free, neither restraining them nor aiding them in their pursuits.*

—THOMAS JEFFERSON—


*The founders of the United States based their design upon the following: Our libertarian rights to life, liberty and property sit above any operation of government; laws cannot be enacted that do away with these inalienable rights.*

—J. A. PATRINA—

*It is true that liberty is precious; so precious
that it must be carefully rationed.*

−VLADIMIR LENIN−


*Democracy is indispensable to socialism.*

−VLADIMIR LENIN−


*Democracy passes into despotism.*

−PLATO−


*Only Americans can hurt America.*

−DWIGHT D. EISENHOWER−


*When I am traveling in a carriage, or walking after a good
meal, or during the night when I cannot sleep; it is on such
occasions that ideas flow best and most abundantly.*

−WOLFGANG AMADEUS MOZART−


*I think and think for months and years. Ninety-nine times,
the conclusion is false. The hundredth time I am right.*

−ALBERT EINSTEIN−

*I know this world is ruled by infinite intelligence.*

−THOMAS EDISON−


*The eyes of that species of extinct Giants, whose bones fill the mounds of America, have gazed on Niagara, as ours do now.*

−ABRAHAM LINCOLN−


*The intellect has little to do with the road to discovery. There comes a leap in consciousness, call it intuition or what you will, and the solution comes to you, and you don't know how or why.*

−ALBERT EINSTEIN−


*With artificial intelligence we are summoning the devil.*

−ELON MUSK−

All of these assorted statements are explained herein.

# CONTENTS

# AUTHOR'S NOTE

*"About the time of the end, a body of men will
be raised up who will turn their attention to the
Prophecies, and in the midst of much clamor and
opposition insist upon their literal interpretation."*

—SIR ISAAC NEWTON—

This book suggests that everything we have heard about ourselves
happened "just recently," and more so, that it all happened much
differently than told. Get ready to be open minded. In this "Author's
Note" segment I will lay out the key findings. Please don't panic!

## What Really Happened?

The "than-told" version has it that primates slowly evolved into
modern-day humans about 200,000 years ago, eventually leaving
East Africa to wander the globe for 70,000 years, only to achieve
a few stone tools, cave paintings, fire, camp dogs and some pottery,
until … "out of the blue," humans began to create and congregate in
cities around 2,200 B.C.

Moreover, the traditional narrative claims that every Homo
Sapient advance started and ended in isolation here on Earth; neither God nor Aliens applied any influence. Apparently, in seclusion,
we suddenly blossomed, and supposedly, we continue to evolve

today—no questions, please. That's the science-community's party-line, especially the "no questions" part.

`The historical chapters of SUBJUGATED contend that around 4,000 BC, the mentioned hunter/gatherer humanoid species was "upgraded" in vitro (via test tube) with *select* Alien DNA strands implanted into fertilized human eggs. This resulted in *us*, the *Homo Sapiens*, effectively the manufactured, intelligent, trainable livestock of Alien overlords. Again, please don't panic … at least not yet! I will provide much to support this.

Besides gaining higher intellect, the new Homo Sapiens emerged conflicted, as traits from the Primates and the Aliens did not sit right with each other, as follows:

> Primate Humans emerged from a communal way of life, with a chief ape ruling over his troop, his subordinates all sharing second-tier status. This subservient trait, still present in Homo Sapiens, underpins today's socialist political model. But now, in our upgraded form, a single strong ape no longer dominates over the others. The modern socialist system operates scalable, employing a "pyramid of command" sitting above common citizens – think China – managed by a hierarchy of elite dominate ape confederates. Still, as in the past, no dissent tolerated.

> Aliens came from an opposite existence, living lives of adventure and exploration, characterized by risk-taking and independent thinking, a tad rebellious. This life of quest and entrepreneurial spirit transitioned into today's libertarian political model, where each pursues their own path. The Alien side, though, being hyper-individualistic, is not as "smooth sailing" as, say, U.S. Navy officers. Historic references show that rivalries, fiefdoms, and warfare existed amongst these liberty lovers, with Homo Sapiens always caught in the middle.

Today these incompatible primate/alien genes fuel humankind's conflicts, mainly our political strife and our mental illnesses. After all, aren't we all affected by some sort of turmoil? What generates this unnatural discontent within a species?

And so, though mostly primate, the reader ought to consider the prospect of having a "bit of alien" in one's DNA—the family tree branch never mentioned!

But please, as I urge, don't panic … yet

## My Damascus Road Experience

An example of competing theories *leading us nowhere* finds many accepting the bible as "the word of God" with evolutionists diametrically opposed to biblical content (hence, the Skopes "Monkey Trial" a century ago). The naysayers see the Book of Genesis as fable. And, as fable, they assume that people such as Adam and Noah— if they indeed existed—did not actually live for 900 years. Instead, these ancient claims surely meant something else, perhaps they meant "900 months," not "900 years"? And all this talk about Sons-of-God impregnating human women causing Nephilim Giants appears even more far-fetched. Forget aliens or Sons-of-God; we evolved from apes and came out of Africa 70,000 years ago.

And as for myself?

After assuming biblical content pagan-like for most of my life, one day I decided to flip this mindset around. Instead of casting biblical passages as parables and fables, I instead recast them as *sincere accounts.*

As Isaac Newton suggested in the quote above, I decided to look for ways—historical constructs—that would support *literal interpretation of these sincere accounts* as the most-likely explanation of what went down … and the best explanation of why we behave as we do today. I rethought many mythical topics – in context of modern knowledge – to consider if other *more likely* narratives could explain … who we are.

# PREFACE
## HISTORY RECALIBRATED UPGRADED NARRATIVES

*" The eyes of that species of extinct Giants,*
*whose bones fill the mounds of America,*
*have gazed on Niagara, as ours do now. "*

−ABRAHAM LINCOLN−

Giants? What is Lincoln talking about? You will find out!

As the decades pass and Humankind slowly penetrates reality with more and more findings – building quasi-awareness – it behooves us to reconsider some of the staid elements of our belief systems.

For instance, at one point we needed to reevaluate our belief in a flat Earth (though some still believe). Contemplate another example—did the reader ever consider that some of the grave mounds of the American giants that Lincoln mentioned above still exist, and that other giants once lived as claimed in the bible? What genes did they possess? Ponder …

*The **Nephilim (giants)** were in the earth in those days,*
*and also after that, when the sons of God came into the*
*daughters of men, and they bore children to them.*

−THE BOOK OF GENESIS−

Years ago, this old testament sentence got me going with the "just recently" and "genetic conflict" frameworks described herein. Historical writings reveal that Aliens lived as gods amongst their respective Homo Sapient workers, until one day some took a few of the women, begetting new creatures, giants, called "Nephilim" in the bible. These were not created *in vitro* under controlled conditions, but resulted from full sexual exchanges of genetic matter between Alien males and the new Homo Sapient females. Ugh!

The event occurred before "The Flood" and I realized that, like The Flood, *Nephilim*—crossbred *Homo Sapiens* and *Aliens*—stand as just one of many unsolved historical legends we brush aside. Indeed, no orthodox researcher considers these when explaining the sudden, dramatic ascent of humankind just 6,000 years ago.

> And once the mainstream deems a legend preposterous, then *the experiences actually reported by ancient people are excluded from historical consideration* … a type of enforced ignorance. Certainly not all pre-civilization proclamations are tall tales, so … shouldn't we be doing a lot better at sorting through them by now?

Efforts to bring mythology to historical equivalence have advanced over the course of the author's lifetime, thanks mainly to the extraterrestrial-theory scholars (referred to later). Yet, even now, no compelling backstory reconciles the competing belief systems. A percentage of people insist God held a direct hand in matters; others assume alien involvement; many believe that evolving primates drove history … with most regarding any attempt to explain our past a futile exercise. By habit, we throw up our hands, unable to connect the ancient puzzle pieces of myth, science, theology, genetics, and archeological relics into a compelling, unified history of pre-civilized humankind, 4,000 BC to 1,000 BC.

In turn, this miscalculation of genetic beginnings results in not knowing who we actually are today, and so libertarians base modern political tactics on a flawed foundation.

They get drawn into diversionary ideological arguments and do not squarely face humankind's genetically determined trajectory. Most people want socialism, no questions asked, after all, we are strongly primate, while "… those who are about to die" still desire alien libertarian ways of life.

## Could Noah Have Lived for 900 Years?

Consider below, for example, a recasting using Einsteinian physics to suggest how Noah could have lived for 900 solar years. But please don't conclude anything just yet. This is a new and astonishing insight, outlined just to get you started, with greater discussion to follow. Using what we now know of physics, there are three retro-constructs.

*Construct 1*—In days past, light photons, electrons, and other *atomic activity* moved much more rapidly than now, and then decelerated as we moved away from the "Big Bang". If so, Noah's body, consisting of trillions of atoms operating closer in time to the Big Bang *likely* generated more amounts of energy *per second* than ours, keeping the ark-builder strong and healthy. Explanation …

> The key to the "atomic speed" construct pictures the immediate instance of the "Big Bang" … the first flash of pure expanding energy and *no* mass. With $E=MC^2$, *when mass was zero*, light speed would need to reach infinity to offset infinite energy. This implies that since then, light and electric particle speeds have slowed from infinity down to today's 186,000 miles-per-second rate, commensurate with the growing level of mass in the universe. Logically, deceleration continues to this day, as more and more dark matter forms (dark matter only conceptualized after Einstein posted $E=MC^2$).

> And so, everything changes. Initially, when universal expansion operated *near infinity*, one billion years of electron cycles at today's "slow" electron speed only took a solar *day* for the

same number of cycles to occur. Likewise, the life force 6,000 years back enjoyed the fuel of many more atomic cycling repetitions occurring each solar year than occur now.

*Construct 2*—This atomic multiple caused plant life on earth to soar, generating far greater amounts of oxygen than today's 21 percent level. Indeed, air bubbles trapped within old tree-resin amber show a 35 percent oxygen level. Noah's high-energy body would have had all the oxygen necessary to fuel his metabolism.

*Construct 3*—Also a factor for living 900 years is Noah's status as only the 10th generation since Adam. Noah's genes accumulated few mutations. Unlike today, where every mutation and accumulated viral parasite since Adam lurks within our gene pool (de-evolution), Noah had no material weaknesses. He lived life high energy, high oxygen, and free of defect.

## Historical Mysteries Can Explain the Then and the Now

This framework on how to live for 900 years exists as just one spoke on the "ancient legends wheel" that begs fresh inspection ...

Hence this book contemplates "What about the dinosaurs? What about giants? What about the flood? What about the races and languages? What about Moses? What about the pyramids? What about the Sumerian and Sanskrit texts, Greek, Chinese, and Mayan myths? What about the source of ideas? What about the dichotomy of Socialism versus Libertarianism, what about ..."

The overarching hypothesis adds up to *a unified theory of divine creation, natural evolution, and alien intervention*, and SUBJUGATED connects these elements, leading us from 4,000 BC to today, revealing the genetic underpinning driving our ongoing political strife. Most importantly, it explains the modern goal of exterminating those *Alien-libertarian* remnants (me), standing in the way of the *Primate-socialist* pyramid-of-control-based society, with most everyone poor but content, sitting on their assigned perch.

Many would say that SUBJUGATED boasts far too much ambition, covering just about everything imaginable in "just one go." But that remains the point. To sum up, everything must hang together in a unified manner, and SUBJUGATED attempts to encapsulate the central truth of our Homo Sapient species into one cohesive narrative.

SUBJUGATED begins with the past and ends with the present, so get ready for a fast … but solid ride!

# 1

# INTERVENTION, THE ALTERNATIVE HISTORY

*"What is Man? Man is a noisome bacillus whom Our Heavenly Father created because he was disappointed in the monkey."*

—MARK TWAIN—

*SUBJUGATED* offers an alternative framework to explain biblical and other ancient passages and connects this updated framework to today's world, even looking beyond into AI. By looking through the combined lenses of divine creation, natural evolution, and alien intervention, we recast the competing narratives of *God micro-managing human affairs* versus *evolution occurring strictly via cellular mutations*, enabling us to ask, "What is going on here amongst these various imperfect mortal beings who suddenly took over the earth, and what are we up to now?"

As a start, if one puts on hold the mindset of God poking his nose into our petty human affairs, one might instead find advanced outside "aliens" trying out all kinds of practical, even nutty things on humans. The bible chronicles these foreign imperialistic actors as gods, devils, and angels, rather than pushy mortals from elsewhere. But once we regard mortal aliens as responsible for the ensuing nonsense, we can no longer blame God!

What mortal aliens?

The Book of Genesis mentions Nephilim, a crossbreed of Homo Sapiens and some "other" species from above. The Old Testament refers to these mysterious "Others" as the *"sons of God,"* and the *Book of Enoch* calls them the *"Watchers."* We will dig into these texts shortly, but to get you started, I re-present the aforementioned quote from the bible.

> *The Nephilim were in the earth in those days, and also after that, when the sons of God came in unto the daughters of men, and they bore children to them; the same were the mighty men that were of old, the men of renown.*

How can one brush this statement aside?

A second biblical quote follows; a report on the Nephilim giants by Joshua upon his return from a spying mission in Canaan:

> *And there we saw the Nephilim, the sons of Anak, who come of the Nephilim; and we were in our own sight as grasshoppers, and so we were in their sight.*

Apparently, these Nephilim (meaning "Giants" in Greek) came about through the crossbreeding of the Sons of God and Homo Sapient women, as follows:

> *Now when men began to multiply on the face of the earth and daughters were born to them, the sons of God saw that the daughters of men were beautiful, and they took as wives whomever they chose.*

Enoch—alive back then, and who we will cover later—has it that 200 or so of these Sons of God "landed" on Mount Harmon in present-day Israel, spread out, and wantonly began taking Homo Sapient women, impregnating them by the thousands.

Though this assault is never mentioned in churches or synagogues, theological intellectuals love to debate whether the aforementioned "Sons of God" were angels, spirits, or (human) men possessed by devils. This debate is slightly irrelevant. The birth of many crossbred Nephilim babies is what's relevant; huge babies, undoubtedly cut from their human mothers' bellies, who would mature into unstoppable sexual beasts and (unless sterile, like a mule) beget even more Nephilim babies.

What a mess.

Apparently, whoever oversaw these 200 interlopers came down hard on them and their mutinous behavior. Here the Bible's New Testament describes the "clamping down":

*And the angels who did not stay within their own position of authority, but left their proper dwelling, he has kept in eternal chains under gloomy darkness until the judgment of the great day—just as Sodom and Gomorrah and the surrounding cities, which likewise indulged in sexual immorality and pursued unnatural desire, serve as an example by undergoing a punishment of eternal fire.*

Though punished for the crossbreeding, the horses had left the barn, so to speak, and the Homo Sapient gene pool now stood corrupted.

One certainly assumes that crossbreeding with outsiders is not good for Homo Sapiens. To start, the resultant Nephilim offspring grew into giants, seven-to-12 feet in height, and they dominated everything, possessing insatiable sex drives. Undoubtedly, the fledgling Homo Sapient species would be squeezed out were nothing done.

The Homo Sapiens, though, have a *Champion* responsible for them— labeled "God" in the bible, but in *SUBJUGATED*, this Champion exists a mere mortal alien with a big job—possibly that of a ship's Admiral— responsible for orchestrating the overall Homo Sapient experiment, now gone sour.

The *Homo Sapient* project began under his direction once the upgrade potential of the *Human* hunter/gathers became apparent. Primitive Humans functioned as capable animals, with large brains, already employing crude language, using some stone tools and crafting simple pottery, living plainly for some 200,000 years. But these attributes represented the extent of the then-current Human gene set.

Nevertheless, a simple genetic *implant* might just bring these rather dull beings up to the next level, the way today, we Homo Sapiens play with genetics to create faster horses and genetically modified "corn." The upgraded Humans could be useful, both as workers, and even as soldiers in the armies of competing Aliens.

These Aliens, who operated at much higher levels than we do even now, knew, for instance, how to power up the mind itself, not just make "corn" disease resistant. The Admiral decided to run the upgrade experiment.

Sure enough, the minds of the resulting Adam and Eve babies impressed all, but at a big cost. Unlike the human parents that sired the Adam and Eve embryos—who both looked the way all animals of a kind appear, each identical, each uniformly beautiful—these genetically modified "Homo Sapiens" all looked different. Few possessed beauty, with many of them anxious, depressed, or worse, psychopaths (no moral or emotional foundation whatsoever), prone to lying and deception.

Yes, the alien doctors knew how to infuse genes, but in doing so, they created the unintended consequence of a destabilized organism, leading to the many flawed physical and mental traits exhibited by Homo Sapiens ever since, unlike any other species on Earth.

But, as any breakfast enthusiast knows, "You can't make an omelet without breaking a few eggs," and so the Admiral kept the experiment going. Sure enough, soon Cain killed Abel, and, for some reason, the project team allowed Cain to live. Mistake upon mistake followed, with yet another mistake: the crossbred Nephilim.

After chaining his bad crew members to "hell" for the crossbreeding debacle, the Admiral, probably to save his job, chose to wipe out the original *Simple Humans*, plus the *Homo Sapient Humans*, plus the vile *Nephilim Humans* by unleashing a devastating flood, leaving no loose ends. He had the technology to effect this, as the very anti-gravity system used to power his ship can repurpose to perform odd jobs on any given planet. The bible puts it this way:

> *Then the LORD saw that the wickedness of man was great upon the earth, and that every inclination of the thoughts of his heart was altogether evil all the time. And the LORD said, "I will blot out man, whom I have created, from the face of the earth—every man and beast and crawling creature and bird of the air—for I am grieved that I have made them."*

But the Admiral's lieutenants—Michael, Raphael, Uriel, and Gabriel— stepped in. All was not lost. They identified a Homo Sapient family not yet poisoned with Nephilim genes: Noah, his wife, his three sons, and his three daughters-in-law stood pure. Rather than starting from scratch after the flood, they could use this family as a quick reboot button.

Indeed, post flood, Noah's decedents started things up again, living long lives, bearing children, slowly repopulating the Tigris Euphrates Valley according to plan. Noah himself lived another 350 years!

But a problem surfaced. Unbeknownst to all, one of Noah's daughters-in-law carried buried Nephilim genes, and soon, some of her offspring yielded new generations of giants who formed kingdoms in Canaan and the surrounding areas of modern-day Israel and Jordan.

The Admiral, who came to and from Earth, operating in different time scales than those fixed on Earth, brooded over the failed flood extermination and needed a new plan. Nephilim abomination against humanity would not stand. At first, he torched two of the worst Nephilim cities, Sodom and Gomorrah, where debauchery stood as a way of life.

But too many Nephilim mixed in, requiring a more surgical approach. The Admiral hatched a second attempt at total extermination, envisioning a military force to do the heartless work. Conveniently, a potential army waited innocently in the wings, the slaves of Egypt, the Hebrews.

The Admiral assigned a trusted lieutenant to act as on-site project manager of this new approach (the lieutenant is called "the Lord" by the Hebrews). His mission? To extract this Homo Sapient horde from Pharaoh and convert them into a military machine able to annihilate Nephilim kingdoms. Over the next 40 years of Earth time, all of the know-how and technology available from the Admiral came to bear for this extermination agenda.

With the promise of land and some very stern management oversight by the on-site lieutenant, the "chosen ones," the former slaves, followed the script, though frustrating "the Lord" every step of the way.

For decades, "the Lord," this on-site lieutenant, traveled with the Israelite horde, boasting his own camp tent (the meeting tent), his own culinary preferences, a personal guard (the Levite tribe), an ability to use gravitational disruptions (the Ark), and demonstrating the temper requisite to recondition the Hebrew population away from their habitual complaining, converting them into a killing machine.

But this assignment tasked "the Lord," and he never pulled punches:

> *The Lord said to Moses, "How long will these people treat me with contempt? How long will they refuse to believe in me, in spite of all the signs I have performed among them? I will strike them down with a plague and destroy them, but I will make you into a nation greater and stronger than they."*

In the coming chapter *The Lord*, we will closely examine how the Lord interacted with Moses, Moses's brother Aaron, and with the Hebrew military captain, Joshua. Later we will deconstruct creation statements in Genesis, factoring in the earlier-mentioned atomic speed theory, while pondering if the Lord likely dictated Genesis to Moses, "the Lord" possibly a witness to part of the Genesis "Day 6" activities.

Throughout the Lord's time with the Hebrews, the Ark's power stood central to the entire Exodus and Nephilim extermination saga. Today, we Homo Sapiens use gasoline-powered cars and dream of electric cars, proud of our underachievement. But long ago—as Sanskrit writings proclaim—Aliens had mastered the mysterious forces of gravity, using variations of anti-gravity technology to propel vehicles and even disrupt natural conditions. This tactical capability would cause frogs to leave the Nile, locusts to swarm, waters to part, quail to fly from marshes to feed the wandering Hebrews, and so on. But most of all, Aliens would use anti-gravity technology to level cities and destabilize tectonic plates.

In the end, around 1,400 BC, the Hebrews leveled 30 of 32 Nephilim kingdoms, leaving few survivors. Hence, they *almost* achieved their designated mission. But not *all* Nephilim fell. Four hundred years later, around 1,000 BC, David fought Goliath, a nine-foot tall Philistine, and so it continued. Alien/Nephilim genes remained on Earth.

But the Exodus books are not unique. Tales of alien "gods," themselves at war with one other, using massively destructive weaponry and Homo Sapient troops, abound in India, China, Mayan lands, North America and elsewhere.

Thus, consider this Alternative History, with a few more things to mention …

First, don't think the above a case for Atheism, the proposition that God does not exist. *SUBJUGATED* instead poses the simple proposition that although God may very well exist, *He* had nothing to do with the violent sagas of the Old Testament nor at other ancient

Homo Sapient outposts in Egypt, Mesopotamia, India, Greece, China, and the Americas … we just *assumed* He had. Blaming God for both the Adam & Eve and secondary Nephilim crossbreeding disasters would compare to today blaming God for the fallout from genetically modified foods, chemical carcinogens, and pollution. *He* didn't do it.

Nor should the reader assume *SUBJUGATED* a case pitting the competing theories of evolution and divine creation against one other.

Evolution and divine creation have nothing to do with what went down once things got rolling during the times of Adam, Eve, Enoch, Noah, Abraham, Moses, and Joshua, nor do creation/evolution theories have anything to do with the current troubles of the Homo Sapient race.

Instead, the biblical players of old are mere Alien and Homo Sapient mortals playing out their destinies using the cards dealt: a new Homo Sapient species just getting started, interacting with superior foreign overlords who possess vast stores of know-how. Together they muddle through the grand Homo Sapient experiment, an experiment that went haywire, requiring repair.

It was never repaired. At some point, the Homo Sapiens were abandoned, and we now crawl all over the planet, eight billion of us—the only species, other than domesticated animals—where everyone looks different. In *Subjugated Volume III – Genetics Drives Political Orientation*, we will unravel how our unnatural genetic makeup has brought us to a final extermination conflict.

One more thing. Nephilim lived elsewhere, whether migrating from the mid-east to other parts of the world or sired by outsiders on diverse continents. This will be covered in the *Evidence from Other Civilizations* chapter, and in the *Bigfoot, Little People and Ohio Giants* sections.

For example, thousands of giant skeletons found in North America during the 1800's cannot be explained. Where did they come from and how and why were these American giants exterminated … and by whom? Likewise, the Incas—who could not write and had not "discovered" the wheel—told the Spanish that giants from a previous era had built the gigantic stone structures found in South America. Considering the relative lack of giants today, it appears most were killed off, but also, as described in the *Genetics chapter*, the Nephilim genes were probably recessive, so that over time, the traits fizzled out of the Homo Sapient population.

As said, it all happened just recently, and not as told. Ok, here goes … step it up.

# 2

# HOMO SAPIENS, HOW OLD ARE WE?

*" I am quite sure that our views on evolution would
be very different had biologists studied genetics and
natural selection before and not after most of them
were convinced that evolution had occurred. "*

—JOHN B. HALDANE, BRITISH GENETICS PIONEER—

Evolutionists believe that humans have evolved forever, with new
versions of "us" bubbling up across the ages, each up-and-coming
revision incrementally smarter, nobler, and better than the previous
edition. They claim today's Human genetically equal to the Humans
coming out of Africa 70,000 years ago, we just know more now.

In contrast, religious adherents believe that God created Humans
on Day 6, perfect from the get-go, made in *His* image.

Evolutionists pitch "natural selection"— millions of spontaneous
cellular mutations occurring over millions of years, some beneficial,

others not, whose collective randomness somehow spawn new species. With natural selection, Homo Sapient traits such as literature and engineering came about by cellular mutation 200,000 years ago—it just took a while for humans to realize they had these abilities.

Yet one ponders, even assuming *incremental evolution* plausible, does it explain Homo Sapient intellect, and why it took 200,000 years to kick into gear?

Homo Sapiens—the ones who behave like us, *who foster civilizations*— have a mere record of only 6,000 years, if that. Civilized beings on Earth, the ones who manage nature rather than have nature manage them, are truly a new phenomenon. All other animals passively exist in specific biospheres, merely reproducing (think sea turtles or cavemen) with some variations occurring *within* each species, but only to help specimens better cope with the *local* environment controlling them. Mankind's intellectual leap, operating above nature and possessing traits needed for civilized society, travel beyond the scope of *incremental evolution*.

*Biblical creationists* explain this unprecedented leap of brain power simply by crediting God for the advanced traits of mankind, an easy out.

Still, a third door exists called *intervention*, a door that most people do not dare to open. Behind it lie ancient manuscripts, such as the Hebrew bible, the Sumerian clay tablets, the Indian Sanskrit records, and many stone carvings showing "gods" teaching humans, "gods" in flying vehicles, and etchings of "humans" with oblong heads, not appearing of the primate branch.

This assortment of tangible historical artifacts argues in favor of disruption of the usual, slow-moving trajectory of evolution, and that intervention *likely* explains our sudden ascent.

Below I list the first human civilizations. I contend that what preceded these might have been *Simple Human*, but not *Homo Sapient Human*, that is, *not yet having a civilization-oriented intellect*. So, what went down? How, without warning, did we jump from our existence as Simple Humans using stone tools and primitive pottery, to become Homo Sapiens, the "wise ones," suddenly able to form civilizations, to write and accrue knowledge, to build buildings, cities, and much more? Here are the founders:

2,200 BC – The Mesopotamians

2,200 BC – The Indus Peoples

2,200 BC – The Egyptians

2,200 BC – The Chinese

These blossomed all at once, and other than cuneiform tablets, the most vivid literary record of early humanity is the bible, putting Adam at around 4,000 BC, and Noah's flood at around 2,400 BC. The above civilizations all came around 200 years post-flood.

So, allowing for some wiggle-room with dimensional dates (e.g. some China scholars believe China was colonized by 2,600 B.C.), it appears that Homo Sapient intellect showed itself in Adam's time, around 4,000 BC, and that Homo Sapient civilization started after the 2,400 BC flood, only blossoming around 2,200 BC., and that before Adam, only crude hunter/gatherer stone tools and pottery existed, nothing else.

Creationists claim nothing came before Adam, not even pottery, sticking with *God made man on the sixth day,* as if that covers it all.

Evolutionists postulate that humans *just like us* existed before civilizations formed—primitive yet whole—first reproducing as simple hunter/gatherers for some 130,000 years in Africa, before spreading across the earth 70,000 years ago. I'm not sure where they get these dates, as carbon 14 dating (upon which half-life calibrations can be made) is reliable for just a few thousand years before all the carbon 14 is depleted. Most people do not know that about carbon 14 dating, and actually accept the six-figure dates given!

But more to the point, even after accepting the made-up dates, evolutionists never discuss why we suddenly moved beyond *environmentally-controlled hunter/gathering* to become builders of cities. They only mentioned *evolution,* as if that covers it all. It covers nothing!

Evolutionists construct various scenarios; consider this one: rather than spending hours gnawing raw food, humans discovered fire, allowing them to cook, requiring smaller "mutated" intestines to digest their food, thereby diverting more body-wide energy to the brain, while also providing more time to think. And with these advantages, humans eventually sorted out calculus, eventually leading to our aerospace program. This is the better-food/more-time evolution theory.

I contend that both the creationist and the evolutionist have quirky, incomplete explanations with many holes and ignored puzzle pieces. SUBJUGATED argues that an interventionist element, a third factor, must account for the sudden appearance of "us," describing who we are, how we "got here" so abruptly, why we behave the way we do today, perpetually upset and at each other's throats.

As you will see, we appear an experiment conducted by outsiders, an experiment that went wrong, with the interlopers ultimately abandoning us. Evidence for intervention appears throughout the bible and in many other ancient sources as well. To get a handle, we will deconstruct the historical record, using interventionist findings to plug evolutionist/ creationist narrative shortcomings.

For example, everyone knows the story of David killing the giant Goliath with a slingshot. The bible describes Goliath as so many cubits in height, which yields nine and one-half feet on today's scale.

But the truth surrounding the saga dwarfs this single incident. The big story: Goliath possessed non-human genes, part human and part something else, making him a crossbreed. Similar to mating a horse and a donkey to make a mule, the bible calls these human crossbreeds "Nephilim," and they stood from seven to 12 feet in height.

As already mentioned, Nephilim, *according to the bible*, were sired by extraterrestrial fathers, the "Sons of God" before the time of Noah, around 3,000 BC. Supposedly destroyed by the 2,400 BC flood, by 2,200 BC the Nephilim returned, forming kingdoms in the current region of Jordan and Israel. Nephilim sects included the Amorites, the Canaanites, the Philistines (Goliath's "people"), and others.

By 1,000 BC, when David killed Goliath, the Israelites had been at war with Nephilim populations for 400 years. One might even say that the Israelites were "chosen" by an interventionist (not God) to fight and exterminate these giants. *Chosen*, as, after all, Moses left Egypt by the interventionist command of "the Lord" and while wandering the desert "the Lord" *chose* Moses to prepare the Hebrews for eventual warfare against the Nephilim in the promised land.

Joshua, *chosen* by the Lord to succeed Moses, conducted the actual battles, exterminating untold thousands of Nephilim, though some obviously slipped through, surviving hundreds of years at least until the David and Goliath era. Later, we'll look at "the Lord" through interventionist glasses.

One might notice that although biblical, none of this Nephilim business is spoken about in Jewish synagogues or Christian churches.

Instead, organized religions channel parishioners into dissecting isolated sentences of the bible, hunting for God's message, not seeing the forest for the trees. But if instead one reads the full texts, supposedly formulated by Moses and Joshua, all of this gritty history describing human origins, its aberrant offshoots, and its interventionist agents lies apparent.

Parallel to religious decoying, evolutionists also lead us by the nose, having us look at old monkey bones, making us believe our human traits accrued bit-by-bit through endless micro-cell mutations.

To protect their fragile dogmas, both evolutionist and creationists battle the other to hoard the *sole* explanation of humankind, with each camp covering up their respective narrative's shortcomings.

And yet by all counts, human blossoming, *the formation of civilization and the accumulation of know-how,* started suddenly around 2,200 BC, a telltale clue that intervention occurred. All written accounts point to this, yet evolutionists willfully ignore the coincidence, and religious minds skillfully chase isolated bible passages, neither school embracing the full recordings of the ancients.

Besides the bible, other rare histories exist for us to tap into, such as the Sumerian tablets and the Indian Sanskrit writings. These speak of a unique time when post-flood peoples—yes, around 2,200 BC—were suddenly enlightened, taught things, and guided by other beings. We will look at these writings later.

The Sumerian/Indian/Chinese accounts and their carved stone works, plus the accounts and works of many others, must be considered in conjunction with the Jewish bible to form a more complete picture of the pre-flood *dawn* of mankind and the post-flood *awakening* of mankind. Undoubtedly, outsiders interfered in the pre-flood period, boosting human IQ, and in the post-flood years they taught these brainy-but-ignorant Homo Sapiens how to build civilizations, only to abandon humanity at some point.

Recall that the written accounts and physical works of many civilizations portray giants, visiting gods, and air travel occurring around the time mankind started to civilize. These will come into play.

And finally, realizing both dull primitive Humans and advanced Homo Sapiens quite adept at eliminating other species, the biblically documented Israelite assault on the Nephilim kingdoms demands a better explanation than *a wandering people finally reach the land of milk and honey*. We will examine the need in 1,400 BC to cull the Nephilim giants, as well as the drive today to exterminate a minority of Homo Sapiens who still exhibit Alien traits.

But first, an assessment of the difficulty to prove historic events, and the need to embrace "more likely" theories, next in Chapter 3.

# 3

## PROVE IT!
## HISTORY REQUIRES IMAGINATION

*"People almost invariably arrive at their beliefs not on the basis of proof but on the basis of what they find attractive."*

—BLAISE PASCAL—

Please do not assume SUBJUGATED to assert proof of extraterrestrial involvement with humankind, any more than Darwin claimed proof of Evolution. SUBJUGATED offers something more realistic, the *plausibility* of extraterrestrial involvement.

Over the years, authors such as *Erich Von Daniken*, who, in the 1960's, first floated aspects of the intervention theory with his *Chariots of Fire* book, have been ridiculed and dismissed by critics who cite the evidence offered as misinterpretation or that other explanations exist or that the good evidence still does not amount to proof. Using dismissal tactics, evolutionists and creationists avoid the evidential challenge these ancient artifacts represent, thus sticking to their own unsupported theories.

Philosophers label this a *sophist* trick, as nothing can be proven when it comes right down to it.

> Descartes at least came up with what is called an *a priori*, self-evident logic proof, such as A = A, and, "I think, therefore I am."

> Scientists say that scientific proof occurs when a physical result occurs over and over without exception, such as all objects falling at 32 feet-per-second$^2$.

> Lawyers speak of "beyond a reasonable doubt" levels of courtroom proof.

Historical proof, though, proves more elusive, not truly possible, especially in the pre-writing era. Only religious and scientific *doctrine protectors* demand absolute historical proof when asked to abandon their versions.

But we are not claiming absolute proof in this document. If you don't like certain bits of evidence or logic, then dismiss these, but piecemeal refutations do not sanctify unfounded trust in creation or evolution explanations, both failing to address many loose ends, therefore lacking unity.

Instead, here we contemplate how best to understand our sudden ascent with the "most-likely" unified explanation, and for a theory to be likely, requires the presentation of some compelling *evidence* and *logic* to explain the phenomenon under consideration.

In the case of evolution, no hard *evidence* exists to prove that new species come about through collective cellular mutations. None. Evolution's *logic* builds from the observation that mutations occur, which leads to the *possibility* that, given time, new species *might form* via collective mutations. Not proven, but it can ring true if not looking closely. But even if true, cumulative mutations do not explain how human hunter/gatherers, using stone tools and making crude pottery, suddenly built cities around 2,200 BC.

*Evolution's* incremental, long-term construct negates itself as the answer to the *historical suddenness* this book seeks to untangle. Evolution offers no hard evidence, and its long-term approach does not even apply within this suddenness conundrum.

As with evolution, *biblical creation* offers no direct *evidence* proving this the way things happened. Instead, creation's *logic* asserts *divinity* essential, as the universe's complexity begs for a divine mind capable of creating it—a circular argument. But even assuming creation via a deity necessary, this does not dictate deterministic micro-management of every detail by the creator.

Other intelligent-design-like natural forces, including physics, chemistry, and evolution manage details. Certainly, God is not party to the price of gold. He created $E=MC^2$, and every other concept and formula out there. And creation need not adhere to a schedule, done in six days, but it can be achieved *through* time, the way I'm creating this manuscript as I type. Creation can also include interventions that cause sharp turns, such as when Europeans arrived in America, or with Aliens arriving from elsewhere.

*Intervention*, though, boasts substantial evidence, both written and literally in stone, and considerable logic to account for the instantaneous step-up of Humans becoming Homo Sapiens. Intervention can speak to how for hundreds of thousands of years, we lived like the other animals locked in nature, until suddenly we behaved as Homo Sapiens, able to accumulate know-how, build civilizations, and control nature itself. *Intervention* is simply the more-likely explanation to complete the puzzle, especially as creationism and evolution, though both partially correct in their respective domains, offer nothing to explain the recent, explosive Homo Sapient phenomenon.

And, *intervention* adds up to one thing: we are part advanced Alien and part simple Human, and as you will see in the *Plato* Chapter, to return to primate-styled socialism, those pining for primate-side domination must obscure this dualism. Hence socialists

41

cling to evolution to explain us. Evolution sidesteps the obvious: that many of our foundation traits are not of this Earth.

And with these introductory remarks made, I invite you to explore, not scoff at, *intervention*, the third leg of the creation, evolution and intervention stool.

But first, meet Moses and "the Lord".

# 4

# MOSES & "THE LORD"...PARTNERS

*"Who am I, that I should go unto Pharaoh, and that
I should bring forth the children of Israel out of Egypt?"*

—MOSES—

This chapter will use excerpts from the first books of the bible to describe "The Lord." Before one might accept that our Homo Sapient behavior stems from genetic unbalance, one must first conclude that our unbalanced selves were not "made" on Day 6 by God. The various chapters in SUBJUGATED dealing with the books of the bible are here for that purpose.

The first five books of the bible—*GENESIS, EXODUS, LEVITICUS, NUMBERS, DEUTERONOMY*—are called The Torah, said to be the Laws of God as revealed to Moses. Whether or not Moses wrote them down or memorized revelations, later telling them to other rabbis for posterity, is not known. He probably wrote them down, as Moses, an Egyptian prince and one of Pharaoh's great warriors (covered later), came out of Egypt, a semi-literate society. The five books contain vast hard-to-memorize detail as to dialogues that once took place, and the likelihood that Moses learned the history of humankind—GENESIS— from his alien mentors also comes later in this work.

The Torah, though, reads more like Moses's camp journal, starting from his first meeting with "the Lord" in Egypt and running until Moses's death 40 years later. Upon the death of Moses, Joshua assumed the journalistic responsibilities with, appropriately, *The Book of Joshua*, describing the conquest of the 32 Canaanite kingdoms. With "the Lord" in tow, similar to Moses, Joshua is provisioned with all the "Lord-like" weapons for which one could hope.

The only non-journal aspect of all the writings is GENESIS, as GENESIS, the first book, took place before Moses's time. Someone must have provided Moses with all the detail, including the actual words spoken by the likes of Adam and Eve, Noah, and Abraham. Most true believers assume that Moses received the GENESIS "backstory" through divine revelation from GOD while up on Mount Sinai.

Others say ancient luminaries wrote the stories on cuneiform clay tablets that survived into Moses's time. Still others claim that priests wrote all of the Torah between the time of David in 900 BC and the Babylonian captivity in 500 BC, suggesting it was all made up.

But a more likely source of the GENESIS backstory is that "the Lord," who, for decades, traveled everywhere with Moses, and regularly conversed with him at the "meeting tent," explained creation in detail to Moses, as the Lord possessed knowledge of the actual process.

Functionally, I describe the Lord as "the onsite project manager," assigned to Earth, working on the Nephilim Extermination project. The Lord, apparently, dwelled in a vessel hovering over a pillar of smoke and fire, set above the meeting tent. The Lord undoubtedly reported to higher-ups, and I call his boss "The Admiral"—the guy running the whole Earth operation.

For the reader to get a feel for this alternative picture suggesting the Torah as basically a journal of camp life, consider some of the mundane dialogue between the Lord and Moses ...

*The Lord called to Moses and spoke to him from the tent of
meeting. He said, "Speak to the Israelites and say to them:
'When anyone among you brings an offering to the Lord, bring
as your offering an animal from either the herd or the flock.' If
the offering is a burnt offering from the herd, you are to offer a
male without defect. You must present it at the entrance to the
tent of meeting so that it will be acceptable to the Lord ..."*

The micromanagement boggles the mind. Below, "the Lord"
speaks to Moses and Aaron while still in Egypt regarding portions
of lamb:

*This month is to be for you the first month, the first month of
your year. Tell the whole community of Israel that on the tenth
day of this month each man is to take a lamb for his family, one
for each household. If any household is too small for a whole
lamb, they must share one with their nearest neighbor, having
taken into account the number of people there are. You are to
determine the amount of lamb needed in accordance with what
each person will eat.*

Further, while in the Sanai desert, "the Lord" proclaimed:

*If you bring a grain offering baked in an oven, it is to consist
of the finest flour: either thick loaves made without yeast and
with olive oil mixed in or thin loaves made without yeast and
brushed with olive oil.*

Pages and pages of food preparation proclamations by "the Lord"
exist; the above is just an isolated sentence.

Separate from these incidental meeting tent conversations about
food stands the singular Mount Sinai experience. What took place
up on Sinai actually appears more like revelation, and less like camp
talk. After all, when Moses went up the mountain, he came back

down with a burnt face. This never happened when discussing food preparation matters with "the Lord."

One can surmise that on the mountain Moses met the higher authority, i.e., the Admiral, the boss of the extermination exercise, the one who knew the whole story from Adam onward. The Admiral, who reported to a home planet probably tiring of the whole Homo Sapient debacle, needed to look Moses in the eye, and set parameters for the venture ahead, the planned invasion of Nephilim territories.

It was a lot for Moses to take in, but because Moses and "the Lord" spoke all the time at the meeting tent, with "the Lord" fully versed in creation astrophysics, with an all-to-clear understanding of the whole Nephilim backstory and the upcoming mission to exterminate Nephilim, well ... "the Lord" probably served as a good editor for Moses as he compiled the segments of GENESIS.

Basically, at the special status meeting up on the mountain, "The Admiral" gave the 10 Commandments to Moses so that the Israelites would *not* adopt the sacrilegious behavior of the Canaanite Nephilim. After all, the Nephilim way of life—complete debauchery—might appeal to some of the Hebrew men. "The Lord," operating the camp, had to ensure the enforcement of the Commandments, hence:

> *The Lord said to Moses, "Speak to the Israelites and say to them: 'I am the Lord. You must not do as they do in Egypt, where you used to live, and you must not do as they do in the land of Canaan, where I am bringing you. Do not follow their practices. You must obey my laws and be careful to follow my decrees. I am the Lord. Keep my decrees and laws, for the person who obeys them will live by them. I am the Lord.'"*

After 40 days on Mount Sinai, Moses came down to face the worst possible outcome: his people had created a golden calf to worship, identical to those the sacrilegious Nephilim Canaanites worshipped.

If the Israelites could worship a cow, they could easily adopt every other bad habit taught by Nephilim society. So, to instill discipline in the Israelites, the "on-site Lord" must quickly instill a fear of his ruthlessness in curbing bad behavior and bad attitude. Below, as example, out in the Sinai desert, "the Lord" punishes a few Israelites who have gone astray:

> *The people complained about their hardships in the hearing (proximity) of the Lord, and when he (the Lord) heard them his anger was aroused. Then fire from the Lord burned among them and consumed some of the outskirts of the camp. When the people cried out to Moses, he prayed to the Lord and the fire died down.*

This kind of thing occurred rather regularly. Someone messed up. "The Lord" freaked out. Moses went in to restore peace.

But more baffling is why "the Admiral" and "the Lord" needed to recruit the Hebrews in the first place. The list of Egyptian plagues that these mysterious ones delivered with the snap of a finger makes you wonder, why didn't they simply destroy the Nephilim directly, rather than go through all of this manipulation? Why engage in all the cajoling, scheming, and detailed instruction that "the Lord" exhibited in directing Moses, aged 80, and Moses's 83-year old brother, Aaron?

Below "the Lord" assigns Moses and Aaron the important job of counting able-bodied men for the army, which either assumes "the Lord" did not know the number already, or that he needed Moses and Aaron to experience the process. "The Lord" goes so far as to pick the men he wants assigned to this project:

> *The Lord spoke to Moses in the tent of meeting in the Desert of Sinai on the first day of the second month of the second year after the Israelites came out of Egypt. He said: "Take a census of the whole Israelite community by their clans and families, listing every man by name, one by one. You and Aaron are to count according to their divisions all the men in Israel who are twenty years old or more and able to serve in the army. One man from each tribe, each of them the head of his family, is to help you.*

47

*These are the names of the men who are to assist you:*

*From Reuben, Elizur son of Shedeur;*
*from Simeon, Shelumiel son of Zurishaddai;*
*from Judah, Nahshon son of Amminadab;*
*from Issachar, Nethanel son of Zuar;*
*from Zebulun, Eliab son of Helon;*
*from the sons of Joseph:*
*from Ephraim, Elishama son of Ammihud;*
*from Manasseh, Gamaliel son of Pedahzur;*
*from Benjamin, Abidan son of Gideoni;*
*from Dan, Ahiezer son of Ammishaddai;*
*from Asher, Pagiel son of Okran;*
*from Gad, Eliasaph son of Deuel;*
*from Naphtali, Ahira son of Enan."*

This type of detail is astonishing, and it goes on for pages and pages, book after book, subject after subject. Below one finds just part of "the Lord's" instructions for skin disease:

*A man who has lost his hair and is bald is clean. If he has lost his hair from the front of his scalp and has a bald forehead, he is clean. But if he has a reddish-white sore on his bald head or forehead, it is a defiling disease breaking out on his head or forehead. The priest is to examine him, and if the swollen sore on his head or forehead is reddish-white like a defiling skin disease, the man is diseased and is unclean. The priest shall pronounce him unclean because of the sore on his head.*

*Anyone with such a defiling disease must wear torn clothes, let their hair be unkempt, cover the lower part of their face and cry out, "Unclean! Unclean!" As long as they have the disease they remain unclean. They must live alone; they must live outside the camp.*

Consider this: After Aaron's sons were burned to death by "the Lord" for approaching "the Lord" incorrectly, Aaron, as father, also found himself on the hot seat, rebuked in detail, as follows:

> *The Lord spoke to Moses after the death of the two sons of Aaron who died when they approached the Lord. The Lord said to Moses: "Tell your brother Aaron that he is not to come whenever he chooses into the Most Holy Place behind the curtain in front of the atonement cover on the ark, or else he will die.*

The Wizard of Oz implied the same for Dorothy.

At some point, "the Lord" decided to create a personal staff to tend to the meeting tent, the tabernacle, the Ark of the Covenant, and "the Lord's" meals. "The Lord" chose the tribe of Levi for this role, and thereafter, the Levite men took charge of "the Lord's" stuff, including transporting it once the Israelites were on the move. The other tribes paid a tax to "the Lord" to support the Levites, as the Levites no longer had their own flocks. In getting this arrangement going, "the Lord" seemed to impose a trade of sorts with Moses:

> *The Lord also said to Moses "I have taken the Levites from among the Israelites in place of the first male offspring of every Israelite woman. The Levites are mine, for all the firstborn are mine. When I struck down all the firstborn in Egypt, I set apart for myself every firstborn in Israel, whether human or animal. They are to be mine. I am the Lord."*

I guess "the Lord" wanted no backtalk about getting a personal staff, and pointed out that when all of the Egyptian firstborn babies were killed, their Hebrew counterparts were spared, thus "You guys owe me!" Once he had a staff, the Lord spoke with further precision:

> *Bring you clear oil of pressed olives for the light so that the lamps may be kept burning continually. Outside the curtain that*

*shields the ark of the covenant law in the tent of meeting, Aaron is to tend the lamps before the Lord from evening till morning, continually. This is to be a lasting ordinance for the generations to come. The lamps on the pure gold lampstand before the Lord must be tended continually.*

"The Lord" also got involved in family squabbles. Below, a full passage showing the methods of "the Lord" in action:

*Miriam and Aaron began to talk against Moses because of his Cushite wife, for he had married a Cushite (an African). "Has the Lord spoken only through Moses?" they asked. "Hasn't he also spoken through us?" And the Lord heard this.*

*At once the Lord said to Moses, Aaron and Miriam, "Come out to the tent of meeting, all three of you." So, the three of them went out. Then the Lord came down in a pillar of cloud; he stood at the entrance to the tent and summoned Aaron and Miriam. When the two of them stepped forward, he said, "Listen to my words:*

*"When there is a prophet among you, I, the Lord, reveal myself to them in visions, I speak to them in dreams.*

*But this is not true of my servant Moses; he is faithful in all my house.*

*With him I speak face to face, clearly and not in riddles; he sees the form of the Lord. Why then were you not afraid to speak against my servant Moses?" The anger of the Lord burned against them, and he left them.*

*When the cloud lifted from above the tent, Miriam's skin was leprous —it became as white as snow. Aaron turned toward her and saw that she had a defiling skin disease, and he said to Moses, "Please, my lord, I ask you not to hold against us the sin we have so foolishly committed. Do not let her be like a stillborn infant coming from its mother's womb with its flesh half eaten away." So Moses cried out to the Lord, "Please, God, heal her!"*

*The Lord replied to Moses, "If her father had spit in her face, would she not have been in disgrace for seven days? Confine her outside the camp for seven days; after that she can be brought back." So Miriam was confined outside the camp for seven days, and the people did not move on until she was brought back.*

One major element of the whole "Lord" saga is that Moses was not to live long enough to lead the people into the promised land, not due to old age, but as punishment for doubting the Lord. It all came about due to the "water from the rock" incident, though I can see nothing wrong in anything Moses did. Here is the event:

*Then came the children of Israel, even the whole congregation, into the desert of Zin in the first month: and the people abode in Kadesh; and Miriam died there, and was buried there.*

*And there was no water for the congregation: and they gathered themselves together against Moses and against Aaron.*

*And the people chode with Moses, and spake, saying, Would God that we had died when our brethren died before the Lord!*

*And why have ye brought up the congregation of the Lord into this wilderness, that we and our cattle should die there?*

*And wherefore have ye made us to come up out of Egypt, to bring us in unto this evil place? It is no place of seed, or of figs, or of vines, or of pomegranates; neither is there any water to drink. And Moses and Aaron went from the presence of the assembly unto the door of the tabernacle of the congregation, and they fell upon their faces: and the glory of the Lord appeared unto them.*

51

*And the Lord spake unto Moses, saying,*

*Take the rod, and gather thou the assembly together, thou, and Aaron thy brother, and speak ye unto the rock before their eyes; and it shall give forth his water, and thou shalt bring forth to them water out of the rock: so thou shalt give the congregation and their beasts drink.*

*And Moses took the rod from before the Lord, as he commanded him.*

*And Moses and Aaron gathered the congregation together before the rock, and he said unto them, "Hear now, ye rebels; must we fetch you water out of this rock?"*

*And Moses lifted up his hand, and with his rod he smote the rock twice: and the water came out abundantly, and the congregation drank, and their beasts also.*

*And the Lord spake unto Moses and Aaron. Because ye believed me not, to sanctify me in the eyes of the children of Israel, therefore ye shall not bring this congregation into the land which I have given them.*

Oh well, the Lord must just have had his own reasons ...

This, then, finishes "The Lord," the on-site "Project Manager" chapter. But stay tuned, for in the later *Moses Moves East* and *Joshua Conquers Canaan* chapters, "the Lord" returns, along with Moses and Joshua. But the above should get you wondering "Was the Lord 'God,' or simply the on-site project manager?

# 5

# GENETICS, ACCOUNTING FOR SUDDEN CHANGE

*" I got a hundred bucks says my baby beats Pete's (Sampras') baby. I just think genetics are in my favor. "*

—ANDRE AGASSI—

Meet the Nephilim: The worst neighbors possible! In order to gauge the meaning of Adam & Eve and then the Nephilim, both exhibiting genetic traits not present in any prior Earth species, we need to dig deeper into genetics, first to envision how a genetic upgrade could be possible, and second, to contrast the great competing theories of Creation, Evolution, and Intervention to see which theory best explains these anomalies.

The introduction to this book made a point of not picking a winner between the evolutionists and the creationists. Instead, two of the book's many mysteries, Adam & Eve and the Nephilim sagas, pose interventionist breeding as more likely explanations. Interestingly, evolutionists, creationists, and interventionists all happen to share the topic of genetics.

The difference? Evolutionists claim genes mutate over time to form new species; creationists believe that each plant or animal type holds a relatively fixed genetic makeup that can vary; and interventionists deduce that only outside intervention can explain sudden, *dramatic* genetic diversions. Let's start with Adam & Eve. Where did they—or the first Homo Sapiens—come from?

According to *creationists*, GOD created man and woman instantly on Day 6, with Adam and the Eve possessing a full set of Homo Sapient genes. I suppose God goofed, also creating our mental illnesses within the gene set. According to *evolutionists*, Humans instead progressed through an evolving chain of primates over millions of years via an endless string of genetic mutations – also resulting in mental illnesses.

Before getting to the third possible factor in generating a new species—intervention—let's look at the big problems with both of the first two options.

With *evolution*, one must explain how mutations in the primate world led to our vast array of intellectual faculties. Yes, chimps use sticks to pry into ant colony mounds, a skill used to obtain a crunchy snack, perhaps, but certainly not a foundation trait able to suddenly mutate into algebra, engineering, chemistry, weapon design, cuisine, etc. Realistically, no core traits exist poised within the primate chain to mutate into the vast list of human faculties. And, more so, who was our predecessor primate, the one who could count, but not do algebra? The *absence of previous traits* is the first gaping hole in a "pure evolution" explanation.

Second, if Humans blossomed 200,000 years ago already in possession of our intellect, then why did it take 200,000 years to begin behaving as we do, controlling nature, accumulating know-how, building cities and civilization structures? Instead, these Humans stayed more or less primate-like. *Stagnation* is the second hole.

This leads to the third gaping hole, the obligation to explain *the massive level of successful mutations needed* in order to jump the immediately prior primate-human species up to our current civilization-oriented level Homo Sapient species. A huge jump, at that. Most cellular mutations end up with a dying cell, as the original cell's gene/switch configuration no longer supports intact operational balance. The jump described would require untold numbers of neuron mutations, all successful, all codependent, in a single instance. *Evolution does not work that way.*

A fourth gaping hole finds no predecessor species that could have mutated. Other than Neanderthals, we have *no sign whatsoever of an immediate prior species* that could mutate into humans. We are only offered monkey bones going back millions of years. Let's consider Neanderthals to make this point clearer.

According to *evolutionists*, Neanderthals lived for hundreds of thousands of years, eventually killed off by the new aggressive Humans. Based upon genetic testing of frozen Neanderthal flesh, today's Homo Sapiens contain remnants of Neanderthal DNA (<1%), suggesting that some minor cross breeding took place once the two species confronted each other. Neanderthals certainly did not mutate into Humans where every gene in the Neanderthal system simultaneously mutated.

But as distant as Neanderthals were to human DNA, consider that across hundreds of thousands of years, Neanderthals never advanced. As with all other animals living *within nature*, they sat stagnant. They used the same five or six stone tools in 40,000 BC that they used in 250,000 BC. And Neanderthals possessed larger brains than ours, so why were they so dull, and why are we so smart? Evolutionists ignore this.

Compare both the Neanderthal and Primate-Human stagnations to the trajectory of Homo Sapiens inventiveness: can one seriously claim that our intellectual faculties resulted from unprecedented, massive, synchronized mutations from some prior primate, when no foundation intellectual traits able to be mutated can be found in any such primate?

Finally, fifth, say one day a mutated child was born with the evolved intellectual capabilities possessed by modern *Homo Sapiens*. How would this brilliance be passed along to all the slower *Humans* who had populated the world over the 70,000 years prior? Did all the Humans mutate together allowing, for example, pyramid building to take place on all continents? Checkmate?

Why is evolution even considered?

Now the *creationists* have a few issues of their own with humans popping into existence on Day 6, and they solve their issues in the most amazing ways …

For example, we only properly fathomed dinosaur bones in the mid-1800's. Once uncovered, and the vast sets of dinosaur species identified, this new puzzle piece somehow needed to factor into the "God created everything in six days" system.

The *creationist response?* Dinosaurs lived with humans, but Noah did not invite them onto the Ark, hence they went down with the flood. Yes, creationists actually go with this, and, as you will find in Chapter 9— Noah, *they may have a case!* According to GENESIS, "all flesh became corrupted …" and for thousands of years, readers assumed this passage to mean human flesh, as contaminated with alien bloodlines. But to answer the dinosaur challenge, it became a blanket statement meaning all animal flesh became corrupted, requiring destruction, though some of the animals, obviously viewed as good, gained a seat on the Ark.

Phew, that explains it!

Adam & Eve, or whoever the first super-intelligent humans were, defy the theories of both evolutionists (mutations) and creationists (human mental illnesses). Now let's look into the likelihood of inter-vention by first reviewing genetics.

Basically, a species, e.g., Homo Sapiens, Cats, or Dogs, has a rela-tively fixed, superset set of genes, with individual genes switched on or off in various combinations to form cell types.

For example, cat heart and cat bone cells hold the same gene set, but their respective genes are switched differently to *express* the functional cat heart and bone attributes.

Likewise, our human bodies, comprising more than 100 types of cells, present a standard collection of human genes *expressed via switch combinations* to meet the role of each type of cell.

The on/off gene switching potential is vast, some of it fixed, and some of it done in real-time in response to environmental and hormonal stimulus.

It is said that human genes for eye color contain dozens of options, and that one's actual expressed color comes from the color switch assigned at one's conception (not the gene, but the switch).

In this instance, based upon the parent's switch settings for eye color—plus a determination as to which parental settings are dominant or recessive—the fetus inherits its color from these parental switch preferences. Internally, humans are fundamentally the same, with each human carrying a spectrum of human eye color possibilities; the switches, not the gene itself, cause the specific outcome.

We can find another example in breeding dogs. One looks for desired traits, and then mates male and female candidates exhibiting these traits so that the switches their offspring inherit trigger the desired trait. But all dogs still carry the basic spectrum of dog trait possibilities. And so, a Chihuahua (with help) can mate with a Great Dane.

Some minor mutations can also be in play, but they do not alter the dog "type."

Out in nature a similar thing occurs, called *Variation Within a Species due to Natural Selection*. Darwin sorted this out while sailing around the Galapagos Islands. He observed the same bird species having longer or shorter beaks based upon the island environment it inhabited. But beak size remains just another switch-setting option within that species.

On "Island X," rather than a breeder choosing traits, a survival advantage for birds with longer beaks causes longer-beaked birds to survive and then mate, causing Island X offspring to inherit the longer-beak *switch settings*.

Conversely, "Island Y" birds, which fare better with shorter beaks, inherit shorter-beak *switch settings* from parents thriving in this preferred shorter-beak setting.

But, as in the dog-breeding situation, all birds of that species carry genes supporting both longer and shorter beaks; beak length is just a parameter determined by a *switch setting*. Read the following report coming out of the University of Washington in 2012:

> *The locations of millions of DNA 'switches' that dictate how, when, and where in the body different genes turn on and off have been identified by a research team led by the University of Washington in Seattle. Genes make up only 2 percent of the human genome and were easy to spot, but the on/off switches controlling those genes were encrypted within the remaining 98 percent of the genome. Without these switches, called regulatory DNA, genes are inert.*

*Creationists* insist that God, in *His* wisdom, provided the plant and animal types with these switch options to help the individual specimens adapt to environmental fluctuations. But, mind you, in the creationist camp, God fixed the plant and animal types up-front, with new gene types not possible.

Conversely, in addition to switch options, *evolutionists* believe that although most cell mutations are minor, that some are not, and that over time, certain *mutation sequences* can lead to improved or sometimes degenerated gene types, e.g., bad eyesight.

So far, even though we humans have come a long way in understanding genetics—having created many, many breeds over the past few thousand years—humbly, we have not taken the possibilities of genetics that far. We only play with the switches. To breed animals and agricultural plants, we orchestrate desired switch combinations, *but no one has ever altered the foundation genes to create a new species.*

Currently, we are deconstructing the gene universe to catalogue all the traits expressed by individual strands of DNA within the genes, even identifying some gene conditions as participants in disease.

For example, a woman with an imperfect BRCA gene (a mutation), has a greater chance of breast cancer because the BRCA gene's job is to manufacture a protein that repairs damaged DNA before the damage leads to a cancer mutation during cell division.

Inferior BRCA means that DNA breaks go unrepaired, resulting in greater opportunity for cancerous mutation.

And yes, we can pass mutations like BRCA down to future generations, thereby making offspring both stronger and weaker, i.e., evolution can also weaken us, but the question remains: do mutations lead to a fundamentally different (new) type of plant or animal?

Although mankind is getting closer to cataloguing gene pool functionality, no one out there is inventing brand new genes capable of introducing breakthrough traits outside of the potential of that type. Therefore, *creationists say evolutionists are wrong*. Each type possesses a relatively fixed set of genes, created by God, not by us. Evolutionist counter claiming that at the very least, old species eventually *splinter* into new types. More on this momentarily …

Let's now consider the possibility of materially affecting underlying genes, the theory touted by the *interventionists*.

To start, just because humans have not cracked gene creation or gene supplementation, it doesn't mean that real genetic engineering with enhanced, replacement genes can't be achieved. I believe it has been achieved, not yet by Homo Sapiens, but by others.

Replacement genetics complements both creation, the first species "type" creation factor, and evolution, the second "splintered" species creation factor. This two-factor system accepts plant and animal types created by God, while allowing types to evolve (devolve?) into splintered species, but only within the limited boundaries of their foundation type. For instance, primates remain primates.

Anything outside of species splintering requires intervention, a third species factor, and the suddenness of "Adam & Eve" anchors this three-factor system.

Primate evolution before Homo Sapiens followed various splintering paths with only minor improvements in intellect accruing over great expanses in time, as two-factor evolution works via incremental change. The human hunter/gatherers—the pottery makers—most likely resulted from this slow, two-factor splintering and nothing else.

These Simple Humans acted as primates, troops led by a dominant male, no individuals allowed.

Today, our Homo Sapient gene pool certainly incorporates much of this two-factor legacy, but unlike previous primates that came about solely via splintering, Homo Sapiens received an infusion of genetic material from outside the chain. Only a three-factor infusion can explain both the vast jump in intelligence apparent in the civilization builders as compared to the older pottery makers, and the suddenness in which we came upon the scene.

GENESIS lists the descendants of Adam all the way through Noah, Abraham, and Moses. This backward chronology fixes the *creationist* date of Adam at 4,000 B.C., meaning *creationists* believe that Day 6 occurred in the year 4,000 B.C. But an *evolutionist* could drop the "Day 6" nomenclature and embrace this start date as well, based upon the following ...

The two-factor thesis begins with humans slowly evolving via the primate chain, arriving as hunter/gatherers in the very 200,000 BC timeframe that the evolutionists like, but suggests these beings as merely 'first edition" Humans, only modestly endowed intellectually, and, like other animals, stagnant in their ways, very much like elephants and Neanderthals.

Then in the 4,000 BC timeframe, outsiders selected this species for a genetic upgrade, not new switch combinations, but new foundation genes, especially in the domain of brain neurons. This 4,000 B.C. laboratory upgrade occurred in Year 4 Billion after the earth's formation (we will ponder what 4 Billion means in the *Time & the Speed of Physics* chapter, and ponder the nature of the neuron upgrade in the *Plato* chapter).

The three-factor "sudden shift" thesis goes on to claim that in 4,000 B.C., Adam & Eve, who were the first Humans given these high-powered neuron genes, became the first Homo Sapiens (meaning Humans with wisdom). Besides potent neuron implants, Homo Sapiens were also engineered to appear similar to the alien species breeding them, just as GENESIS points out: humans were made "in the likeness of God." Overall, the natural, two-factor humans "kind of" looked like the aliens in the first place; we looked "cool," but we were pretty stupid. We just needed some upgrades.

So, liking what they saw in the natural two-factor hunter/gatherer Humans, the Aliens decide to try an upgrade. And it "kind of" worked. The new but emotionally volatile Homo Sapient human suddenly possessed the many intellectual faculties we enjoy today, but this came with the aforementioned mental health drawbacks. And also, by starting from scratch, it would take many generations for Homo Sapiens to collect the significant amounts of know-how to match up with their new IQs. These three-factor Humans – the Homo Sapiens – possessed intelligence, but they knew not how to apply it. Things like Noah's Ark would be taught.

And so, upon reflection, it looks as though humankind has remained fairly ignorant ever since, and probably still is, considering the infinite potential of "know how" (touched upon in the *Plato* chapter). From the time of Adam in 4,000 B.C., a lot of wandering took place, and it took until the 2,200 B.C. timeframe for the city building to begin. The Homo Sapiens probably needed a lot of help to get started, hence the Sumerian legends of gods teaching masonry, the wheel, arithmetic, etc., described later.

And once we established the first civilizations, it appears our interlopers abandoned us, probably before the reign of the Incas. Without help, we needed another three thousand years to build enough momentum to break through on our own to what we now experience as the scientific era, (or, maybe they taught us again, but indirectly).

In the *Plato* chapter, the book will describe the theory that our Homo Sapiens imagination links to a greater universe of ideas, explaining our continued ascent.

Indeed, mankind accumulated most of our scientific knowledge only from the 1800's to today. Remember, we revered Ben Franklin for his simple key-on-a-kite experiment only as recently as the 1700's. Plate tectonics—the movement of the continents—only emerged in the 1960's—yes! For more on modern know-how, read Bill Bryson's book *A Short History of Nearly Everything.*

And so, humbly, ever since inception, and through this day, humankind basically plodded along under the weight of immense ignorance. Just imagine the ignorant minds of the smart three-factor Homo Sapiens in the first few thousand years of their journey.

Undoubtedly, at the onset, Homo Sapiens (on Day 6, or Year 4 billion, take your choice), had great imaginations, yet no data, yielding to fear and superstition, especially fear of the superior Aliens they then considered gods. An ignorant mind is a dangerous mind, filling in the blanks with made-up stuff.

To make matters worse, soon after Homo Sapiens arrived upon the scene, a second shoe dropped—the Nephilim—bringing more terror into the world. Can you imagine living back then?

Similar to the advent of Homo Sapiens, the subsequent Nephilim outbreak also occurred having nothing to do with micro-mutations. The Nephilim phenomenon instead points to undisciplined cross-breeding of these new three-factor Homo Sapiens and the other species, a vast genetic interplay. Let's consider the gravity of this ...

These Aliens, though superior to us in the know-how department, were in a sense "human, all *too* human," and the bible says that some of the alien crew members suddenly pined for the improved, "fun-to-be-with" Homo Sapient girls. Boys *will* be boys. This saga will bear itself out in gory detail later when we look at the *Book of Enoch* chapter.

GENESIS says the renegade Aliens—called the Sons of God—took the girls. But as with the horse and a donkey, their respective genes did not totally match up, and so, the offspring—the Nephilim—came out as big, brutal, sex-starved, amoral psychopaths. As mentioned, the Nephilim offspring probably had recessive genes. In the future, to get a Nephilim baby, both parents would need to carry a recessive Nephilim gene and both parents would need to pass these switch options down at conception. Over time, the possibility of finding two parents able to do this would dwindle. Therefore amongst the

Philistines, only Goliath and his brothers were giants, the others having standard Homo Sapient traits.

From that juncture, every bit of GENESIS deals with this horrible situation: the casting down of the rogue crew members by Michael the Archangel, the subsequent corruption of all flesh, the selection of Noah as genetically pure, the building of Noah's Ark, the Flood, the repopulation of Earth, the separation of people via language and the diaspora of Noah's grandchildren across the planet after the tower of Babel, all leading up to Abraham and then Moses. Genesis 11, below, describes Babel:

> *And the LORD said, Behold, the people is one, and they have all one language; and this they begin to do (building the tower): and now nothing will be restrained from them, which they have imagined to do.*
>
> *Go to, let **us** go down, and there confound their language, that they may not understand one another's speech. So the LORD scattered them abroad from thence upon the face of all the earth: and they left off to build the city. Therefore is the name of it called Babel.*

Hmmm … what is meant by "let **us** go down" mentioned above?

We cover Babel and the diaspora of people across the earth in the coming *Noah* chapter.

After Babel, say, 200 years post-flood, the Homo Sapiens scatter to the different ends of the earth, morphing into diverse races, cultures, and language systems *simply via natural selection gene switching,* as quickly as we breed dogs.

But what about the post-flood Nephilim? The flood ought to have destroyed both the remaining two-factor, natural-but-stupid humans plus the grotesque Nephilim, leaving the coast clear for Noah's enlightened offspring. It seems the flood eliminated the natural first-edition humans, including all those spread out across the earth, but though also destroyed by the flood, the Nephilim returned. How?

Following the diaspora after the Tower of Babel crisis, Noah's grandson Canaan settled in the Dead Sea area. It was Canaan's father Ham, who before getting onto the Ark, mistakenly took a wife assumed to be genetically pure. But she was not pure. Her gene set held Nephilim traits, and the buried, *recessive* genes would switch on down the inheritance line, so long as both parents carried Nephilim traits. The so-called post-flood Nephilim described in the bible ascended through this recessive gene path.

Please note, so far, none of the chaos and terror described has anything to do with God, and one ponders that if a God wanted to rid the world of Nephilim he could have achieved this with a blink of an eye, even without a flood.

And so, the rigor-moral of the flood, followed by the failure of the flood to achieve its extermination goal … shows the whole thing to be a botched operation performed by mortal Aliens. The folly presented by GENESIS proves with evidence that God was *not* in the middle of this. Instead, fallible alien decision-makers, the interventionists, stood at the helm of both the Adam & Eve and the Nephilim genetic debacles.

All of this historical complexity bled into modern times.

## A Footnote on the Scopes Monkey Trial of 1925
## Socialism Finds Evolution

### The Historical Circumstaces

I add this relatively modern-era footnote to remind the reader that between 1870 (Charles Darwin), and 1970 (Eric von Däniken), the musings of our rapid Homo Sapient ascendency became a brawl between creationists and evolutionists. Yet neither camp had evidence, let alone proof … both just ran on supposition. This fighting-in-ignorance approach peaked during the famous 1925 "Skopes" trial – the one about the school teacher who taught evolution, saying we evolved from monkeys.

Hard to fathom, but back then, genetics was still unknown to the sure-minded evolutionists claiming the moment. And of course in 1925, the pious creationists were still operating on blind faith. Hence, both the evolution and creation warriors of the day argued based upon guessed propositions. And more, trapped within this "prism of just two possible choices", no player back then could think outside of the box to envision, for example, Alien intervention as the more likely missing link explaining us.

Without any direct evidence, life on earth was seen as a massive random mutation cauldron. Creation in six days was the fool's errand of the "deplorables".

This was just 100 years ago, and though today, almost all of our modern Democrats assume evolution "settled science", in 1925, millions of fiercely-divided Democrats clashed over the evolution/creation issue. Accordingly, at the Scopes trial, two opposing democrat party "super elites" volunteered, one to prosecute and one to defend John Skopes. Republicans went "missing".

## Case Background

*John Skopes*, a substitute teacher in Dayton Tennessee, introduced "evolution" to his students, and upon doing so agreed to be arrested for violating a Tennessee statute forbidding the teaching of evolution. The "progressive", secular democrat *Clarence Darrow*, the top attorney in the land, became Skope's defense attorney. Darrow agreed to waive his fee ($1 million in 2023 money).

And for the prosecution, "the common man's" democrat, *William Jennings Bryan* volunteered to lead the Christian attack. Bryan, a three-time Democrat candidate for the U. S. Presidency, always a fierce advocate of a Christian America, saw this showdown moment as "his destiny". He would die of heart failure just days after the trial.

With these two powerhouse lawyers entering the ring, the Skope's trial became a nationwide battle between Christians and Secularists. Here is how the key players thought:

> Skopes: *"Although not a trained scholar, I thought Darwin was right. It was the only plausible explanation of man's long and tortuous journey to his current mental and physical development."*

> Darrow: *"Education was in danger from the source that has always hampered it ... religious fanaticism."*

> Bryan: *"Darwinism represents man as reaching his current perfection by the operation of the law of hate – the merciless law by which the strong crowd out and kill the weak"*

## My Take On The Scopes Event

Over the 100 years since 1925, the Democrat party morphed into a socialist tribe that pined for evolution. Why? Because evolution preaches "survival of the fittest", the ugly terror just postulated above by William Jennings Bryan. To counter this ever-present "existential" threat against individual survival, a socialist state was needed to protect the people from evolution's cruel dynamic. Ta da ... the envisioned "primate-leaning" socialist state would shield anyone victimized by *inadequate life survival skills* from everything, especially from the competitive, gung-ho, alien-leaning Homo Sapiens.

But this "safety" utopia required uncontested Socialism to counter the *"winner take all – free for all"* pass that evolutionary theory conferred upon humankind's scary overlords. And so, by declaring evolution "settled science", socialism became the "settled solution". By obediently sticking together inside of the troop, one's individual shortcomings no longer pose a danger to one's survival.

Yet as mentioned in SUBJUGATED's "Prove It" chapter, scientific proof requires repetitive observable behavior in nature, of which *evolution* – Darwin's "what if" proposition – offers none. Yes,

Darwin noticed *natural selection* while sailing the Galapagos Islands (birds with different beak lengths), but he assumed this was caused by specie mutations, and not simply by the activation of alternative traits already housed in the bird's chromosomes.

During the Scopes trial, those advocating evolution were ignorant of both genes (not understood until the 1950's) and genetic trait switches (published by Washington State University only in 2012). Hence, all of the guessing that went on back then becomes understandable.

But through presumption, these die-hard 1925 evolutionists misunderstood species variation altogether. They assumed that, over time, mutation chains were constantly morphing beings into fundamentally new species. Yet the modern science of natural selection merely shows that species mainly adapt to diverse environments simply by expressing alternative built-in traits. And whenever a trait works, the surviving parent passes this winning genetic switch advantage onto the next generation. *Constant* mutation chains are not in play.

And even if a random mutation can cause a new genetic trait, as probable, a complete species transformation can only occur through innumerable mutations compounded over great expanses of time. This slow-go aspect of evolution cannot explain how Homo Sapiens, out of nowhere, suddenly began building cities in 2,000 B.C..

If one juxtaposes the subsequent 4,000 year trajectory of Homo Sapient achievement against the primitive Humans living for 200,000 years *in an endlessly stagnant world* of camp fires, camp dogs, simple pottery and six stone tools ... then you will see us – Homo Sapiens – to be a separately designed species.

### Conflating Natural Selection

The Skopes Trial incorrectly conflated natural selection (living things expressing various built-in switch options) with the wholesale generation of new species via massive numbers of supposedly-random, yet cohesive, operationally-intact mutations, a phenomena not yet observed in nature.

Today, many safety-enthusiasts willingly conflate the two topics, as half of society relies upon the "survival of the fittest" boogeyman in order to justify a "safe" managed socialist operating model, one that protects some, by enforcing primate obedience on all.

This ends the chapter on genetics. Ask yourself, *what's more likely:* Are we two-factor or three-factor beings? And, could recessive Nephilim genes still be floating around amongst the earth's eight billion Homo Sapiens?

> **Interesting Note:** Apparently, evidence exists that other primates, like Baboons, raise dogs both as pets and to stand guard over the troop. So genetically, this "camp dog" trait clearly comes from the primate line. Likewise, the vast list of Homo Sapient intellectual faculties – mathematics, literature, etc., obviously come from elsewhere, not from primitive humans.

The Baboon evidence (amazing film clips) can be found on You Tube. Next, we explore Enoch, Noah's long lost grandfather. Here is the genealogy:

| | | |
|---|---|---|
| Adam | Born 4,000 B.C., | Lived 930 years |
| Seth | Born 3,870 B.C. | Lived 912 years |
| Enosh | Born 3,765 B.C. | Lived 905 years |
| Cainan | Born 3,675 B.C. | Lived 910 years |
| Mahalalel | Born 3,605 B.C. | Lived 895 years |
| Jared | Born 3,560 B.C. | Lived 962 years |
| **Enoch** | **Born 3,378 B.C.** | **Enoch the Taken One** |
| Methuselah | Born 3,313 B.C. | Lived 969 years |
| Lamech | Born 3,126 B.C. | Lived 777 years |
| Noah | Born 2,944 B.C. | Lived 950 years |

# 6

# ENOCH & THE BOOK OF ENOCH, THE WATCHERS

*" You may force me to say what you wish;*
*you may revile me for saying what I do. But it moves. "*

—GALILEO—

Before heading back to Moses and "the Lord," let's glean what we can from Enoch about the mortal players operating pre-flood.

Enoch, the grandfather of Noah, born seven generations after Adam around 3,400 B.C., once had his account of the pre-flood era included in the Jewish bible. Enoch's account was almost lost after rabbis removed it at one point. Old Ethiopian bibles found in the 1800's still included Enoch, and these relics saved the day. Enoch, therefore, is no slouch in the annals of history, and writings attributed to him – however still intact – should not be brushed aside.

Those wishing to discredit the Enoch accounts particularly rail against Enoch's claim that he "was taken," quite often, by superior

Aliens aboard their vessels, giving him a bird's eye view over the whole operation.

Enoch did not refer to these Aliens as "the Sons of God" as did others. He referred to them by function, calling them "the Watchers." Their job? To monitor the progress of the Homo Sapient project.

Instead, some of the Watchers messed up, taking unsanctioned "shore leave" to meet Homo Sapient "babes." Sailors will be sailors! Back in the day, they called guys like this *scallywags*.

Why Enoch rose to such fame eludes me, but GENISIS says the Watchers revered him so that they finally took him for good, not to return. This meant that Enoch ascended, alive, into "heaven".

To Enoch, it probably meant that he permanently signed up for duty with the high command of the Watchers—the Admiral and his lieutenants—Michael, Uriel, Raphael, and Gabriel—whom Enoch spoke of before his disappearance.

This said, obviously Enoch and his alien friends grated against both the proponents of the Bible's old and new testaments, which insist biblical content the opinion of God, not of mortals. Hence, in order to protect entrenched institutional agendas, Enoch was never canonized (approved of ) by any of the Jewish or Christian authorities. But there he is in print!

And so, the whole Nephilim phenomenon, and its non-religious implications, though sitting in plain sight within GENESIS, and reinforced by ENOCH, remains buried, never presented whole via the Book of Enoch to the layperson at temple or Sunday school.

The great mystery makes one wonder "Who wrote the Book of Enoch?" as Homo Sapiens did not write in the pre-flood era. Was the following all told to Moses some 1,500 years later, *after* the events occurred?

Consider the following excerpts from the Book of Enoch, actual written accounts by the ancients we are told to ignore!

Enoch describes Semiazaz, leader of the 200 fallen angels:

*And Semjâzâ, who was their leader, said unto them: "I fear ye will not indeed agree to do this deed, and I alone shall have to pay the penalty of a great sin." And they all answered him and said: "Let us all swear an oath, and all bind ourselves by mutual imprecations not to abandon this plan but to do this thing.*

*Then swear they all together and bound themselves by mutual imprecations upon it. And they were in all two hundred; who descended in the days of Jared on the summit of Mount Hermon, and they called it Mount Hermon, because they had sworn and bound themselves by mutual imprecations upon it.*

The names of the fallen angel captains are given:

*Araqiel, Râmêêl, Kokabiel, Tamiel, Ramiel, Dânêl, Chazaqiel, Baraqiel, Asael, Armaros, Batariel, Bezaliel, Ananiel, Zaqiel, Shamsiel, Satariel, Turiel, Yomiel, Sariel.*

This results in the creation of the Nephilim or Anakim/Anak as described in the book:

*And they became pregnant, and they bore great giants, whose height was three hundred ells: Who consumed all the acquisitions of men. And when men could no longer sustain them, the giants turned against them and devoured mankind. And they began to sin against birds, and beasts, and reptiles, and fish, and to devour one another's flesh, and drink the blood.*

Enoch discusses the teaching of humans by the fallen angels:

*And Azâzêl taught men to make swords, and knives, and shields, and breastplates, and made known to them the metals of the earth and the art of working them, and bracelets, and ornaments, and the use of antimony, and the beautifying of the eyelids, and all kinds of costly stones, and all colouring tinctures.*

*And there arose much godlessness, and they committed fornication, and they were led astray, and became corrupt in all their ways. Semjâzâ taught enchantments, and root-cuttings, Armârôs the resolving of enchantments, Barâqîjâl, taught astrology, Kôkabêl the constellations, Ezêqêêl the knowledge of the clouds, Araqiêl the signs of the earth, Shamsiêl the signs of the sun, and Sariêl the course of the moon.*

Michael, Uriel, Raphael, and Gabriel appeal to "God" to judge the fallen angels. Uriel is then sent to tell Noah of the flood and what he needs to do:

*Then said the Most High, the Holy and Great One spoke, and sent Uriel to the son of Lamech, and said to him: Go to Noah and tell him in my name "Hide thyself!" and reveal to him the end that is approaching: that the whole earth will be destroyed, and a deluge is about to come upon the whole earth, and will destroy all that is on it. And now instruct him that he may escape and his seed may be preserved for all the generations of the world.*

God Commands Raphael to imprison Azazel:

*The Lord said to Raphael: "Bind Azâzêl hand and foot, and cast him into the darkness: and make an opening in the desert, which is in Dûdâêl (God's Kettle/Crucible/Cauldron), and cast him therein. And place upon him rough and jagged rocks, and cover him with darkness, and let him abide there forever, and cover his face that he may not see light. And on the day of the great judgement he shall be cast into the fire. And heal the earth which the angels have corrupted, and proclaim the healing of the earth, that they may heal the plague, and that all the children of men may not perish through all the secret things that the Watchers have disclosed and have taught their sons. And the whole earth has been corrupted through the works that were taught by Azâzêl: to him ascribe all sin."*

72

God gave Gabriel instructions concerning the Nephilim and the imprisonment of the fallen angels:

*And to Gabriel said the Lord: "Proceed against the biters and the reprobates, and against the children of fornication: and destroy [the children of fornication and] the children of the Watchers from amongst men [and cause them to go forth]: send them one against the other that they may destroy each other in battle ..."*

The Lord commands Michael to bind the fallen angels:

*And the Lord said unto Michael: "Go, bind Semjâzâ and his associates who have united themselves with women so as to have defiled themselves with them in all their uncleanness. And when their sons have slain one another, and they have seen the destruction of their beloved ones, bind them fast for seventy generations in the valleys of the earth, till the day of their judgement and of their consummation, till the judgement that is for ever and ever is consummated. In those days they shall be led off to the abyss of fire: (and) to the torment and the prison in which they shall be confined forever. And whosoever shall be condemned and destroyed will from thenceforth be bound together with them to the end of all generations."*

The Book of Enoch continues, with Enoch explaining his visits aboard the ship of the Watchers, and his various trips to different parts of the globe. No wonder the rabbis and priests voted Enoch out in compiling the books of the bible ... the grandfather of Noah knew too much!

Was all of Enoch, page after page, made up? Contrived?

Ok, let's move forward 1,500 years and get back to Moses and Joshua, to see what "the Lord" has in mind for them.

*Moses Moves East* is next.

# 7

# MOSES MOVES EAST, THE ASSAULT

*" What shall I do unto this people?*
*They are almost ready to stone me. "*

—MOSES—

This chapter covers the initial extermination battles that took place in modern-day Jordan, east of the Dead Sea, while Moses still lived, before Joshua took over to lead the subsequent campaign in Canaan.

One unsettling claim of the Exodus story holds that after leaving Egypt, the Hebrews wandered for four decades before launching the attack on Canaan. The wandering seems to have lasted for 38 years, with most of the famous events happening within the first year of the Exodus, including the Red Sea and the Ten Commandments incidents. Then came the wandering of which little is written, followed by the final big year when the Hebrews left the dessert and in full-warfare mode, marched east of the Dead Sea up through Jordan, arriving north on the Jordan River to attack Jericho. As commented upon, the written detail of year one and year 40 appear very journal-like, so why did the journaling stop altogether for almost four decades?

The only things mentioned about the 38 interim years are a) Joshua's spying mission on the Canaanites, where he reported that the Hebrews appeared like grasshoppers next to the giants, and b) an early attempt by the Hebrews to attack southern Canaanite towns, which failed due to fortifications. Nevertheless, these two noted incidents frame what came next.

First, due to Joshua's resolve that the giants could be beaten, the Lord appointed Joshua the designated leader of the eventual campaign, and second, it was decided that attacking from the south was out, and that a long end-around march north to Jericho was the better strategy. Below, Joshua urging the people on:

> *Joshua son of Nun and Caleb son of Jephunneh, who were among those who had explored the land, tore their clothes and said to the entire Israelite assembly, "The land we passed through and explored is exceedingly good. If the Lord is pleased with us, he will lead us into that land, a land flowing with milk and honey, and will give it to us. Only do not rebel against the Lord. And do not be afraid of the people of the land, because we will devour them. Their protection is gone, but the Lord is with us. Do not be afraid of them."*

And so, in year 40, the Hebrews set out moving east. Yet the land east of the Dead Sea held a few proud kingdoms, and the Hebrews could not simply walk through uninvited, hence the pre-Canaan troubles with the Edomites, the Moabites, the Amorites, and the Ammonites.

But before digging into these precursor conflicts, we should dimension how big the Hebrew horde stood. After all, they had no transportation other than walking, no supply lines other than their flocks, and the women, children, and old folks traveled with the army. And so, the logistics seem impossible, one of the reasons naysayers consider the whole Exodus saga an invented mythology.

SUBJUGATED, however, keeps to its premise: what was written stands true, so we need to determine what was written about numbers to gauge reasonableness.

Before writing SUBJUGATED I had heard that two million Hebrews left Egypt, with 600,000 men of military age, and I never extrapolated these numbers out to see if they made sense. They don't! The column of marching people would be hundreds of miles long, and the flocks of animals needed to sustain the horde would reach 20 million or more. Water and sanitary measures out in the desert could not be managed. Plus, whenever Moses delivered a big speech, it seems *all* the people could gather 'round and hear his words.

Beyond these points, one must consider Hebrew population growth during their short captivity in Egypt. Only some 70 Hebrews—the descendants of Abraham—arrived in 1,700 BC and lived in the Nile Valley for 215 years. So, all told, how many people are we realistically contemplating?

Exodus never said two million. It used the word "eleph" to quantify numbers of people. This word has two usages. *Eleph* can mean a clan unit, or *eleph* can mean 1,000. One thousand *elephs* might therefore equate to 30,000 people using the clan translation (at 30 people per clan) or 1,000,000 people using the 1,000 translation. So, this *eleph* dilemma sits as the starting point of the controversy, further debated based upon the already practical matters described above.

For example, those advocating that indeed two million Hebrews left Egypt, argue that numbers like these exist in cities today—such as Manhattan, NY having two million residents—so they find it all quite reasonable. By the way, Manhattan achieves that number vertically—via skyscrapers—not via the tent city used by the Hebrews. On the other hand, on 9/11 while residing in Manhattan, I sat and watched hundreds of thousands of my fellow city dwellers choke the avenues, fleeing the city in about six hours' time, so practical, modern-day abstract arguments carry on both sides.

However, considering also that in 1,500 BC the worldwide population—including India and China—amounted to just a few million, it is unlikely that the Hebrews accounted for two million of the total. Modern-day Israel comprises only six million Jews. Overall, I side with eleph meaning "a clan unit," with the Hebrew horde sitting between 10,000 and 30,000 people. *Plus, they had the Ark!*

Let's move on to the defeat of Sihon and Og, the two Jordanian kings.

With their end-around strategy to assault Canaan by initially moving east and then north, Moses and Joshua intended to strike the Canaanites above the Dead Sea at Jericho, but they first had to contend with Sihon and Og.

Yet before getting to the cities of Sihon and Og, other kingdoms stood in the way, but these more southern people were related to the Hebrews way back from the time of Abraham. So the Lord instructed the Hebrews not to fight the Edomite and the Moabite cousins, but disclosed that the cities of Sihon and Og – which bear the names of their respective Nephilim kings – required extermination. Why?

Sihon and Og were giants, that's why! Og stood some 13 feet tall, had lived for more than 1,000 years, and upon his death by the Hebrews, they took his 16-foot bed with them and held onto it in Jerusalem for another thousand years, until Babylonia leveled Jerusalem in the 500 BC era. This Babylonian assault, by the way, was the event in which the Ark, too, was lost.

Here are some related bible passages regarding Sihon and Og:

*Israel sent messengers to say to Sihon king of the Amorites:*

*"Let us pass through your country. We will not turn aside into any field or vineyard, or drink water from any well.*

*We will travel along the King's Highway until we have passed through your territory."*

*But Sihon would not let Israel pass through his territory. He mustered his entire army and marched out into the wilderness against Israel. When he reached Jahaz, he fought with Israel. Israel, however, put him to the sword and took over his land from the Arnon to the Jabbok, but only as far as the Ammonites, because their border was fortified.*

Next came Og of the Ammonites:

*So the Lord our God also gave into our hands Og king of Bashan and all his army. We struck them down, leaving no survivors. At that time we took all his cities. There was not one of the sixty cities that we did not take from them—the whole region of Argob, Og's kingdom in Bashan. All these cities were fortified with high walls and with gates and bars, and there were also a great many unwalled villages. We completely destroyed them, as we had done with Sihon king of Heshbon, destroying every city—men, women and children. But all the livestock and the plunder from their cities we carried off for ourselves.*

After this, the Hebrew horde sat across the Jordan river in front of Jericho, their first true "milk and honey" target, and it represented the end of the road for one of the great figures of Homo Sapient history: MOSES. According to his best friend THE LORD, Moses would not cross the Jordan into the promised land due to that ridiculous incident of the water and the rock back in the Arabian desert. Dutifully, Moses died on a mountain top on the Jordanian side of the Dead Sea.

But before leaving Moses behind, the reader should learn what some surmise about him and his 120 years on earth. No one knows for sure, but again, taking written words at face value, it appears that Moses loomed larger than even the Exodus, a titan of Egypt in his youth, as follows …

Today, Homo Sapiens—the truly productive ones, anyway—deliver that productivity for a mere 30 years, from age 25 through 55. Moses led the Hebrews until the end at 120 years of age and launched the Exodus at age 80. Before that, he had time to do much more than modern Homo Sapiens can dream of. What might he have accomplished in his first 80 years?

Recall that he was rescued by Pharaoh's sister and raised a prince in court. Some say that "Moses" is not a name but a title meaning "presumptive Pharaoh—the next in line." Some historians connect Moses as general to Pharaoh's military campaigns farther south in the Sudan, which Egypt conquered in Moses's time. The theory goes that Moses—then called Tuta-Moses—emerged the conquering general. After the success of the campaign, he set up an administrative city to govern this vast expanse (the Nile runs 4,000 miles long), which Moses operated extremely well, so well that he outshone Pharaoh himself. This led to Moses fleeing to Media, across the Persian Gulf from Saudi Arabia, where he married a Cushite "African" woman and lived for 40 years before daring to return to Egypt at age 80, upon his first Pharaoh's death.

Only here, at age 80, does the Exodus saga begin. And when Pharaoh sent his chariots to slaughter the Hebrews at the Red Sea, Pharaoh lost his entire army. Records show that shortly thereafter, Egypt itself was conquered by counter-forces (the Shepard's), probably from the Sudan. I believe that Moses and his overall impact on the region was greater than we can envision.

His final recorded speech at the gates of Jericho before his death follows:

> *When the Lord your God brings you into the land you are entering to possess and drives out before you many nations—the Hittites, Girgashites, Amorites, Canaanites, Perizzites, Hivites and Jebusites, seven nations larger and stronger than you— and when the Lord your God has delivered them over to you and you have defeated them, then you must destroy them totally. Make no treaty with them, and show them no mercy. Do not intermarry with them. Do not give your daughters to their sons*

*or take their daughters for your sons, for they will turn your children away from following me to serve other gods, and the Lord's anger will burn against you and will quickly destroy you. This is what you are to do to them: Break down their altars, smash their sacred stones, cut down their Asherah poles and burn their idols in the fire. For you are a people holy to the Lord your God. The Lord your God has chosen you out of all the peoples on the face of the earth to be his people, his treasured possession. The Lord did not set his affection on you and choose you because you were more numerous than other peoples, for you were the fewest of all peoples.*

It is clear in Moses's final resolve that Nephilim genes required extermination.

# 8

## TIME & THE SPEED OF PHYSICS: HOW MUCH GETS DONE PER SECOND

*" Nature is relentless and unchangeable, and it is indifferent as to whether its hidden reasons are understandable to man or not. "*

—GALILEO—

### Unchangeable? We'll See

According to this book, we Homo Sapiens exist today in our present form due to three interrelated factors: creation (energy, mass, and light formation), "organic evolution (splintered primate genetics) … and Alien intervention (in vitro alien genetic implant). Here in Chapter 8, we'll focus on *Creation.*

Creation poses three main questions: First, who *is/was* the creator and why did the creator trigger creation? Second, how did creation physically unfold once the whole thing got rolling? Third, after the formation of things such as particles, atoms, suns and galaxies, what established life structures?

The *who and why* of the creator is, of course, unknowable, a claim solely held through belief and/or claims of revelation. And for thousands of years *how* creation unfolded also remained a mystery, but finally this functional question became fathomable once scientists framed the laws of physics and chemistry, able to envision these laws playing out within the various stages of the "Big Bang." The source of life remains hidden.

The Big Bang is very much a creationist construct. Though the deity figure launching the Big Bang remains anonymous, the idea of a *launch* by some entity sits at the heart of the Big Bang. Proponents claim that all the potential energy and matter that would become the universe exploded in one instant, super-hot, expanding outward, eventually cooling, forming the universe we see today.

Two men—and their work—"bookend" the mentioned advances in physics and chemistry. First, Isaac Newton and his insights with gravity and light in the 1700's, and second, Albert Einstein, when he envisioned $E=MC^2$ in 1905. Many, many others contributed along the way, collectively forming a unified view on *creation, time*, and *the speed of light*. This understanding of *creation, time, and the speed of light* might just represent the intellectual pinnacle of Homo Sapiens so far. Consider the following implications of Einstein's work …

According to Einstein's reasoning, as a space vessel accelerates away from its liftoff site, time elapsed on the space craft is less as compared to the expenditure of time at the liftoff site. And should the escaping vessel achieve the speed of light, time expenditure actually stops on the vessel, although it continues to flow at the launch site! Einstein imagined this via contemplation; the math equation came later. We will discuss the contemplation phenomenon in the *Plato* chapter.

And so, applying Einstein's maxim, if aliens could travel close to lightspeed, they might journey from Earth to their home planet in a week, though the Earth aged, say, 100 years during that time. Time simply indicates an abstract measurement of "how many atomic cycling (electron orbits) occurred." In the case of the Alien rocket, only one week's worth of atomic cycling occurred inside of the Alien bodies, whereas back on earth, 100 solar years of electron cycling occurred in local cells during the Aliens' absence.

Indeed, to prove this, relying upon our own humble "human" space program, we have conducted clock experiments, using two clocks.

One clock sits on the ground, the other in the space craft. When the space craft returns from its Journey, the clock that traveled shows slightly less time expended than the clock on the ground. Less atomic stuff happened in space then happened on earth, so less "time" elapsed.

Therefore, *NASA has empirically proven time relativity,* yet it remains the most difficult thing to cope with, as, day-to-day, we only experience "slow-motion time," with no one coming and going on spacecrafts to illustrate the more significant relativity dynamic. And to make the understanding of time even more difficult, consider this: time is dynamic in yet a *second* way.

The first way (just described) demonstrates that time—atomic cycles completed—moves relatively slower as an object travels away from another object, but the second time factor claims that overall, *time—photon/electron cycle speed—has been slowing down ever since the Big Bang.* Even Einstein assumed light constant at 186,000 miles per second.

This chapter digs into the implications of time—cycle speeds— slowing ever since the Big Bang. Assuming the theory true, we will suggest how the faster atomic times of yesteryear affected getting stuff done, things such as the formation of solar systems and the evolutionary processes of living organisms.

But first, before getting into Einstein's physics, please indulge the author and consider my anecdotal, yet telling, time observation. I will use it later to make a point regarding the *productivity of time.*

In the 1960's my family moved from the New York area up to Connecticut. It seemed that other than town centers and housing developments, an endless, sprawling forest covered all of Connecticut. Walking through these forests, I encountered vast stone walls built by farmers living there before the Civil War, some 100 years prior to my explorations.

Before the Civil War, 90 percent of Connecticut's land stood clear, endless farms with stone walls bordering fields. After the war, two things happened.

> First, easterners discovered that the Mississippi Valley offered deep soil without rocks, so those bent on farming might just as well go west ...
>
> Second, those who stayed put in Connecticut took jobs in the many hundreds of riverside factories that participated in the industrial revolution. Farms faded.

And in just those 100 years from the end of the Civil War in 1865 to when I moved to Connecticut in 1964, all the forests grew back. But in 1964, the only animal life I ever saw in these great forests comprised squirrels, possums, skunks, and raccoons. One had to visit special fields at dusk to spy deer.

Then an amazing thing happened. In the subsequent 50 years a comprehensive population of animals moved in, including coyotes, bears, moose, bobcats, fisher cats, foxes, mountain lions, turkeys, geese, and wolves. In just 150 years, nature reclaimed its territory.

Experiencing the speed of reclamation, I can only imagine what might have occurred in 1,000 years, or 3,000 years, or in the 4,000 years that have passed since Noah's flood. And I ponder further, what more could have been achieved back then, assuming time more efficient, allowing much more *natural atomic advancement* in each solar year than now possible?

With the conceptual table set thus, pondering the power of time to get stuff done based upon atomic cycling speeds, let's dig deep into the physics of *atomic processes slowing down*.

We'll start with Einstein's breakthrough, E=MC², which asserts that units of Energy (E) and units of Mass (M) can be exchanged: *different forms of the same thing, akin to ice, water, and steam* (solid, liquid, gas). But based upon the *Law of Conservation*, the total of both can never be destroyed or increased (this law is soon challenged below). The C² parameter, though—the speed of light squared—remains the more interesting topic.

As mentioned, when Einstein envisioned his E=MC² formula, he assumed the speed of light constant at 186,000 miles per second, with E and M implicitly conserved. But how could this be, considering the extreme condition of no mass existing at the launch, *with light speed the only variable able to offset infinite energy?*

In the 100 years since Einstein's breakthrough, many scientists found different ways to measure the speed of light (C), and found it slowing down, though erratically. What can explain this erratic slowdown?

The explanation: units of mass (M) in the universe must be increasing *without* energy (E) proportionally decreasing, thus instead requiring light (C²) to fall in order to balance off the MC² side of the E=MC² equation. In other words, not only can (E) and (M) be exchanged, but so can (C), the speed of light, as mass increases. Contrary to the Law of Conservation, the overall mass + energy sum can increase, as long as light slows. Sacrilegious, but if true, the speed of light suddenly comes into play as an offset to growing mass.

But how is mass growing?

Most agree that mass has grown bit-by-bit ever since the Big Bang. But they assume the proportionate reduction of energy, not light, made this happen.

But in the first moments of creation, with only energy in play, no mass yet existed—no subatomic particles, no atoms, nothing but expanding energy. In this brief setting, energy expansion (E) reached near infinite levels, with no mass (M) whatsoever to balance the equation. Instead, in place of mass (M) as offset, the speed of light ($C^2$) needed to approach infinite speeds to balance the extreme energy (E) levels then in play. Light back then moved at vastly greater (near infinite) speeds than today's mere 186,000 miles per second.

I consider this "creation launch moment" an *a priori* (self-evident) proof that the speed of light *need not be constant* and that it functions relative to the combined quantities of mass and energy ... not just due to objects accelerating away from each other, but also due to the quantity of mass in the universe. The fact that lab data backs this up impresses me even more than *a priori*. For more, look into Barry Setterfield on YouTube.

Ok, this speaks to the speed of light once traveling incredibly faster, but if there were no mass (M) at first, how did mass form?

Before providing an answer, please realize that since the Big Bang, mass has accumulated in vast proportions, including visible mass (galaxies), and invisible mass (tiny, preatomic particles filling every nook and cranny of the universe, including dark space and the space in which electrons travel while orbiting an atom's nucleus). Mass (M), today, is everywhere, clogging up space itself. But this still poses the question "How does energy (E) + light (C) become mass (M)?"

On one hand, we know how to turn mass into energy. Burning logs in my fireplace accomplishes this. But how is mass created from energy, the way plants grow using light photons? What exactly creates these tiny mass particles that have come to clog up every imaginable gap in the universe's fabric?

According to one construct, the generation of mass occurs when energy waves collide, effectively neutralizing speed.

This causes the weightless photon particles, no longer moving at the speed of light, to matriculate into mass, and to suddenly possess weight. Something akin to water freezing, a different state of the same entity.

Let's carry the thought forward. After the Big Bang, energy waves began to collide all over the place (at first with each other), and particles with mass formed. The gravitational and electro-magnetic properties inherent with mass-laden particles allowed them to pull together to form atoms.

After atoms, it was off to the races, and I mean *the races*, as light and electron particles moved so quickly back then that all of this mass generation, including the formation of galaxies, potentially happened in just a few "solar" days' time, as per GENESIS.

In the space of what we experience as one solar day, atomic processes operated *billions of times faster* than they do now, getting a lot more done.

The overall efficiency of time (gauging how much gets done per second), therefore, is a function of the speed of underlying atomic processes, which always operate at the current speed of light. When light zoomed, a lot got done. As light slowed, atomic processes slowed, and less got done each year.

But the Big Bang dynamic never stops; time will get slower still. Energy waves continue to collide everywhere. Mass particles form prolifically. More and more, mass saturates space, and the speed of light decays in inverse proportion to the ever-growing level of accumulated mass. None of the components—energy (E), mass (M) or light speed (C)—stays constant. Contrary to what we once thought, the Law of Conservation applies to all three.

But as reported, changes to the speed of light appear erratic. Why? My hypothesis: light speed collapses only after enough particle build-up accumulates to tip the scale. This need for critical mass to trigger the next jump occurs elsewhere in physics.

Water, for example, can only turn into ice or steam after losing or infusing a huge build-up of calories at the zero-degree Celsius and 100-degree Celsius borders. A watched pot never boils; resistance points are how some things—including light, energy and mass—work when changing form.

We next move to the question of how did things work when light and time moved with much more productivity than they do now?

As background, one should know that in referring to light, we really refer to all forms of non-mass radiation such as x-rays, gamma-rays, radio-waves, etc., of which light waves are just one type, the only radiation waves visible to our eyes.

As with ocean waves, radiation waves have an up-and-down motion called amplitude, with each radiation class having its own amplitude shape. For example, each light color has a specific up-and-down amplitude, X-rays have yet another amplitude, radio waves yet another.

But with the ocean, water swells up and down. What about radiation, what stuff goes up and down?

After a few hundred years of scientific bickering, Einstein stepped in and sorted out that light waves consist of particles called photons, which flow up and down at the speed of light. At that speed, the photons have no mass. More so, anything traveling at the speed of light becomes both weightless and timeless. Einstein said so.

Much greater expressions of energy therefore once sat within each atom. Let's apply this boost in atomic energy to living things.

Humans have around 100 trillion cells, with each cell holding around 100 trillion atoms. That's 100 trillion cells multiplied by 100 trillion atoms, which equals "a number of atoms in one's body so vast we cannot fathom it": 10,000,000,000,000,000,000,000.

Now take these atoms and boost their atomic speed by 10 and you get one pumped-up living being able to operate at a level we can't imagine, with internal systems humming, bodies virtually unable to get sick, and slow to age.

These super beings include the first *10* generations of homo sapiens, starting with Adam through Noah, each living for 900 years. These people lived for more than 10 times our current life expectancy! That is why I, at age 65, sit here typing sluggishly. My atoms are tired.

Ok, but what about other plants and animals?

Well, if in today's slow-motion time, nature could retake Connecticut in 150 years, then a 10-speed advantage would mean that an ancient jungle could reestablish itself in 15 years, not 150. Evolutionary *natural selection* changes within species might only take a few decades, and some animals, e.g., dinosaurs, could grow to enormous size.

Following the Tower of Babel diaspora of people in 2,200 BC. the Homo Sapiens could quickly morph into the current human races as they relocated around the planet.

Time (physics) back then was very, very different. "Back then," to reiterate, still required 365 days for Earth to complete one orbit of the sun (solar time), *but at the atomic level,* 10 times more atomic stuff took place in that year than takes place nowadays (atomic productivity, or how much stuff got done per unit of time).

This leads to a few suppositions regarding Noah's flood …

The first supposition envisions the amount of pre-flood plant and animal stuff growing within this high-yield hot house. An unimaginable abundance of organics explains the vast stores of coal, oil, and dinosaur bones found today, buried and compressed in mass graveyards by the flood just 4,600 years ago.

The second implication envisions the world's prolific ability to bounce back from the flood. The speed upon which the plants and animals retook the planet and then splintered into hundreds of sub-species could total many times our current expectation. The scene during GENESIS must have resembled the playback of a time-elapsed video!

The third implication is that higher atomic speeds drove higher plant metabolisms, creating higher levels of oxygen. Noah's body had fast atoms and his lungs had plenty of oxygen to fuel his cells.

Plus, fourth, being only the 10th generation, Noah's ancestral line had accumulated far fewer genetic disease mutations then we carry today. There was nothing wrong with him at all!

No wonder he lived so long …

Ok, with all of the above to set the stage, let's next dig into more detail on the flood and the post-flood time of Noah, but factor in this variable light-and-time optic.

Noah is next..

# 9

# NOAH'S ARK, THE FLOOD, BABEL & THE DIASPORA

*"Seven days from now I will send rain on the earth for forty days and forty nights, and I will wipe from the face of the earth every living creature I have made."*

—GOD—

One of the more astonishing findings of my research places Noah's flood at 2,400 BC, not even 5,000 years ago. The inductive conclusion for this date (no other explanation of the evidence makes sense) is the simultaneous formation of civilizations around 2,200 BC in Mesopotamia, Egypt, India and China, all—as we will see—by the grandsons of Noah.

The short timeframe of, say, 200 years between the flood and the major settlements, foots with the Hebrew claims of Genesis, with the Egyptian legends, with the Sumerian creation tablets, with the Indus Sanskrit texts, and with ancient Chinese written history.

The *Evidence from Other Civilizations* chapter will present these details.

For now, by accepting 2,400 BC as the flood date, and 2,200 BC as when the world's first civilizations formed via the forced clan migrations of Noah's grandsons, there were only a few Homo Sapiens on earth—all spread out. Since then, we grew from just 1,000 people to almost eight billion in 4,000 years (yes, we've become a problem!).

As the tiny clans spread out, they traveled with their Alien overlords, the Aliens themselves looking for new domains to possess as private kingdoms. An Alien trait appears to embrace "unfettered ambition".

Because the bible is so precise in notating the generations from Adam to Noah to Abraham to Moses to David, we can place Adam & Eve at around 4,000 BC, just 6,000 years ago, leaving 1,600 years from Adam to the flood in 2,400 BC. SUBJUGATED from the get-go has promised that everything we know happened just recently, and not as told, and this *Noah* chapter exemplifies the point.

*Noah's Ark, The Flood, Babel & The Diaspora* covers the geological causes of the flood itself, the ability of Noah to build an ark, the return of life on Earth, the slow growth of Homo Sapient population after the flood, the population level at Babel 200 years post-flood in 2,200 BC, the diaspora of the various grandsons of Noah, the main settlement areas of the Nile, the Tigris Euphrates, the Indus and the Yellow River valleys, and the morphing of these settlements into races. Here is a quote from Jesus:

> *"For as were the days of Noah, so will be the coming of*
> *the Son of Man. For as in those days before the flood*
> *they were eating and drinking, marrying and giving in*
> *marriage, until the day when Noah entered the ark, and*
> *they were unaware until the flood came and swept them*
> *all away, so will be the coming of the Son of Man."*

−MATTHEW 24:37-39−

Let's start with a condensed version of GENESIS 6-9, to see what it claimed, literally …

*So, the Lord said, "I will wipe from the face of the earth the human race I have created—and with them the animals, the birds and the creatures **that move along the ground**—for I regret that I have made them."*

*Two of every kind of bird, of every kind of animal and of every kind of creature that moves along the ground **will come to you** to be kept alive. You are to take every kind of food that is to be eaten and store it away as food for you and for them."*

*Pairs of all creatures that have the breath of life in them **came to Noah** and entered the ark.*

*On that day **all the springs of the great deep burst forth**, and the floodgates of the heavens were opened. And rain fell on the earth forty days and forty nights.*

*But God remembered Noah and all the wild animals and the livestock that were with him in the ark, and he sent a wind over the earth, and the waters receded.*

*At the end of the hundred and fifty days the water had gone down, **and** on the seventeenth day of the seventh month the ark came to rest on the mountains of Ararat.*

*The waters continued to recede until the tenth month, and **on the first day of the tenth month the tops of the mountains became visible**.*

*By the first day of the first month of Noah's six hundred and first year, the water had dried up from the earth. Noah then **removed the covering from the ark** and saw that the surface of the ground was dry.*

*By the twenty-seventh day of the second month the earth was completely dry.*

*After the flood **Noah lived 350 years**.*

The mission of SUBJUGATED assumes these types of passages "sincere accounts." Enlightened historical constructs are needed that explain what's going on. But before we consider the explanatory constructs below, I'll offer a few comments about the ark story. Generally, my comments comprise practical musings, such as "What about sewage, and water and air supply for thousands of animals locked up in a waterproof vessel for a year?" Another point: GENISIS refers to two of each kind ... Genetically this means two *dogs*, period, not two of *every* dog breed, the same for horses, sheep, etc. And rather than all of these animals, another explanation finds Noah carrying fertilized eggs of animals, supplied to him by the Alien doctors. Either way, after release from the ark, the kinds would easily "switch" (as discussed) into breeds and eventually splinter into sub-kinds. These things said, let's get to the explanatory constructs.

It starts with *Pangea*, the solo continent sitting astride the "water planet."

Before the flood, envision the earth's land masses joined together as one gigantic continent. Theorists call the single continent *Pangea*, and many accept that Pangea existed, as North and South America appear to have once fit snuggly with Europe and Africa. Chances are that at first water completely covered the earth, and Pangea formed only after a massive projectile collided with Earth, deeply rupturing the crust, creating the greatest singular "volcanic eruption" ever, probably dislodging matter resulting in the moon.

In this construct—years later—the intentional breakup of Pangea came about through the injection of anti-gravity forces into Pangea's fragile fault lines by our friends, the agitated Aliens. By accepting the existence of Pangea, we can explain multiple mysteries of Earth's past ...

First, it explains why North and South America fit perfectly with their eastern counter-continents, Europe and Africa. Hey, that in and of itself is significant.

Second, it provides the likelihood that Humans co-existed with dinosaurs ... Yes! Most do not know that 90 percent of dinosaur fossils are found in the Americas. China comes in a distant second. This leaves only a scattering of remains across the other 80 percent of Earth.

So, humankind, including the Simple Humans from Africa and the first Homo Sapiens from either Africa or Mesopotamia, may have enjoyed seclusion in separate biospheres ... and so, with how many dinosaurs did they actually share real estate?

Third, should the Americas North and South suddenly separate from Pangea and slide westward into the vast waters of our orb, what would result? Let me help you envision what transpired. From *Geology.com:*

*On the night of July 9, 1958, an earthquake along the Fairweather Fault in the Alaska Panhandle loosened about 40 million cubic yards (30.6 million cubic meters) of rock high above the northeastern shore of Lituya Bay. This mass of rock plunged from an altitude of approximately 3000 feet (914 meters) down into the waters of Gilbert Inlet. The impact generated a local tsunami that crashed against the southwest shoreline of Gilbert Inlet. The wave hit with such power that it swept completely over the spur of land that separates Gilbert Inlet from the main body of Lituya Bay. The wave then continued down the entire length of Lituya Bay, over La Chaussee Spit and into the Gulf of Alaska. The force of the wave removed all trees and vegetation from elevations as high as 1720 feet (524 meters) above sea level. Millions of trees were uprooted and swept away by the wave. This is the highest wave that has ever been known.*

A pile of rocks did this. Entire continents driving into the sea would cause waves tens of miles high. And the continents slid for *thousands* of miles, their momentum *incalculable* until finally they collapse against what we now call the Pacific Plate, as the Rocky and Andes mountains emerge, a vast buckling of the earth's crust. Who can deny this?

Fourth, examine North America's geological deposits. Once the continents let go, a series of slap-back waves swarmed across the sliding crust. Geologists cite six deposit layers in North America. Evolutionists believe these deposits occurred over millions of years; flood advocates explain the deposits over the course of weeks as follows:

> The most telling aspects of the six layers ties back to the fossil record, including fossil layers from aquatic animals up to Tyrannosaurus Rex. The first layers hold fossils of marine life, and these first layers stretch across both the western and eastern sides of North America, leaving an untouched corridor from New Mexico up to Montana. But each successive wave begins to close the corridor down, depositing hundreds of feet of silt, until the final sliver of America is submerged. All of the famous dinosaur deposits are found beneath this last silt deposit, as if, like Buffalo or Wildebeests, they stampeded north through the corridor looking for safety until the last. Whole herds of dinosaurs found buried together. Who can disregard this evidence?

Fifth, the landscape. And when the waters receded, great inland seas remained, temporarily trapped behind by the sediment layers. But water always seeks the lowest level, and after the flood, great quantities of water finally escaped, cutting a Grand Canyon through the landscape on its way home.

> **Side Note:** The ancient Chinese history book, the *Shu Jing*, cites that great areas of water were trapped inland and that

a great engineer, Emperor Yu, living in the days of Abraham, circa 2,000 BC found ways of draining the waters without causing damage to the dry areas.

Sixth, India. Universal belief holds that during the breakup of Pangea, India swept up from lower Africa and crashed into Asia, forming the world's tallest mountains, the Himalayas. Likewise, Africa's shift north form the Alps and the Caucuses.

Seventh, the aftermath. When the waters receded, many sea creatures undoubtedly survived, some plant life remained intact, but animal life? Gone. Dinosaurs? Gone. Insects? There are missing pieces, but the above explanation stands "most likely."

Assuming this the most likely explanation to explain the above, what could have come next? GENESIS says that Noah planted a grapevine as his first act and gives us no further information. Too bad. Noah, though, did have three sons and 16 grandsons, and the Genesis 10, Table of Nations, chronicles that much, as follows.

## The Table of Nations

*This is the account of Shem, Ham and Japheth,*
*Noah's sons, who themselves had sons after the flood.*
*These are the clans of Noah's sons, according to their*
*lines of descent, within their nations. From these the*
*nations spread out over the earth after the flood*

—GENESIS—

The sons and grandsons, and where they settled, are listed below:

### *JAPHETH*

Gomer—Europe Magog—Ukraine Madai—Iran
Javan—Greece

Tubal—Georgia
Meshech—Russia
Tiras—China/Japan

## HAM

Cush—Ethiopia Mizraim—Egypt
Phut Libya
Canaan—Palestine

## SHEM

Arphaxad—Chaldea/Hebrews
Lud—West Turkey
Aram—Syria

Either all of this was made up, or it is a "sincere account." To help support the above claims, consider evidence still present on earth:

Today, Ethiopians still call themselves Cushites (e.g. Moses's wife).

The old name for the Welsh language is Gomeraeg, from their ancestor, Gomer, whose descendants began to populate the British Isles from the mainland.

Mechech is the old name for Moscow, Russia, and one region called the Mechech Lowland still holds the original name today.

Libya is still referred to as The Land of Phut.

The languages of north and east Africa are Hamatic – after Ham – Noah's son.

Assuming a historical founding, we need to envision what became of this budding race of flood survivors. It starts with Noah living another 350 years to age 950, and his sons lasting only 400 years. After the flood, things changed, lifespans shrank, perhaps oxygen levels fell due to decreased vegetation and to new weather patterns that led to an ice age covering a third of the globe. But no matter, it all happened recently. If so, Noah still lived in Abraham's time, circa 2,000 BC. And so, the flood survivor mentioned by Gilgamesh, circa 2,200 BC makes sense.

> **Side Note:** The Aboriginal peoples of Australia, who spoke of a global flood and how only eight people escaped in a canoe do not seem farfetched.

Nevertheless, back then, after the flood, atomic processes still hummed as compared to now, and life took off again. Assuming Noah's clan held together until Babel, as reported, and that this repopulation expanse lasted just 200 years, then how many Homo Sapiens do we have in Babel, by 2,200 BC, considering eight souls in 2,400 BC?

According to the internet growth calculators I tried, the answer comes to around 1,000. That's it. After Babel, the clans of 100-odd people split up, settling in a few river valleys in the east and in the west, with the north still covered with ice. At some point population growth exploded, but not at that point, not yet. But 700 years post flood in Moses's time, millions were likely (five to seven million), some in Mesopotamia, some along the Nile, the Indus, The Yellow and Yangtze rivers, plus smaller scatterings elsewhere. A few would make it to Australia and to the Americas.

The takeaway? We are all descendants of Noah, it only matters what grandson and what daughter-in-law bore that grandson and to where they drifted ... The various locations settled by the Noah peoples are listed in GENESIS. You can look yours up, but the point remains: our common ancestor stands just 4,000 years back. Like dog breeds, Homo Sapiens are the same, just switched differently!

For more on the science of the Flood, visit *Genesis Apologetics* on YouTube.

## The Babel Diaspora, Pygmies and the Little People

Possibly the best, though least factored-in evidence of the 2,200 B.C. Babel *diaspora* of Noah's grandsons … is today's African Pygmies, who still live in equatorial jungles surrounded by the taller, very distinct Negro races. Pygmies are **not** small Negros.

The most illuminating aspects include Pygmy memories, genetics, language and religious beliefs, all intact from ancient times. Through mitochondrial DNA analysis (from the eggs, tracing the mother's inheritance line), they are considered one of the oldest unadulterated races on earth.

*Time/History* – As a marker, the Egyptian Pharaoh, Pepi I – certainly an Alien reigning soon after the diaspora from Babel – used tomb hieroglyphics to write about a Pygmy dancer transported 4,000 miles from the source of the Nile up to his Egyptian court. Pygmies apparently influenced and entertained the Egyptians for centuries, but the Pygmy people themselves – always cloistered in the jungle – were never internally disrupted. Even after Stanley – of "Doctor Livingstone I presume" – encountered the Pygmies in the A.D. 1870's, they kept their world private.

*Language/Race* – The Pygmies, who call themselves *The People of Ete*, claim their ancestors "white men". They possess a "Hamite" derivative language (from Noah's son Ham, and Ham's sons who colonized Africa), derived initially from the true root language of Babel which, in turn, drove many if not all of the languages on earth. For example, the Efe word for "my" is MAI, French MA, Spanish MI, Persian MIAY,

German MEIN, Norse MIN. There are hundreds of other examples like this, showing that Homo Sapiens once shared a common language.

*Religion* – The Efe believe in an eternal God who once lived with them (i.e., their Alien escort following the diaspora). "When he lived with us – HIM, giving his orders, and us obeying HIM – we were happy, we were powerful and strong, we were the masters". In their "original sin" tradition, they say that when a woman violated the word of God at the fruit tree, God departed, introducing death to humankind.

*Little People* – Today's Efe Pygmies, standing at four-and-a-half feet in height, are not to be confused with the legendary three-foot humans – *The Little People* – spoken of throughout all of humankind's folk legends, though Little People and Pygmies may be a hybrid.

Legends that Little People interacted with Homo Sapiens reveal the Little People night owls who squinted in broad daylight, hard workers, great implementors of earth and stone concoctions, like Stonehenge and the thousands of mounds built within the Ohio River basin, and firm in turning away from Homo Sapiens who mistreated them.

Legends also talk about **Pan,** the original pre-flood home land of the Little People in the Pacific Ocean, part of **Pan**gea, off the coast of today's Ja**pan**. Were the Little People a separate Alien experiment run before the Homo Sapient model? If so, they too were saved during the flood, and were subsequently dispersed by the Aliens, just as both the animals and Noah's sons were intentionally resettled.

Note: If this Little People/Pygmy topic interests you, research the various Jean-Pierre Hallet mid-1900's works on the Pygmy tribe he lived with in the Congo, and read Susan B. Martinez's "Lost History of the Little People" – a great linguist.

And certainly become aware of the Tennessee Little People of North America. In the mid-1800's, the New York Times reported that in Tennessee, 75,000 human skeletons of 2 ½ to 3 feet were uncovered by farmers just west of the Cumberland gap. These were adult skeletons, with molars and ground down teeth. Many newspaper reports from the time period can still be examined.

Note: Read Fritz Zimmerman's "Encyclopedia of Ancient Giants in North America" for nineteenth-century articles on both the Tennessee Little People and the Ohio Giants.

## A Time Aspect of Aliens

If the speed of physics theory is true, though 14 billion years of atomic activity occurred since the big bang, it all happened in a relatively short period … maybe not six days as claimed in Genesis, but in short order nonetheless.

As for advanced aliens, it does not take that much time for intelligent species to scientifically evolve. Look at us! Our alien friends might be no older than 10,000 years, providing plenty of time to develop their anti-gravity and medical advances.

Perhaps they are not better than us, just older.

# 10

# LANGUAGE, BEFORE 1,000 BC, A SLOW START

*" Every now and then a man's mind is
stretched by a new idea or sensation, and
never shrinks back to its former dimensions. "*

−OLIVER WENDELL HOLMES−

Before delving into Joshua's conquest of (almost) 32 Canaanite kingdoms around 1,400 BC, one must understand the primitive conditions of the time, especially in the areas of language and writing.

Pre-Homo-Sapient humans (before Adam) likely used a language of *some* sort, meaning that, in part, they communicated using words, and I say "in part" as many animals use means other than words to communicate. But the exchange of specific, spoken words certainly marks a first-ever earthly breakthrough, and it could have been taking root in primitive forms for some time, even true with the Neanderthals who came before the pre-civilization humans.

Neanderthals, those big dopey lugs, just may have had a small vocabulary, who knows?

As will be argued, language and writing in particular are the means to collect and store know-how, creating a platform to launch further concepts. The role of writing in establishing a knowledge warehouse operates as a prerequisite to civilization. But when Adam & Eve were advanced in IQ, making them Homo Sapiens, their offspring initially lacked the ability to write, greatly limiting their hidden potential.

Let's start this chapter by looking at language itself, realizing language is not a black-and-white phenomenon with all languages the same. Languages are systems of words, and some systems offer more efficient communication than others. The more efficient, the better the language works toward organizing thinking, allowing imagination to move current ideas forward to the next level.

That said, despite the high IQs of early Homo Sapiens, their lack of know-how and moreover, their lack of efficient written language certainly held them back, until taught communication fundamentals by their alien "caretakers" around 2,000 BC (3,000 years after Adam & Eve).

To make my language point, I *dare* propose *English* the best language so far, considering the following comparisons:

*English versus Oriental*—English uses an alphabet of 26 letters, a mixture of vowels and consonants that can be assembled to represent any spoken word. Many words are spelled similarly to the way spoken, though English spelling idiosyncrasies abound, easily tripping one up. But Chinese, Japanese, Korean, and Vietnamese languages are far more problematic, using discrete pictures for each word. One needs to learn and then draw a series of pictures to communicate in this manner. And in modern times, as new concepts and words race into play, the cavalcade of new Oriental pictures designed to "underwrite" scientific concepts has little hope of keeping up with the times, certainly nothing reflecting the spoken sound of the new words. Instead, they use English and mix it with picture words!

As described below, original Sumerian writing was also picture based, later copied by the Orient and by Egypt. And then somehow, alphabet systems replaced Sumerian picture methods, capable of enough words to support storytelling, a new ability just becoming available to early dignitaries such as Abraham, who lived in the Tigris-Euphrates region during the 2,000 BC written-word era.

But for some reason in the Far East and in the Americas, picture methods took root and they remain in force even until now. Overall, language locked into picture methods bears many shortcomings. English words: 400,000 (using just 26 letters)—Oriental pictures: more than one million, and the individual must learn English anyway to compete internationally.

Next, let's examine the European Romance languages that rose following the Roman Empire.

*English versus Romance Languages* (French, Italian, Spanish, German)—The relatively older Romance languages have two large inefficiencies. First, subjects and adjectives are gender defined, though this offers no communication value, only baggage. Does it really help to memorize a "tree" as being masculine or feminine?

Also, Romance languages have verb conjugations all spelled and pronounced differently, although some of this variation is also present in English conjugations, but not to the same degree. English: He *left*; He might have *left* earlier; He would have *left* … Notice that "left" stays constant.

*English versus German*—Though both use an alphabet, German often builds new adjectives by combining old adjectives, causing long, redundant words, plus it incorporates inverse, jagged sentence structures.

English typically creates a fresh word for every new idea or description, so that the meaning is precise, and English sequencing—subject, verb, result—clues the receiver in sooner. English words: 400,000—German words 300,000 (many German words also requiring gender baggage). Consider this:

> **English:** "We have a long way to go
>
> **German:** "Vielleicht ist unser weg noch weit," literally, "perhaps is our way yet far."

The above provides a quick look at how languages stack up now. You are free to reject what was just presented, but it still raises the question: "Who knows how language operated with the Neanderthals 200,000 years ago, with pre-civilization humans 20,000 years ago, or even with post-civilization Homo Sapiens 5,000 years ago?"

Undoubtedly, language stood relatively imperfect at all points in time, stifling communication and clarity. And for sure, one cannot easily overcome one's core language deficits. So, if spoken language has issues, then what about writing ... the function of recording complex ideas, the real foundation making intellectual advancement possible?

> Written languages outside of Sumer, robust enough to record history, did not exist until around 1,000 BC. Before that, crude Egyptian hieroglyphics and Sumerian cuneiform pictures existed on a very limited scale, these percolating around 2,200 BC. (post flood). Noah did not write. Adam did not write. No one wrote, except possibly the one called Enoch—ancestor of Noah, supposedly trained by extraterrestrials. We covered him earlier.

Early writing attempts were mere precursors, mainly used to keep warehouse inventory counts, with Egyptian hieroglyphic symbols amounting to only 900 "words" and Mesopotamian cuneiform about as many. A picture of a bird, a picture of a cow, etc., all virtually useless in conveying anything of complexity.

Let's delve into the Mesopotamians, of the so-called fertile crescent, to fathom the ascent of writing.

## Mesopotamian Civilization 4,000 BC (Adam) To 550 BC.

Considered the oldest civilization, the Mesopotamian historical arch consists of six major eras across 4,000 years, including Pre-flood People, and Post-flood Sumerian, Chaldean, Akkadian, Assyrian, and Babylonian eras.

These peoples spoke Akkadian and used cuneiform figures—notches in clay—to communicate in writing. At first very limited, around the noted 2,200 BC timeframe (200 years, post flood), cuneiform advanced as a workable language. Rather than using a picture of say "a noble man," a picture representing the condition "noble" surfaced, and this abstraction (separating adjectives and nouns) continued to evolve, resulting in a more fluent language. The Sumerians say they were *taught* to make this leap in approach.

To achieve this, cuneiform, once consisting of 1,000 pictures, is next reconstituted to around 600 "letters" which a writer combines to make words. Six hundred letters is a long way from the tidy 26 letters found in today's modern English, but still a big step toward efficient written communication.

Once cuneiform advanced in these ways, long-standing Akkadian folk legends, passed along until that point by word of mouth, could finally be notated, resulting in the first major work of literature known to mankind, titled *The Epic of Gilgamesh*. Noah *and* Abraham, both still living, and later Moses, *likely* inherited these stories and the underlying ability to write from whoever first instructed the Homo Sapiens.

King Gilgamesh of Sumer, who ruled circa 2,000 BC. (around the time of Abraham) had many recorded adventures within his written epic. In one, he meets an old man (Noah?), a survivor of the flood. This important literary find, of course, dovetails nicely with the Jewish flood version, which gives some credence that the flood occurred in 2,400 BC, or even later.

Some 3,400 years post flood, in the 1800's, *The Epic of Gilgamesh* was discovered on clay tablets in Uruk (Iraq). Since then, other Gilgamesh copies have been uncovered along with other stories recorded in this manner, some written around 1,800 BC, others as late as 500 BC. Written legends include the interaction of "gods" who taught humans things such as construction, irrigation, and writing. These relics speak volumes.

Also, many stone carvings still exist depicting the "gods" instructing the humans, with gods wearing what appear to be watches—perhaps timekeepers, communication vehicles, or even time-travel devices. The gods are big, the humans small. Don't discount these images.

Cuneiform writing was used by the successive empires mentioned above but dropped around 300 B.C., replaced by the Greek language once Alexander the Great conquered the Mideast. Isaac Newton postulated that the Greeks learned writing from *Cadmus*, who came out of the Mideast in the 1,000 BC timeframe (more on Isaac Newton later).

Considering that the Gilgamesh epic was written down in 1,800 B.C., and that Noah's descendants, including Abraham, came from the region in that time period, there may have been lasting cuneiform texts of Genesis and Enoch available in the time of Moses – just 500 years later in 1,500 B.C. – from which Moses crafted GENESIS. This stands another alternative to either divine revelation or "the Lord as editor" versions of GENESIS mentioned earlier.

Next in line is the Egyptian language (Coptic) which lasted from 2,200 BC to AD 1700, when Arabic ultimately replaced it.

## Egyptian Civilization 2,200 BC to 1,700 AD

*Coptic*, a four-thousand-year language, only survives today in the Christian churches of Egypt. Complementing Coptic speech, hieroglyphic writing began later, around 2,000 BC, remaining in use until AD 400, replaced, once and for all, by Roman Latin, and then by Arabic in the post-Mohammad AD 650 era.

At that point Egypt hieroglyphic meanings were forgotten, unde-cipherable until the discovery of the *Rosetta Stone* in 1799 containing parallel hieroglyphic and Greek texts.

Some historians believe that the very idea of reflecting subjects in picture-writing came from Sumer, and that Egypt followed suit, creating its own hieroglyphic concoction. The same may hold true of the Far Eastern picture languages that surfaced after 1,500 BC in China's Yellow River Valley, and later in the American picture lan-guages of the Mayan, Aztec, and Inca peoples, these lasting beyond Cortez and Pizarro until AD 1,700. Some peoples never moved beyond pictures …

But primitive language aside, the two inexplicable aspects of ancient Egypt remain: the pyramids and the shape of the Pharaoh heads— yes, their elliptical heads. To some, these two things go together as the Pharaoh heads seem alien, not primate, and hardly anyone believes that humans, just recently engaged in pottery, could suddenly have built the pyramids.

A plausible correlation is that *alien Pharaohs* directed humans to build the monuments, using the mentioned anti-gravity energy systems to move 70-ton granite stones around. No, the stones were not pulled hundreds of miles using ropes, rolling them on palm tree logs. Only a diehard "evolution or bust" type, decrying intervention, would go around explaining the construction of both Egyptian and American pyramid structures as a function of human propulsion. The same conclusions tilt true with Stonehenge and the Easter Island statues (I have personally touched both).

Even if massive human efforts could move these stones, why would people do this? Yes, today we build skyscrapers, but the human effort to do so is minor. If we did not have our machines, we simply would not attempt to build beyond our means. The ancients did not operate differently.

The elongated heads, though, are quite something. Evolutionists, rejecting aliens, claim the heads were constricted from infancy onward the way the Chinese once bound a girl's feet to keep them small. But we are not talking feet, we are talking brains, something not readily toyed with ...

More so, examples of elongated heads appear in both Egypt and in the Americas. Believe what you want, but no necessary purpose, such as indicating nobility, resides in restricting and shaping the growth of the heads of one's children. Nobility has been demonstrated repeatedly through other means, especially clothing. Wear a crown, but leave the skull beneath it alone.

The point: strange stuff went on in Egypt in the post-flood era, with people using a 900-character picture language articulating little or nothing. Some postulate that engineering is mathematical and not verbal, inferring that the Egyptians might have been good at math, not words. Yet all engineering, physics, and chemistry originate with verbal concepts, next translated into mathematical expressions ... just ask Newton and Einstein. Egyptians acting alone with their narrow picture-writing and worship of the sun simply could not have fostered ancient Egypt.

## Sanskrit: Let's Look at India

Sanskrit is the language of ancient Indus valley peoples in India. Its written form appeared pre-1,000 BC, the same time frame in which Hebrew and Greek writing coalesced.

> Sanskrit did not emerge from a picture-based system. The Indus race was Aryan, the same racial stock forming the Greek and Latin cultures in Europe, those who gravitated to letters. In India, the writing system called *Devanagari* evolved, still used today in more than 100 modern languages, including Sanskrit. Devanagari script has 47 primary characters, including 14 vowels and 33 consonants—not quite as lean

as English, but approaching English efficiency. Devanagari, though, has no letter case, and spelling flows closely with pronunciation, a fairly efficient system. Regarding numbers, India later adopted the Arabic digits, including zero, in the AD 700 timeframe.

The Indus people eventually adopted Hinduism as their core religious practice, a multiple-god, multiple-class view of existence featuring reincarnation, and the reassembly of old souls in each lifetime.

Here, a modern writer, Gregory David Roberts, explains an old Sanskrit explanation of how one recognizes one's reincarnated mate:

*"The ancient Sanskrit legends speak of a destined love, a karmic connection between souls that are fated to meet and collide and enrapture one another. The legends say that the loved one is instantly recognized, because she's loved in every gesture, every expression of thought, every movement, every sound, and every mood that prays in her eyes. The legends say that we know her by her wings—the wings that only we can see—and because wanting her kills every other desire of love."*

Ok. What else did these Indian ancients think? We will cover the Indian legends of aliens in the *Evidence from Other Civilizations* chapter and contemplate the many Sanskrit writings regarding *Vimana's*, the various flying saucers used by aliens back in the day. Among the things described:

*The secret of constructing aircraft, which will not break, which cannot be cut, will not catch fire, and cannot be destroyed. The secret of making planes motionless. The secret of making planes invisible.*

*The secret of hearing conversations and other sounds in enemy planes. The secret of receiving photographs of the interior of*

113

*enemy planes. The secret of ascertaining the direction of enemy planes approach. The secret of making persons in enemy planes lose consciousness. The secret of destroying enemy planes.*

These guys must be taken seriously. As they shall.

## Greeks ... let's look at the Greeks

Similar to the Indus Valley people, the Greeks are a branch of the Aryan race, just one more offshoot of Noah. Aryans skipped the picture-based language approach and probably learned to strive for an alphabet-based system using letters to approximate the spoken word, i.e., "phonics."

The modern Greek alphabet evolved around 1,000 BC, in the same timeframe as Indian Sanskrit and Hebrew (a prior Greek alphabet was lost to historians). Other regional peoples, such as the Etruscan and Latin groups in Italy next adopted the Greek approach, and, much later, the Celtics, Russian and Germanic peoples.

Overall, this written alphabet breakthrough allowed for the recording of complex stories and ideas, building a growing base of know-how. The dates of the Trojan War stand somewhere in the 1,250 BC timeframe, but likely the *Iliad* and the *Odyssey*, written by Homer, came later, in 700 BC, when Greek writing matured beyond poetic writing toward analytical prose.

The Greek philosophers who opened the door to many of mankind's advanced ontological, mathematical, political, and moral concepts came hundreds of years after Homer, in the 400 BC era after the Greeks had mastered analytical prose. We now consider these reason-oriented writings and their intellectual breakthroughs the starting points of the modern Homo Sapient trajectory leading to us, such as we are.

Ok. In those olden days, the new Homo Sapient peoples appear born with high IQs, though limited in application. But that's not all. Few of them existed, and limited population, as with limited communication, factors in understanding the ascent of the early Homo Sapiens.

## Isaac Newton Footnote

Which brings us to Sir Isaac. Most readers of this book know who Isaac Newton was—already mentioned as a foundation physicist in the *Time* chapter—but Sir Isaac also specialized in sorting out ancient history between the dates of 1,500 B.C. and 300 B.C., essentially from Moses to Alexander the Great. Newton spent a lifetime on this, with his book *Revised History of Ancient Kingdoms* published following his death in A.D. 1727.

This amazing work endeavors to accurately date activities in the mentioned time frame by correlating the diverse figures of history across Greek, Egyptian, Hebrew and Assyrian civilizations. If, say, an Egyptian writing claims that a certain pharaoh lived during the time of a certain Greek king, then Isaac would have a cross-footed reference to fix a date upon. The gist of his findings claims that prior to 1,000 BC, Homo Sapiens were but few in number and scattered about, forming tiny, so-called cities here and there. More, according to Isaac, the known historical events happened "more recently" than once assumed. Isaac, for example, calculated that the Trojan War occurred in the 900s B.C. timeframe, not in 1,250 B.C. as others believe, and that the Pyramids of Egypt are from that same era, not before. He showed that the Egyptians exaggerated the reins of each Pharoah.

He also claimed written language not introduced into Greece and Italy until 900 B.C. Isaac does mention Cadmus as the father of the Greek alphabet, but Cadmus, the founder of Thebes, lived around 1,400 BC, so I would need a one-on-one to nail this down.

Unfortunately, Newton could not dig further back to the flood civilization dates of 2,400-to-2,200 B.C. era, as the evidence needed for analytical purposes from that period only surfaced via archeological finds in the 1800's, 150 years after Isaac's death.

Still, I credit him for establishing strong historical markers, especially in the realm of written history.

Writing is the keystone to advancement!

*The increase of known truths stimulates the investigation, establishment, and growth of the arts.*

−GALILEO−

And now beyond writing, we have the Internet. Consider:

*The internet has been the most fundamental change during my lifetime and for hundreds of years. It's the biggest thing since the invention of writing.*

−RUPERT MURDOCH−

And now beyond the internet, we have Artificial Intelligence.

*You have to talk about 'The Terminator' if you're talking about artificial intelligence.*

−GREY SCOTT−

Ok, with the primitive nature of pre-1,000 B.C. Humankind established, let's check in with the boys, Joshua and "the Lord," operating circa 1,400 B.C.

# 11

# JOSHUA, 1400 B.C., THE EXTERMINATION OF NEPHILIM IN CANAAN

*"No one will be able to stand against you all the days of your life. As I was with Moses, so I will be with you; I will never leave you nor forsake you."*

—JOSHUA—

Upon the death of Moses at age 120, Joshua, probably 80 years of age himself, took charge of the Exodus project, working directly with "the Lord" to carry out their plan to exterminate the "crossbred" Nephilim giants still living in Canaan.

Back in *Moses Moves East*, we left the Hebrews traveling on the Jordanian side of the Dead Sea, quietly circumventing their distant relatives from Abraham's time, the Edomites and Moabites. But farther north, Moses's army went all out to surgically strike the two

Amorite kingdoms of Sihon and Og (both Nephilim Kings), killing every man, woman, and child in the region.

Then Moses died. And now, under Joshua, we resume the story, with the Hebrews massed on the Jordan River directly across from their next target, Jericho, a big "milk & honey" city. The people of Jericho cower in fear, with reports of the feats of the Hebrew horde having spread throughout the land.

After Moses died, Joshua made an opening speech to his people, reminding those younger members of the community of the proud events transpiring since leaving Egypt 40 years ago:

> *I know that the Lord has given you this land and that a great fear of you has fallen on us, so that all who live in this country are melting in fear because of you. We have heard how the Lord dried up the water of the Red Sea for you when you came out of Egypt, and what you did to Sihon and Og, the two kings of the Amorites east of the Jordan, whom you completely destroyed. When we heard of it, our hearts melted in fear and everyone's courage failed because of you, for the Lord your God is God in heaven above and on the earth below.*

Next, Joshua and the Lord prepare for the assault on Jericho by formulating a plan for crossing the Jordan river:

> *Early in the morning Joshua and all the Israelites set out from Shittim and went to the Jordan, where they camped before crossing over. After three days the officers went throughout the camp, giving orders to the people: "When you see the ark of the covenant of the Lord your God, and the Levitical priests carrying it, you are to move out from your positions and follow it. Then you will know which way to go, since you have never been this way before. But keep a distance of about two thousand cubits between you and the ark; do not go near it."*

This "do not go near it" command proves most revealing. What force of energy did the Ark house that would soon annihilate 30 of 32 Canaan kingdoms in short order? Joshua outlines what will transpire:

> Joshua said to the Israelites, "Come here and listen to the words of the Lord your God. This is how you will know that the living God is among you and that he will certainly drive out before you the Canaanites, Hittites, Hivites, Perizzites, Girgashites, Amorites and Jebusites. See, the ark of the covenant of the Lord of all the earth will go into the Jordan ahead of you. Now then, choose twelve men from the tribes of Israel, one from each tribe. And as soon as the priests who carry the ark of the Lord—the Lord of all the earth—set foot in the Jordan, its waters flowing downstream will be cut off and stand up in a heap."

Thus the second instance—after the Red Sea—where the Ark of the Covenant projects an anti-gravity wall to stem water.

> So, when the people broke camp to cross the Jordan, the priests carrying the ark of the covenant went ahead of them. Now the Jordan is at flood stage all during harvest. Yet as soon as the priests who carried the ark reached the Jordan and their feet touched the water's edge, the water from upstream stopped flowing. It piled up in a heap a great distance away, at a town called Adam in the vicinity of Zarethan, while the water flowing down to the Sea of the Arabah (that is, the Dead Sea) was completely cut off. So, the people crossed over opposite Jericho. The priests who carried the ark of the covenant of the Lord stopped in the middle of the Jordan and stood on dry ground, while all Israel passed by until the whole nation had completed the crossing on dry ground.

Next a most telling statement, one claiming that the Hebrew army consisted of 40,000 men armed for battle, a number that dovetails with my previous estimate of only 10,000 to 30,000 men, women, and children having left Egypt 40 years prior.

*Now the priests who carried the ark remained standing in the middle of the Jordan until everything the Lord had commanded Joshua was done by the people, just as Moses had directed Joshua. The people hurried over, and as soon as all of them had crossed, the ark of the Lord and the priests came to the other side while the people watched. About forty thousand armed for battle crossed over before the Lord to the plains of Jericho for war.*

This "supernatural" crossing alone reinforced the dread of all the kingdoms within Canaan.

*Now when all the Amorite kings west of the Jordan and all the Canaanite kings along the coast heard how the Lord had dried up the Jordan before the Israelites until they had crossed over, their hearts melted in fear and they no longer had the courage to face the Israelites.*

The assault on Jericho foretold all that would come to the subsequent 32 kingdoms. As the people of Jericho waited in terror inside the city walls, Joshua's men marched around the city with the ark, told to circle quietly. Why? After a few days of this, Joshua commanded his horde to shout and stamp, all at once. The sound waves collapsed every brick within Jericho, the city crumbled, and the Hebrews rushed in to kill any survivors. Obviously, the ark slowly destabilized the molecular cohesiveness of the brick material, allowing the sonic shock wave to serve as the final trigger. Below appear the commands of Joshua:

*March around the city once with all the armed men. Do this for six days. Have seven priests carry trumpets of rams' horns*

120

*in front of the ark. On the seventh day, march around the city seven times, with the priests blowing the trumpets. When you hear them sound a long blast on the trumpets, have the whole army give a loud shout; then the wall of the city will collapse and the army will go up, everyone straight in." But Joshua had commanded the army, "Do not give a war cry, do not raise your voices, do not say a word until the day I tell you to shout. Then shout".*

Joshua's journal—the Book of Joshua—describes the lead-up to the collapse:

*Joshua got up early the next morning and the priests took up the ark of the Lord. The seven priests carrying the seven trumpets went forward, marching before the ark of the Lord and blowing the trumpets. The armed men went ahead of them and the rear guard followed the ark of the Lord, while the trumpets kept sounding. So, on the second day they marched around the city once and returned to the camp. They did this for six days.*

*On the seventh day, they got up at daybreak and marched around the city seven times in the same manner, except that on that day they circled the city seven times. The seventh time around, when the priests sounded the trumpet blast, Joshua commanded the army, "Shout!". For the Lord has given you the city! The city and all that is in it are to be devoted to the Lord. All the silver and gold and the articles of bronze and iron are sacred to the Lord and must go into his treasury."*

*When the trumpets sounded, the army shouted, and at the sound of the trumpet, when the men gave a loud shout, the wall collapsed; so, everyone charged straight in, and they took the city. They devoted the city to the Lord and destroyed with the sword every living thing in it— men and women, young and old, cattle, sheep and donkeys.*

So that's how they did it.

From Jericho, many other events transpired as the kingdoms fell, but the common denominator of the campaign bore the complete destruction of entire populations. For example, read Joshua's report on the city of Ai, which fell following Jericho:

*When Israel had finished killing all the men of Ai in the fields and in the wilderness where they had chased them, and when every one of them had been put to the sword, all the Israelites returned to Ai and killed those who were in it. Twelve thousand men and women fell that day—all the people of Ai.*

In many locations, the local king reigned a giant, a Nephilim byproduct of insemination by the Watchers in the time of Enoch, 1,500 years back. And now, via the army of the Exodus, these genetic bloodlines finally ended.

But the mystery remains … why did Joshua stop at 30 kingdoms when two more remained, Jerusalem and that of the Philistines? The Philistine territory stood south, between Canaan and Egypt, a known Nephilim society. Some 400 years later David would fight the nine-and-one-half-foot-tall Philistine Goliath, and Goliath had brothers of this same stature, so … what gives?

The overall conclusion of this chapter considers the failure of both the Flood and the Exodus to rid Earth of the Nephilim-crossbred bloodlines, showing these efforts as the flawed design of mortals, not God. But with that said, what happened to the Nephilim between the time of King David in 900 BC and today?

I propose that their recessive genes would finally run out of mating partners, but not for a long time.

As presented shortly, many escaped to America, settling in the Ohio valley, eventually killed by Mongolian tribes (the so-called indigenous American Indians) coming across the Alaskan land bridge.

# 12

# EVIDENCE FROM OTHER CIVILIZATIONS

*" Mockery ends where understanding begins. "*

—ERIC VON DÄNIKEN—

In the upcoming quote, check out the battle that evolutionist Carl Sagan wages against Eric von Däniken, an alienist advocate …

*… That writing as careless as von Däniken's, whose principal thesis is that our ancestors were dummies, should be so popular is a sober commentary on the credulousness and despair of our times. I hope books like his Chariots of the Gods are used in high school and college logic courses as object lessons in sloppy thinking. I know of no recent book so riddled with logical and factual errors as the work of von Däniken.*

**Written by Carl Sagan,** in his foreword to *The Space Gods Revealed*—a book specifically written to refute von Däniken

This 1960s rivalry between mainstream astronomer *Carl Sagan* and outside provocateur *Eric von Däniken* is par for the course. Sagan's technique was to get the common man amazed at the scope of the universe, using his trademark "billions and billions" nomenclature to emphasize space's magnitude. This made him a "rock star", selling books and videos, and garnishing many TV appearances where he explained the majesty of science and evolution. *Eric von Däniken's* technique was the opposite, suggesting that startling events involving aliens happened right here on earth, and rather recently. *Eric von Däniken*—the alternative alien story teller—needed to be silenced by the mainstream.

Dr. Sagan was one of many famous scientists making their mark over the prior hundred years, and to get to the top as he did, was quite an achievement. But *Eric von Däniken*, Sagan's nemesis, was the first of his kind advocating Aliens, and in his *Chariots of the Gods* book published in 1968, he threw in the kitchen sink, claiming all kinds of firm evidence of alien contact. Subsequently, some of Eric's pronouncements were found wrong or flawed, allowing people like Sagan to craft *put down messages*, and more, to use the put downs to dismiss the whole proposition of alien visitation all together.

But for all the push back von Däniken absorbed for his audacity and a few rushed errors, the quest to understand alien involvement in our past was launched, and thousands of von Däniken disciples rose up over the subsequent decades including great authors like David Hatcher Childress and Giorgio A. Tsoukalos. These researchers explored every scrap of evidence on earth—writings, formations, relics, carvings—and filmed their work as documentaries, broadcast both on commercial TV, Amazon Prime and YouTube. Over my lifetime, the body of work cataloguing ancient physical stuff has become vast. And so have the findings of astronomy and the efforts of UFO theorists. I urge you to dig into all of these on your own.

**But note, neither Sagan nor von Däniken went as far as this book, which poses more than Alien visitation.**

Besides being taught a few things by Aliens, SUBJUGATED proclaims alien intervention at the genetic level, causing both our very being while simultaneously sowing the seeds for our very demise. Carl Sagan—RIP — would really not go for this extended proposition!

Another related topic includes UFOs. There is so much out there regarding UFOs that I will not try and catalogue or judge the evidence or lack of evidence here. Obviously SUBJUGATED starts with the premise that Aliens—able to master time and gravity—exist.

SUBJUGATED's unified explanation of Homo Sapient evidence "inductively" calls for, but cannot prove, alien existence. Though there are no dead alien bodies to view, thereby ending the debate, no other unified explanation exists that speaks to the genetic and historical riddles covered in this book.

*Evolution* stands **not** the viable "riddle solver" it claims to be, for all of the reasons already given. The exaggeration of evolution's role in the sudden ascent of Homo Sapiens just 6,000 years ago, only creates more riddles. Conversely, *genetic intervention* solves historical riddles, including: our sudden ascent, our ancient myths, the earth's geography, our ability to grow knowledge, our unnatural biological characteristics, our mental unrest and our political propensities.

With that said, this chapter touches upon a few more *sincere accounts* from ancient times that reinforce SUBJUGATED's intervention theme. Let's start with the Sumerians and branch out from there.

## Sumerian Creation Tablets

Sumerian tales of mankind's creation are held on seven clay tablets discovered in the late 1800's in Mesopotamia, now housed by the British Museum, London. These tablets are tedious to read, first because some of the cuneiform writing is missing, and second, due to the archaic poetic cadence of the pronouncements. Luckily many academics have devoted their lives both towards deciphering these and finding other fragments that shore up the missing bits. Some of the translated statements are given below.

As I wrote this book, people I discussed it with often wondered "why would Aliens go to the trouble of genetically producing the

Homo Sapient species?" The answer: according to the Sumerians "to produce workers capable of doing the hard labor of industrial projects like the mining of raw materials"—think King Solomon's mines.

The cuneiform tablets claim that before creating Homo Sapiens, the Aliens (the gods) had colonized Earth for such purposes, and that initially Alien beings assigned to do the dirty work, objected to and rebelled against it. To fix the unrest, the upgrade of primitive humans to become Homo Sapient humans was decided upon, thereby establishing a trainable work force—think China today.

Here is the Sumerian passage concerning the initial Alien work colony.

*When the gods like men*
*Bore the work and suffered the toll*

*The toil of the gods was great,*

*The work was heavy, the distress was much.*

In order to achieve the genetic implant, one of the Aliens was sacrificed to act as donor. This Alien's genes, therefore, sit within all of us.

*You have slaughtered a god together With his personality*

*I have removed your heavy work*
*I have imposed your toil on man.*

. . .

*In the clay, god and man*
*Shall be bound,*

*To a unity brought together;*
*So that to the end of days*
*The Flesh and the Soul*

*Which in a god have ripened –*
*That soul in a blood-kinship be bound.*

It is interesting that other Sumerian tablets also declare the first man created in Eden, a Sumerian word which means 'flat terrain'. In the Epic of Gilgamesh, "Eden", mentioned as the garden of the gods, is located somewhere in Mesopotamia between the Tigris and Euphrates rivers, though another theory places Eden in central Africa.

The original Sumer— meaning land of the civilized kings— surfaced 500 years after Adam, around 3,500 BC. It was a collection of small "cities", each city loyal to their own sub-set of Aliens (gods), who trained the new Homo Sapiens in the ways of civilization, mainly agriculture and craftmanship. It was in this era of interactive coexistence between Alien overlords and fledging Homo Sapiens that the illicit cross breeding occurred resulting in the Nephilim. This is also when Enoch, Noah's grandfather, lived.

## The Greeks

The Greek classics—the *Iliad* and the *Odyssey*—plus the earlier *Argonauts* saga (circa 1,300 B.C.), contain ongoing references to the Greek gods Most of the readers of SUBJUGATED have read these accounts and probably assumed them exotic fantasies. To put these tales in proper context, be reminded that there are two Greek eras, the "modern" one from Socrates' birth around 500 BC to Alexander the Greats death in 323 BC, and a much earlier one from 2,200 BC to 1,200 B.C. and a lot of years lost in the middle.

The older period claims Heracles, Jason, Achilles and Odysseus as leading characters, all battling it out with various gods like Zeus, and demi-gods (crossbred children of Zeus). In this *Mycenae* era, Greece had populated Sicily and the coast of Turkey, where ultimately it fought with its Trojan cousins around 1,250 B.C. (Newton says 900 B.C.).

This early Greek civilization had a writing system since lost, replaced by the Greek system that morphed into the various languages of Europe. The mentioned sagas were written down in modern Greek 600-to-700 years after they occurred, so there is room for error, to say the least.

But consider this. The ancient Greek tales of giants and gods parallel others of that era. Just as the Sumerians had specific gods (aliens) dwelling in each city, Greece may have had a similar interaction with alien overlords, including cross breeding—as both Heracles and Achilles are said to have come from a "God" and a human mother.

These Olympian aliens operated like this for 1,000 years. Overall, I put the Greek sagas high on the "most likely" scale for sincere accounts.

Zeus, for example, lived from around 1,500 B.C. to 1,200 BC. He first battled his alien kin … the Titans and the Giants … before taking the reins of Olympus. Zeus was born in Crete, and is buried there, after retiring following his third war, Troy. Why did he disappear?

He left once his kingdom disintegrated due to family squabbles underpinning Troy. Apollo, his son, had built Troy and its gigantic walls, using anti-gravity to assemble the stone works, as done in Egypt and around the world. So when the Greeks attacked, certain Olympians sided with Apollo and Troy, while others sided with Athene, (Zeus' favorite) and Greece. Zeus hated the whole dynamic. After the war, some of the Olympians, embittered, abandoned Zeus, though the Iliad does not explain where they went.

Odysseus, one of the Greek kings, was against the war from the get go, complaining that Homo Sapiens were being used by the "gods". In returning home, he was sabotaged by certain Trojan backers like Poseidon (Zeus' brother). Unmoved during this ten-year period, Odysseus maintained his criticisms of the gods, urging Homo Sapiens to abandon their worship of them. This political attack against Zeus, and the loss of Zeus's family became the last straw. A worn out Zeus went back to Create around 1,200 B.C. Even aliens get old.

Of note, Heracles, "son of Zeus", operated just before Troy, living perhaps over 200 years from 1,500 B.C. to 1,300 B.C. He was the right hand of Zeus during the war with the giants, and became the first Homo Sapient who helped carve civilization in an unchartered world about to be inherited by the Homo Sapiens, once the final Olympians left around 1,200 BC.

Likewise, Jason, the Argonaut, who lived in the latter days of Heracles, became the first Homo Sapient explorer. In 1,300 BC, we were "on the march!" Jason, BTW, had come from a family line that had alien roots.

## Chinese Writings

China was only colonized by Noah's descendant *Tiras* after the diaspora of 2,400 B.C. China's oldest writing – *The Classic of Mountains and Seas* – sets 2,200 BC as the start of the Hsia Dynasty.

Aliens appeared to have led Homo Sapiens to China, probably to set up shop elsewhere on the planet. Here are some of the Chinese *sincere accounts*.

The *Yellow Emperor,* considered the father of Chinese civilization, a demi-god (something greater than man, but less than god—sounds like an Alien), taught the hunter gathering peoples many things. Many historians place the Yellow Emperor at around 2,200 B.C., 200 years post flood, as above, yet others slightly earlier, in 2,600 BC.

In the ancient book of *Huangdi Sijing, or the Yellow Emperor's Four Classics (just archeologically discovered in 1973)*, the Yellow Emperor's lessons are listed, including: building shelters, taming animals, the five grains, carts, boats, clothing, music, mathematics and medicine. These are echoed in the already mentioned ancient Chinese book called, *Classic of Mountains and Sea*, both writings *sincere accounts*. I surmise that the Yellow Emperor taught acupuncture, as it seems an unlikely art uncovered by trial and error.

And like the Indian Indus River accounts of warfare amongst the "gods" using advanced technology (coming up next), the Yellow Emperor too engaged in warfare with other mighty opponents. He conquered all enemies but *Chi You*, who had thwarted the Yellow Emperor in nine straight battles. Finally, a woman goddess, the *Enigmatic Lady*, came to the rescue, delivering weaponry that caused

gigantic fogs and pounding rainstorms. One weapon she brought triggered by the pounding of eighty battle drums brought down enemies
of the Yellow Emperor, similar to Joshua's use of "the shout" to level
Jericho after it being destabilized by the Ark.

Finally, like Enoch, the Yellow Emperor, when 117 years old,
ascends to heaven in a "dragon" that housed 70 of his closest advocates. As said, these are sincere accounts.

> Note: The "Great Flood of Gun-Yu" ought to be mentioned.
> This took place a few hundred years after Noah's world-wide
> flood. An inland sea, left from the world flood that fed the
> Yellow River, broke free, devastating the land for a decade
> all the way to the ocean. Gun-Yu had a "canal" dug, to divert
> the water away from the cities.

After the Yellow Emperor's time, further Chinese *sincere accounts*
continued. Here is just one of many as told by Chinese witnesses.
This abduction account comes from a manuscript called the Da Li
Gu Yi Shu Chao, dated 1528 A.D.

> *On the seventh year of Jia Jing, of the summer of the fifth month
> and day three, there was a "guest star" which appeared, flying from
> the southeast towards the northwest, bright and shaped like a giant
> wheel, sometimes hovering high and low, and sometimes moving
> and stopping, and it was witnessed by more than a thousand people.*

> *At midnight, it appeared again, returning along northwest at Lu
> Tao village in Diang Chang Mountain and descending in the
> village. There was a stonemason by the name of He Geng in the
> village, working at the foot of the mountain, and seeing the light
> from the scaffoldings. There was an object shaped like a grinding
> wheel, yet big as a house, having all kinds of colorful illumination,
> which resembled men, but not quite men. They captured He Geng
> and brought him into the structure of blinding light.*

*Within, they extracted the heart from He Geng to observe, yet he was unhurt, and not bleeding. They spoke but were unintelligible. After which He Geng lost consciousness. In his dream, he was in a celestial realm, that was not of mortal, in view of the cosmos, of an empty void, with no familiar dwellings. There were people but not resembling men, like humanoids, with three eyes, and all of them, did not wear human-like costumes or spoke human-like languages. As he observed, it just got very confusing.*

*When he woke, he was at the work site, and when he returned home, he realized one year had passed, and family members thought he had been devoured by beasts. They came and observed him and found a red scar on his chest, which bore no pain.*

This observer had no agenda, no sci-fi movies to egg him on, and no scientific framework to guide him, and yet he reported this in such a straight-forward manner.

Moving on to India …

# India

From the Indus Valley, in the Sanskrit Samaraanganasutraadhaara it is written:

*Strong and durable must the body of the Vimana be made, like a great flying bird of light material. Inside one must put the mercury engine with its iron heating apparatus underneath. By means of the power latent in the mercury which sets the driving whirlwind in motion, a man sitting inside may travel a great distance in the sky. The movements of the Vimana are such that it can vertically ascend, vertically descend, move slanting forwards and backwards. With the help of the machines human beings can fly in the air and heavenly beings can come down to earth.*

This sincere account of Vimanas—flying ships—says it all. Who would make this up? How could someone in 1,500 BC make it up without witnessing it?

From the Indus River Valley, in the Mahabharata, alien warfare is described.

> *Gurkha flying in his swift and powerful Vimana hurled against the three cities of the Vrishis and Andhakas a single projectile charged with all the power of the Universe. An incandescent column of smoke and fire, as brilliant as ten thousand suns, rose in all its splendor. It was the unknown weapon, the Iron Thunderbolt, a gigantic messenger of death which reduced to ashes the entire race of the Vrishnis and Andhakas.*

This sounds like another Sodom and Gomorra nuclear incident. Is it all made up?

By the way, while in Afghanistan, *Alexander the Great* purportedly gave a description of "dozens of silver disk-like objects" entering and leaving the Jaxartes River in 337 BC. Alexander, so the story goes, then became obsessed with the craft and spent many hours in a primitive diving bell searching for them.

Overachiever!

Now to Mesopotamia …

## Mesopotamia

In Babylonia—central Mesopotamia—from the Hakatha Laws it states:

> *The privilege of operating a flying machine is great.*

> *The knowledge of flight is among the most ancient of our inheritances. A gift from 'those from upon high'. We received it from them as a means of saving many lives.*

From Chaldea—southern Mesopotamia – the "Sifrala" contains over one hundred pages of technical details on building a flying machine. It contains words which translate as graphite rod, copper coils, crystal indicator, vibrating spheres, stable angles, etc.

Then Egypt …

## Egypt

In Egypt, From the Zep Tepi saga (the First Time saga), When Gods Ruled the Nile:

> *It was a golden age, during which the waters of the abyss receded, the primordial darkness was banished, and humanity, emerging into the light, was offered the gifts of civilization.*

The Egyptians also referred to intermediaries between gods and men—the Urshu—a category of lesser divinities whose title meant 'the Watchers'.

The construction of Egypt's stone works clearly speaks to the existence of aliens and anti-gravity technology. Here is a summary:

The Pyramids by Graham Hancock

How Was The Pyramid At Gisa Built?

No one knows. It is one of the biggest mysteries ever.

The great Gisa Pyramid weighs 6 million tons.

Its footprint covers 13 acres.

Its length along each side is 750 feet, and 481 feet tall.

Half a million blocks were used in its construction.

There are supposedly 144,000 casing stones, all highly pol-ished and flat to an accuracy of 1/100th of an inch, about

100 inches (or 8 feet) thick and weighing about 15 tons each with nearly perfect right angles for all six sides.

More importantly than its size, is its mathematical precision and its earth-grid coordinates locking it in to cardinal True North, so precise within 3/60th of a single degree!

The pyramid incorporates the astrological dimensions of the planet.

When you take the **height** of the Pyramid and multiply it by 43,200, you get the Polar Radius of the Earth!

When you take the **base** or perimeter of the Pyramid and multiply it by 43,200, you get the Equatorial Circumference of the Earth! So, for thousands of years, this amazing monument has encoded the precise dimensions of the planet on a scale of 1 : 43,200.

This is not a random ratio. It is indexed to the Earth's wobble, and the Precession of the Equinoxes that accounts for 1 degree of movement every 72 years, (and 72 is a factor of 43,200, that is, it is divisible into this number by 600 times).

It also relates to the number of seconds in a day which is 60 x 60 x 24 = 86,400, which is double this number of 43,200. Where did this space-age data and precision come from?

For these many reasons, it is farcical or even stupidity to think that slaves built the pyramids.

The average stone block was about 2.5 tons, but some blocks were actually over 70 tons. How could slaves have raised these large blocks 300 feet above the ground?

The conclusion is that there must be a lost civilization that we have either forgotten about, or our history books have censored, as this knowledge threatens the current and misinformed archeological reality.

We are sadly missing some important chapter of the Human Story.

Sourced and transcribed from a Facebook video by Graham Hancock on "How The Pyramids Were Built." Authors Note: Ditto for the ancient stone work found all around the world.

And in the America's ...

## The Mayans

As described in the *Language* chapter, the Mayans – a two-thousand-year civilization – from 1,000 B.C. to 1,000 A.D. – used hieroglyphics and did not have a phonics-based system to record their detailed thoughts. Still, the Mayans offer four types of evidence for Alien interaction.

First, many carved figures show elongated skulls and large almond-shaped eyes.

Second, for a hieroglyphics-based people, they somehow possessed great astronomical know-how of the planets—*even the invisible ones*— and the pace of their respective revolutions around the sun, leading to an accurate calendar projecting solstices out to the year 2012. Go ahead and try it!

Third, their pyramids, which, regardless of the many far-fetched explanations claiming hordes of laborers built them, contained rare elements like mica and mercury, used in electrical and signaling contraptions.

Fourth, the *Popol Vuh*, a history dictated to Spanish missionaries in the 1500's by Guatemalan Mayans, portrays the Mayan *Genesis* rendition, example:

*Men came from the stars, knowing everything, and they examined the four corners of the sky and the Earth's round surface.*

135

This body of evidence is so compelling that government officials in Mexico claim alien intervention the most likely explanation. There are over 50 Maya and Aztec pyramids in central America, and the Aztecs told Cortez they did not build them, they just occupied them.

In 2002, I went south to Belize and took a two-hour dirt-road trip through the jungle to visit an un-excavated Mayan city. Only one side of the city's giant pyramid was cleared, the jungle still growing on the other three sides. Climbing to the top, I saw bulging lumps in the jungle five miles in all directions. These were the other covered buildings of a once-thriving city, miles in diameter.

When the Aliens were amongst them, the Maya thrived. After 1,000 A.D. with no further Alien contact, *millions* of Mayan people suddenly vanished. This is one of the great mysteries of Homo Sapient history. Legends of warfare amongst Mayan gods (kings) amongst each other, might explain the sudden death of 20 million people.

## On Easter Island

`In 1991 when I visited, only one dirt road penetrated the island. I borrowed an off-road Wrangler and literally toured the whole island in cross country fashion to view the volcanoes and the giant statues, the Moai. Could locals have carved gigantic blocks of stone from the volcano beds, sculpted them, dragged them, and stood them up throughout the island? Unlikely, but why? Why devote a society's skimpy resources to something like this?

Today, yes, as we have trucks and cranes that match our aspirations, but then, manually? I doubt it. I surmise anti-gravity commonplace in the Alien world. We simply haven't caught up yet (though funding for anti-gravity research has been provided by multiple governments since World War II).

And so, as I stood in front of the 1,000 Moai dispersed through-out Easter Island, and stared up at those almond-eyed, other-worldly monstrosities, my gut said "Aliens and anti-gravity".

## Stonehenge

I have visited Stonehenge multiple times, as well as experiencing many other stone formations in England, Scotland, Ireland and Karnak, France. Stonehenge is different. In comparison, all the other formations are dwarfed in scale, able to be built by the people of the time using their technology—physical hauling. But the Stonehenge blue stone components are 30 feet high, weighing 25 tons each, mined from a quarry 20 miles north. These, like the Egyptian pyramids, are positioned so precisely as to align with various planetary cycles. Quite simply, Alien participation is the more likely explanation for a project happening post-flood around 2,200 BC.

Stonehenge may not represent "beyond a reasonable doubt" proof of alien influence, but alien participation rings more plausible when staring at 25 ton rocks.

## Peru – The Paracas Skulls – "Hiding in plain sight"

In the 1920's, elongated skulls with intact DNA were discovered in Paracas, Peru – the Paracas skulls. Over time, six findings surfaced: 1) mitochondria DNA from the skulls (inherited from one's mother), is neither human nor primate, 2) the skulls are 30% larger than human skulls, 3) rather than the multiple skull plates humans carry, the Paracus forehead plate connects to a single skull encasement. 4) The skulls carry wavy red hair not found in other native Peruvians. 5) The skulls are only 3,000 years old, and 6) similar DNA has been uncovered within elongated skulls found in the Black Sea region.

Apparently, no one in mainstream science is digging into this collection of skulls held at the National Museum of Archaeology, Anthropology and History in Lima, Peru. Look these up on the internet.

## Summary

Of note, during Magellan's famous world navigation of 1520, a scribe, Antonio Pigafetta, was hired to journal Magellan's Voyage, a book still in print today. He reported ten-foot giants living on the coast of Brazil, and tiny two-foot people living in the Philippines. Renegades from somewhere.

There are many recorded descriptions from ancient times that speak to these kinds of experiences, and so one can only assume that the world of mainstream academia actually works in denial of what they are directly told by ancient peoples. Voices from the past contradict evolution's narrative of evolution-alone causing Homo Sapiens. Mainstream academics label alien advocates "conspiracy theorists", but it is they who run a conspiracy against written and relic-sourced history.

One should ask, am I to reject every ancient sincere account and stick to evolution as the total answer, or should I solve ancient riddles with more likely explanations, the explanations described in writing by the historic witnesses?

Ok, the above listing gives you an idea. But there is more coming out of America. Next.

# 13

## RENEGADE PRIMATE/ALIENS THE BIGFOOT SPECIES

*" Small shifts in your thinking, and small changes in your energy, can lead to massive alterations of your end result. "*

–KEVIN MICHEL–
MOVING THROUGH PARALLEL WORLDS

Having just covered ancient writings that focused on Homo Sapiens, we should not make the mistake of believing ourselves the only version of Primate/Alien genetics. In the next chapters we will visit with three of our relatives: Bigfoot, The Little People, and the Ohio Valley Giants.

We start with the Bigfoot race.

Today, one assumes the African gorillas the only remaining large primates other than ourselves. But the fossil record throughout Asia shows that species, like Gigantopithecus, once inhabited the vast Asian landscapes not yet populated by Homo Sapiens. It is postulated that these great apes along with The Neanderthals were terminated by Homo Sapiens.

But before their demise, Gigantopithecus may likely have been the baseline species that led to today's mysterious Bigfoot primate, explaining how Bigfoots communicate, and their extreme, almost magical, illusive nature.

Based upon recent sound recordings, like dolphins and whales, Bigfoots communicate, not with words, but through frequency variations, extending into high pitched registers. To hear a Bigfoot – sounding like a siren – visit BigFootBase.com. Link below:

*https://bigfootbase.com/bigfoot-evidence/sounds/#:~:text=In%20 1994%20Finding%20Bigfoot's%20Matt%20Moneymaker%20 recorded%20a,used%20to%20this%20day%20for%20 "Bigfoot%20call%20blasting".*

Similar to when Aliens upgraded primitive Humans into Homo Sapiens, foundation Gigantopithecus embryos were likely infused with alien neurons, but this time with a different blend. The neuron genes included an alien ability to slightly shift time, a fourth dimension.

Today, us Homo Sapiens navigate in just three dimensions – up, down and sideways – and cannot accelerate or rewind our movements in time like digital TVs. And though Homo Sapiens enjoy links to the world of ideas, and to other dimensions, such as those of intuition and ESP, we are fixed in time.

Sasquatch, the first Bigfoot, would not be so encumbered.

Why? Energy operates differently than matter. Energy particles, like electrons and light photons, have no weight. Each energy packet exists as a spread-out wave – like ripples in a pond. This is why one cannot pin point the location of an electron. Potentially it resides simultaneously in many locations across the span of the wave form. Today, we call this kind of thinking *quantum physics* – the physics of energy and time.

And though Homo Sapiens only began to explore quantum physics in the days of Einstein, our alien parents have lived by it in perpetuity. And not just in designing their time/space travel apparatuses, able to avoid missile attacks by "ducking into time", but also in operating their own organic selves.

By slightly shifting energy wave forms within, those with this ability can shimmy out of current time into an adjacent time cell. To someone stuck in time – like ourselves – the Bigfoot suddenly disappears.

The theory goes, that the Yellow Emperor of China (the Alien who escorted Tiras and the Homo Sapiens out of Babel to China), decided to try this faculty out on the Gigantopithecus primates. Accordingly, male and female Gigantopithecus embryos were manipulated. Out of this came the first enlightened Bigfoot male and, the first female … the Bigfoot versions of Adam and Eve.

And it worked, except for one problem. Once the Bigfoot offspring mastered this "time shimmying" ability, they decided to use it to hide from their overlords, an unintended consequence of bestowing the ability within the primate line. What is more, the hybrid Bigfoot species also inherited the independent streak that aliens are known for. Yes, libertarian Bigfoots were afoot!

And so, as the brood multiplied, like all liberty lovers, the Bigfoots wanted to separate from both the Yellow Emperor and the Emperor's Homo Sapient slaves.

As the escaped plan unfolded, some fled into the Himalaya mountains – becoming today's abominable snowmen. But most of the Bigfoot clan crossed the Asia/Alaska land bridge into North America.

Here they live today, known as Bigfoots, though American Indian legend calls them Sasquatches.

At first, the small clan settles in the Pacific Northwest, where they easily multiply and spread out across the continent. Existing alone for centuries, eventually American Indians coming in from Mongolia, moving east from the Pacific coast, and later Europeans moving west from the Atlantic coast, encroach Bigfoot's world.

As mentioned, recently Bigfoot voices have been recorded – jesting with those who dare invade their wilderness domains, with footprints sometimes found. But it is their ability to disappear in time with that slight energy shift which keeps them isolated, safe from the Homo Sapient race.

Through biological stealth, Bigfoots can live in many North American regions. Tempestuous creatures who can lash out at and intimidate invaders, and even take Homo Sapient wives, revered as preservers of nature, and sometimes connected to UFO sightings, … they, like Homo Sapiens, accumulate knowledge and history which they employ for their well-being in their own way.

Today, their instinct for danger is so refined that by using time shifts they can evade bullets the way their alien ancestors evaded missiles. Yet, a website called SasquatchChronicles.com lists 35 reported Bigfoot killings between A.D. 1800 and now. Link:

*https://sasquatchchronicles.com/forums/topic/list-of-bigfoot-shootings-in-chronological-order/*

If all this is not sufficiently bizarre, there have been many reports of UFO crafts taking Bigfoots on board. To look into this, visit MysteriousUniverse.org. Link:

*https://mysteriousuniverse.org/2021/05/bizarre-cases-of-bigfoot-and-ufos/*

These are not kidnappings but what appear to be scheduled meetings. If Bigfoots are part Alien, then why couldn't they have a particular interaction with modern Aliens, especially if both the Bigfoot and Alien beings share quantum physic attributes?

Don't forget, like the Sun, the Planets and all the Stars revolving around Earth, Homo Sapiens crave being at the center, the sole story. And so, even when considering if Aliens exist on Earth, this possibility can only pertain to us, the Homo Sapient.

# 14

## RENEGADE PRIMATE/ALIENS
## THE LITTLE PEOPLE

*" Sometimes their drums are heard in lonely
places in the mountains, but it is not safe to follow it,
for they do not like to be disturbed at home. "*

—CHEROKEE SAYING—

Where to start? First off, the *Little People* were not some sort of
Homo Sapient mutation – like dwarfs with mis-proportioned heads
– they were a separate, elegant race trying to survive alongside the
Homo Sapiens. At some point, they came to America. Consider their
plight according to the ancients:

### Pliny of Rome's Natural History

*"In the most outlying mountain region of Sythia we are told of
the Pygmae who do not exceed twenty-seven inches (2 ½ feet)*

*in height. This tribe, Homer of the Iliad has also recorded as being beset by cranes. It is reported that in springtime their entire band, mounted on the backs of rams and she-goats and armed with arrows, goes in a body down to the sea and eats the cranes' eggs and chickens, and that this outing occupies three months."*

### Aristotle's History of Animals

*These birds [the cranes] migrate from the steppes of Scythia to the marshlands south of Egypt where the Nile has its source. And the story is not fabulous. There is in reality a race of dwarfish men, and the horses are little in proportion, and the men live in caves underground.*

The tiny beings mentioned are not to be confused with today's Pygmies of central Africa who, at 4 & 1/2 feet, inherited the "Pygmy" moniker from the original pygmies-of-legend who roamed the earth thousands of years ago.

Folk law abounds about this lost race inhabiting earth before the spread of Homo Sapiens. The "Little People" as called, were everywhere, tiny human-looking, red-haired beings just two-to-three feet tall, living in caves, mainly vegetarian, with squinty eyes, generally operating at night, willing to help, but quick to find fault, and often playing the role of tricksters. This undisputed description of them is universal, and so we must not ponder their existence, but instead explain where they came from and how and if they ended.

Legends insist that they lived before the Homo Sapiens, making the Little People a first edition Alien experiment – primates upgraded into a usable species of underground mine workers. And though different from the second edition *Homo Sapiens*, genetically, *Little People* might have been close enough to cross breed with us, hence the modern day Pygmies of the Congo jungle.

But what of the original 3-foot species? Thousands of folk legends from every culture say the Little People slowly retreated to find remote virgin pockets to survive in. As a species, they ultimately clung to just a few places – such as Indonesia and the Americas. Until then, they overlapped with Homo Sapiens, sometimes cooperatively, sometimes via interbreeding, sometimes as slaves and sometimes by being slaughtered.

But do not overlook that both the Little People and the Homo Sapient primates shared an important link; they were both part Alien.

Still, as interesting as the Little People "genetic design" turned out, ultimately they were not what was hoped for by their alien scientists. Little People hated the sun, they lived underground, and they remained obstinate, timid primates, overly dependent upon their environment, not showing enough of that "alien spunk".

Oh well, we'll do better next time with our improved concoction: the aggressive Homo Sapiens, who will want to dominate nature.

Besides the shout out in the Iliad, it also was written that around 1,400 B.C., Little People in Libya climbed onto a sleeping Heracles trying to "tie him down", though the makeshift bonds were easily discarded once the hero awoke. What pests they were!

As well, Saint Augustine of A.D. 400 – the super intellect of Christianity – who pondered the world's disparate human forms in his **City of God** book, by asking *"Whether Certain Monstrous Races of Men Are Derived From the Stock of Adam or Noah's Sons"*, never contemplated that some of these known aberrant beings were simply genetically produced either by alien design or by random cross breeding of alien-designed beings. What a mess!

And here is the big shocker: Certainly Noah and his sons were not the only ones saved from the flood. Many Little People who originally resided in "Pan" – a landmass part of **Pan**gea east of Ja**pan** *(notice the "pan")* – were saved when Pan sunk during the flood.

Once saved, the Little People – mainly vegetarians who could immediately survive without meat – were quickly re-instated by the aliens upon the rapidly recovering earth. Conversely, Noah's offspring had no choice but to give the animal kingdom time to re-establish itself, needing to wait 200 years beyond Babel for Homo Sapiens to spread out to the Earth's corners.

Because Homer's *Iliad* – that mentions the Little People – places the Trojan War occurring sometime around 1,250 B.C., it must be after this time, say 1,000 B.C., that, in earnest and fear, the Little People race started its defensive migration out of Eurasia, ultimately depositing themselves in South East Asia, the British Isles and ultimately America, and of all places – in Tennessee. Yes, they could have walked to Malaysia, but the question is, how did they get to Tennessee and how did they end there? You may be asking for proof of this Tennessee story line.

In 1875, the *New York Times* printed an extensive article reporting that since 1820 thousands of shallow graves with "little people" had been dug up by farming ploughs near Sparta Tennessee, right beyond the Cumberland gap. First considered the graves of children, scientists from the Smithsonian and elsewhere eventually confirmed them small-bodied adults with mature, ground-down molars. But due to shallow graves and scientific neglect, the remains were plowed under.

An estimate of 75,000 Pygmy graves were destroyed by local Tennessee farmers. Next, throughout the 20th century, in both North Carolina and Tennessee, many underground dirt tunnels 4-feet in height leading to underground chambers were uncovered – their humble abodes.

Fortunately, in modern times, another find was made. Enter: *Homo floresiensis* – the real-life "Hobbits" of Indonesia. Found in A.D. 2,000 preserved in a cave on an isolated island, this ancient race was discovered with intact skulls and stone tools, also 2-to-3 feet in stature, deemed "pre-human" and called Hobbits by some and *Homo floresiensis* by anthropologists who – as is the want of today's geologists and anthropologists – claimed them a million years old.

Nonetheless, somehow, the Indonesian branch of tiny travelers, mentioned by Magellan in 1520, must have gotten there, even if by boat.

And let one not forget that Little People abound in Irish, Welsh and Scottish legends, who for hundreds of years lived cooperatively with the Celts until the Celtic crossover to Christianity took place in the A.D. 500 era. After that, the Little People were hunted down, not just in the British Isles, but throughout all of Europe out to the Ural Mountains of Russia.

Yet they may still survive. In 1820, the official census of Kauai Hawaii – where I visited – listed 65 "Menehune", 3-foot Little People, the descendants of Pan, as part of the official population, who according to Kauai legend, lived there in the Nepali coast valleys (which I visited in 1991) even before the Polynesians.

And so, one needs to assemble a more likely explanation for all of this besides it being fodder for U.K. fantasy films or it being used as invented "descent of man" evidence cited by the many enthusiasts of Darwinian evolution.

Back in 1,000 B.C., the Little People still had many relocation choices. The Celtics of the British Isles would not arrive for many centuries, the Orientals from Asia had not reached the thousands of islands of Indonesia, and the Mongol tribes coming across the land bridge into North America would not move east *from* the Pacific Coast for a thousand years or more. Instead these Mongolian immigrants at first drifted south into Central and South America. In 1,000 B.C., the Little People were still safe.

Later, as **Mongolian-American** tribes finally made contact with these American renegades, they gathered stories like the following about the Little People:

The Mohegans describe small people who lived below Mohegan Hill in Connecticut. They were not to be spoken about during the summer when they were active, and not to be stared at; otherwise, they would freeze you and steal your things. In return for the food and respect, they taught how to grow corn and use healing plants.

The Eskasoni in Canada say that little people lived on a hill in Nova Scotia. Children were told not to go near it, lest they be stolen.

The Shoshone tribe in the Rocky Mountains tell of little people who used bows and poisoned arrows to keep trespassers away.

The Choctaw called them Kwanikosha, who supposedly kidnapped boys to test them and figure out their nature.

The Cherokee tribe believed in three different types of Little People: the Laurels, the Rocks, and the Dogwoods. They ranged from being good and helpful to being purely *malicious*.


The question becomes, did the American Little People emigrate from Ireland or from Indonesia? Considering that they settled near the Cumberland Gap, a guess says they came across the Atlantic, found the North American eastern seaboard, marched inland through the Gap and hid amongst the Allegheny mountains.

Considering their size, and wondering how they could cross a vast ocean, one can also guess that they walked across the Alaska land bridge and made their way east across an empty American land not yet populated by dangerous Mongolian-Americans.

No matter how achieved, any Little People migration path represents an extraordinary epic showing immense skill and grit.

Once in Tennessee, finally in a secure isolation, they would live for 2,000 years before the Cherokee moved east to greet them in the A.D. 1,200 time frame. But there may be another path-to-Tennessee.

As will be seen in the subsequent Ohio Giants' research, during the just-mentioned 2,000 year American chapter, the 3-foot Tennessee Little People somehow lived in peace adjacent to the Ohio mound-builder Giants, who reached 7-to-9 feet in height.

Considering that global legends of the Little People claim them hyper-productive builders, to survive, the Little People obviously had some meaningful alliance with the Giants, probably as the nighttime labor force constructing the thousands of earth works built from the Great Lakes down through the Ohio and Mississippi river valleys. A labor exchange for food arrangement.

Which leads to this likely explanation. When the Nephilim Giants escaped Israel and later abandoned their British Isle outpost, they brought some of the Little People with them. In America, Little People and Giants coexisted until the Giants were rubbed out by the Iroquois, and the Cherokees arrived to create new cooperative alliances with the Little People. Cherokee folk law describes the Little People as follows.

Said to remain invisible most of the time, watching humans from afar, inhabiting the most remote mountain peaks and darkest caves. Known to appear to the Cherokee during times of need, fiercely protective of the tribe, and would rally together with forces of invisible warriors to drive away enemies.

They constructed elaborate townhouses underground or within mountains. Humans who were lost or injured often told of being brought to these subterranean homes to be nursed back to health, and some Cherokee were said to even go off to live with them permanently.

The Little People were capable of doing good deeds for people who treated them with respect. However, to look upon one was bad luck, potentially resulting in premature death. Usually, those who encountered the Little People were warned by them not to tell others. It is also considered bad luck to even speak of the Little People.

When humans built homes near the Little People, it was important to leave food for them and not to block any of their paths. If the little beings were pleased, they did chores

149

at night, like plowing fields and harvesting crops, as the Little People once did in Ireland. Sometimes the people in the house heard the work being done, but knew not to look outside.

When the Cherokees were driven out of the Cumberland area in the 1830s – during the dreadful *Trail of Tears* clearances – supposedly a few Little People families went with them, but most were left behind. After this, no further mention of the American Little People surfaced.

Yet according to Cherokee legend, the Little People, like Sasquatch, have the ability to duck into adjacent time cells. Possibly they survive, hidden away in their underground biospheres.

Next, we meet the unlikely partners of the Little People, the escaping Nephilim giants coming out of Palestine.

# 15

# THE OHIO GIANTS

*" Springfield, O., April 7.—A giant skeleton of
a man has been unearthed on the Woolverton farm.
It measures eight feet from the top of the leg to the
ankles, the feet being missing. The skull Is large enough
to fit as a helmet over the average man's head. "*

—OHIO NEWSPAPER, 1800'S—

Finally, the just mentioned Ohio Giants ...

Moses, Joshua and their Exodus exploits took place circa 1,400 B.C., with the Hebrew army attempting to kill every crossbred Nephilim man, woman and child living in Jordan and Israel ... including King Og, the 13-foor giant, and all others across 32 kingdoms. How many escaped?

1,400 B.C. was just 1,000 years after the separation of Noah's grandsons out of Babel. In 1,400 B.C., few people lived on earth, possibly only a few hundred thousand, and so there were plenty of places where one could hide from the aggressive Homo Sapiens.

Also at the time, a retreating ice age still held sea levels down, and vast, open shore lines served as pathways allowing one to quickly move from place to place. More, in 1,400 B.C., the British Isles were connected to mainland Europe by a valley called Doggerland. The sea waters would only rise up over the next 1,000 years creating the islands we know today.

And so, back then, one could walk to Ireland from the Mideast along the open coast, unperturbed by others.

Stonehenge, said to be built by the "Beaker People" circa 2,200 B.C., is the world's most famous circular soil and rock "henge". The Beaker People were a branch of the Little People, just explained above. Recall, that the Little People specialized in mining and earth-oriented work, were actually bred to do so by aliens before the start of Homo Sapiens in 4,000 B.C. timeframe. Later, henge building became the passion of the Britannic Little People.

Since the flood of 2,400 B.C., the Beaker's, therefore, were able to cultivate the British Isles their way, and across many centuries they built henges – temples to the sun – throughout the reaches of Beaker territory. But their isolation ended when this race of 3-footers suddenly met a race of 8-footers walking up their beach! The Nephilim had arrived.

But the two races find common ground. Nephilim giants appreciate the work ethic of the Little People, and the Little People appreciate the higher civilization benefits of agriculture and sea travel brought in from Mesopotamia. The two races live in harmony in Britannia for six hundred years from 1,400 B.C. up until the 800 B.C. Celtic invasion of the Islands.

By then, Nephilim giants had already explored the North American coastline, the Saint Laurence River and the Great Lakes, aware of copper deposits in the Great Lake region. To this day, the remnants of their mine still stands on a Great Lake island. No housing or graves are found at the site, so copper mining proved a seasonal, once-a-year adventure made by the hardiest Giants and any hardy Little People who worked for them underground in the mines.

For more on the copper mines, visit GreaterAncestors.com

*https://greaterancestors.com/great-copper-mines-of-michigan/*

This site by Chris L Lesley is a gold mine!

And so, once the Celtic hoards swarmed the western islands – coming in from Spain and France – many of the British Giant/Little People families decided to move their clans west across the ocean into the empty but familiar lands of the Ohio.

How do we know this?

The henges of Ohio and the skull remains found inside of the Ohio henges generally match the henge designs and the remains of the Beaker era people of Britain and Ireland.

Once in America the two races continue to work symbiotically, but the Little People set up their own territory further south against the Smoky Mountains of Tennessee, with mountainous terrain their preferred natural environment for housing the families. But still, every spring, as in the days of seafaring copper mining, young Little People travel north to work the mines and the henges that they still build for sun worship, but now also purpose as towns and burial tombs for the Nephilim Giant chiefs.

And so it was, for 2,000 years, from 800 B.C. until A.D. 1,200, as only in A.D. 1,200 did the Mongolian-American tribes from the west come across the Mississippi. Many, many tribes arrived, none of whom wrote, with all of their history regarding the Ohio Giants verbally passed generation to generation.

Verbal history is fragile. Furthermore, by A.D. 1,900, the tribes themselves begin to melt away into the modern era, and so, even oral history dried up. Only the notated A.D. 1,800 exchanges between European settlers and older Indians remain to tell the story.

They report the Giants white people with red and sometimes yellow hair, many around 6-foot, but the noble families, even the woman, standing 7-to-9 feet in height. For generations, the Giants held their own against the incoming Iroquois-Mongolian tribes, but

A.D. 1,700 Indian folk law says that the Ohio Giants were finally exterminated "some 300 years prior", around A.D. 1,400. It was then that the Cherokees slipped in south of the Iroquois, forging an alliance with the now abandoned Little People.

So what did the English American settlers think of all of this?

*The eyes of that species of extinct Giants, whose bones fill the mounds of America, have gazed on Niagara, as ours do now.*

–ABRAHAM LINCOLN–

Back in Lincoln's time of 1838, as the English stock of America pushed into the wilderness, they routinely found skeletons of buried giants, 7-to-9 feet in height, usually found in burial mounds. It was common knowledge that another race had dominated America before the more recent Mongolian-American tribes moved in, tribes such as the Iroquois, etc.

Most of the skeletal remains found inside the mounds were reported by local newspapers (articles still intact), faithfully sent by locals to the Smithsonian Institute in Washington D.C. But by 1900, the thousands of skeletal remains sent to Washington all "disappeared", and thereafter, the Smithsonian denied their existence altogether.

This about-face regarding America's history came from the top of the U.S. government. As a policy statement, in 1889, John Wesley Powell, the head of the Bureau of Ethnology at the Smithsonian Institute in Washington, D.C., pronounced:

*"Artifacts found prior to Christopher Columbus's arrival, would be considered illegitimate by the Smithsonian. Only the savage Indian culture would be observed."*

Since then, as the modern generations came and went, the very idea of giants faded from the American mind, and in more recent

154

years even the mention of giants causes a backlash of ridicule by the scientific community. The "giant thing," in America, was successfully shuttered— no remaining evidence, no remaining memories.

Yet hundreds of A.D. 1,800's newspaper accounts survive.

Legend has it that at the end, the Iroquois encircled the last Giants on Sand Island, beneath the Ohio river falls, exterminating the nine-foot chief and all of his clan. The American Nephilim were no more.

However, their "Michigan copper" from the Great Lake mines – having singular impurities – does show up in archeological prizes found world-wide. The copper survives, and yet the Ohio Giants are never mentioned.

Why are all of these back story examples ignored by modern academics?

# 16

## COLLUSION—HISTORY SUPPRESSED, PRIMATE CONTROL OVER NARRATIVES

*" Faith is believing in things you know ain't so. "*

—MARK TWAIN—

Below we unravel the purpose of this "deception via omission," tactic used by the primate-socialist to distort reality, but first, a look at the old and new testaments of the bible, themselves byproducts of institutional agendas.

We already covered The Book of Enoch earlier. Besides this work, other works such as the Book of Jasher and the Book of Jubilees were specifically excluded from the old testament. Who knows what else came and went over the thousand years between King David and the time of Christ?

Besides Jasher and Jubilees—which are the more well-known works— other lesser ancient Hebrew *titles* are also mentioned in the bible, yet their content sits aside from the official Old Testament version. Works such as the *Book of the Wars of the Lord*, the *Book of Samuel the Seer*, the *Book of Nathan the Prophet*, and the *Book of Gad the Seer*. Also, the *Acts of Rehoboam* and the *Chronicles of the Kings of Judah*. We also know that Solomon composed more than a thousand songs, yet only two are preserved in the book of Psalms (72 and 127).

In the New Testament, bishops attending the Council of Nicaea in AD 325 debated various written works about Jesus Christ and decided what to officially include within the New Testament. Much was left out, including writings of Jesus as a "hot-tempered" boy— making him appear too human. Since Nicaea, the Christian narrative has coasted along without disruption, reinforced by Christian intellectuals such as Saint Augustus in A.D. 400 (already mentioned), and Saint Thomas Aquinas in A.D. 1.200.

Overall, with both the Old and New Testaments, great efforts were made to clean narratives up, to steer us away from mankind-oriented storytelling to deity-oriented sagas. Things like Aliens, Nephilim, and Giants are scarce, mainly found in the ancient scripts of unfiltered writers, such as the Sumerians and Chinese.

These censoring operations should not come as a surprise. A premise of SUBJUGATED finds that ever since our creation in 4,000 BC, a tug-of-war has waged between primate socialist forces intent on controlling the Homo Sapient troop using any means possible – including spinning reality – and the opposing alien libertarian forces who try to dig deeper into actual reality to optimize their wellbeing and their independent way of life.

Most Alien-sourced Libertarians want nothing to do with institutions, and so, for the most part, primate-sourced Socialists fill the religious, scientific, medical, and government ranks. These institutional types can't help themselves and need to keep everyone in the dark as much as possible to maintain discipline within the pyramid, a "need to know" operation controlled by elites.

Today, in this most recent era of Primate Socialist intent, while pursuing their agenda to subjugate Alien Libertarians, institutional specialists have infiltrated all pockets of America's operating institutions, including:

Large Corporations – like Google and Facebook,

Universities – professors and administrators,

The Judiciary – prosecutors and judges,

Medical Schools – the FDA, the CDC,

Government's unelected Deep State agents,

Show Businesses writers, actors, and moguls, and

The News Media's endless minions.

Socialist-primates work inside the system to enforce obedience, a main tenant of Saul Alinsky's *Rules for Radicles* program.

> *Any revolutionary change must be proceeded by an attitude toward change amongst the mass of our people. They must feel so frustrated, so defeated, so lost, so futureless in the prevailing system that they are willing to let go of the past and change the future. To bring on this reformation requires the organizer work inside the system.*

–SAUL ALINSKY–

Today, mainly Primate Socialists hold the insider operational posts. Alien Libertarians are left to run privately controlled companies, big and small, including mom-and-pop concerns, the trades, plumbers, electricians, truckers, with many common-citizen Libertarians simply employees trying to stay strong.

This mosaic of narrative control underway since the beginning has been perfected just in the last 20 years, allowing the socialist narrative to echo through the corridors of all chambers of the civilization.

This is not conspiracy theory; this is how things are.

Entire books can be written on systemic suppression of history, but for now, I invite the reader to access videos on Ancient Giants that catalogue the global findings of this lost Nephilim race. By the way, the American Giants found in the mounds, lasted until AD 1,200 or AD 1,300, just recently. And don't forget the 75,000 Little People graves found in Tennessee! Also, for good measure, read the lost books of the old bible, and the discarded works from Nicaea.

The "fight over humanity" between the primate-socialists and the alien-libertarians, is presented in SUBJUGATED – Volume III – *"Genetics Drives Political Preference"*, coming up soon.

Now, let's turn the page, and learn a thing or two from Plato. In *Plato*, we dig into the nature of the genetic implant which elevated primate humans into Homo Sapient humans.

It is not what you imagine.

# 17

## PLATO & THE WORLD OF IDEAS

*" I know this world is ruled by infinite intelligence. "*

—THOMAS EDISON—

Finally, we examine the Alien gene implanted in us.

Plato's famous *allegory of the caves* teaches that we constantly misinterpret what we experience, that our circumstances often result from something of which we lack awareness or don't understand, such as solar eclipses witnessed in primitive times.

Using an allegorical storytelling form, Plato has cave dwellers sitting, facing a wall, their backs to a fire, with puppeteers projecting shadows onto said wall. The cave dwellers assume the shadows a final reality, neither realizing physical objects cast the shadows nor that puppeteers direct the movements of the masquerade.

Plato's allegory goes on to describe how enthusiastically the cave dwellers weave explanations around misunderstood experiences, coming up with all kinds of elucidations for the shadows, and how they stick to any cockeyed reason once it sounds good enough.

Apparently, Plato concluded that self-deception resides prominently within the human condition.

And so, the reader should wonder about the three themes of this book: *Creation, Evolution and Intervention.* Which aspects of each are real and which parts shadow? Overall, misinterpretation slows humanity down, leaving us saddled with inaccurate operating models, such as assuming the world flat because it *looks* flat. But occasionally we overcome shortsightedness, such as when Copernicus envisioned planets revolving around the sun, challenging the "Earth-centric" way things appear in the sky.

Over time, this ability to gradually uncover deeper realities has built up our many faculties including—get ready—mathematics, physics, chemistry, biology, geology, music, painting, sculpture, dance, cloth design, photography, theater, radio, film, sports, architecture, engineering, aerospace, toolmaking, energy harnessing, agriculture, animal husbandry, cuisine, weapon making and warfare, medicine, psychology and drug making, building, vehicle and communication equipment-making, not to mention philosophy, ethics, morality, theology, politics, law, finance, business administration, history, anthropology, and writing itself, et al.

Yup, we cover the lot, and no original primate Humans from the past demonstrated *any* sign of these possibilities. More so, no Earthly species extrapolated beyond what stood immediately in front of them, and hence no species ever developed a faculty for *anything!* Except Homo Sapiens. This ability to accumulate know-how is our true evolutionary track.

Most notably, the pre-Homo Sapient primate Humans and the Neanderthals lacked this knack for discovery. For hundreds of thousands of years they drifted, discovering nothing to lift them above their hunter/gatherer ways. Controlling fire—their claim to fame— was not a discovery; it was good fortune, and regardless, it did not matriculate simple Humans beyond the aforementioned stone tools, pottery, a simple vocabulary, cave art, and having a few domesticated camp dogs. On Earth, only Homo Sapiens constantly accumulated "know-how," a flow of progress referred to as a *teleo-logical progression.*

*What and why is this?*

The reader might simply assume that Aliens caused a genetic boost of our IQs, and that this newfound intelligence explains humankind's ongoing story. But IQ just projects the shadow on the wall, a mere tool, and not the heart of our propensity to discover. Something more profound sits right behind it … but *what?*

Plato advocated a world of ideas sitting out there that we tap into. For example, we did not invent the *circle, the triangle,* or the *square.* These have sat within the world of ideas forever. The world of "forms," as Plato put it, exists somewhere, very much like an internet cloud database, but spiritually, not physically.

The universal recognition of circles, triangles, and squares presents an *a priori* (again, self-evident) proof that the world of ideas exists, a database, an "ontological encyclopedia of real and imagined beings." Certainly, all of these abstractions are not stored in our local *tabula rasa* genes, any more than the content of the whole internet resides on our smartphones. The smartphone fetches stuff from "above." We operate the same in connecting to "God's" mind. And I recommend the reader get religious about this!

In ancient times, we could not begin to realize the implications of the universe, its physical and spiritual dimensions, and thus the entry of Jesus Christ, the Buddha, and Mohammad, trying their best to use revelation to discover what lay beyond.

The world of ideas travels far beyond the housing of shapes. As with the humble circle, everything recognized (discovered) by Homo Sapiens during the past 6,000 years already sat waiting for us within the world of ideas. We just tapped in, and reciprocally, revelations occurred—as one must *try* in order to get a response! Homo Sapiens invented nothing on their own, including $E=MC^2$.

"Hey!" you might complain, "What about unicorns? Didn't we make these up in our heads?"

No! We made up nothing. Everything that we *recognize* was revealed.

Sorry to burst your bubble ... Atheist evolutionists hate this explanation. Evolutionists want neither God nor Aliens in the picture. They maintain that Humankind alone dragged itself from the jungle to where we stand today, and we did it our way, operating as loyal socialist primates, evolving slowly through mutations.

But contrary to evolutionary doctrine, a combination of Divine knowledge made accessible by Alien "tap-in" telepathy brought us here. Besides a few specific lessons taught to us by Aliens—such as the wheel, and how to make bricks—our interventionist Aliens gave us something much more important, a genetic implant that connects us to the mysterious world of ideas. Biologically this amounts to an organic transceiver in our neurons, an antenna of sorts. I'll expound by using a personal reference.

I am a songwriter, something for which I pined for my entire life, and achieved late, in my 50's. The breakthrough came when I "opened the idea channel."

The idea channel feels a bit like revelation, as it occurs in a mild trance. The fresh idea (music in my case) arrives as an initial inspiration, followed by bite-sized information bits. You must remain open, fiddle with the incoming sounds and lyrics, and *yearn* for more bits so that you can *assemble* the whole thing. It's an elevated but uncomfortable, tedious state of mind and one needs deep motivation to stay at it.

Most artists operate like this, as do physicists such as Einstein. Albert claimed he would disappear into one of his thought escapades where a fuzzy understanding of something slowly became more apparent until finally, he could assemble it whole. $E=MC^2$, for example, stands as an assembled representation of his vision. My songs came to life as the assembled representations of what I was shown.

Sometimes it takes many sessions to collect the entire set of components required for final assembly. Bruce Springsteen says some of his songs hung around forever before he finally completed them. Once, *Rolling Stone* magazine asked Bob Dylan if "...he had written any new songs lately …" and Bob, well, expressed his dismay at the ignorance of the question, the reporter oblivious of the whole process. According to Bob, "No one writes a song unless they have to." It's that uncomfortable.

Michelangelo would let a block of marble sit in his studio for months until he finally saw the trapped "form" within. Then he would chisel away to discover the details, the "figure."

A songwriter might receive a song's chorus first, and the verses later. Or might get a guitar lick first that totally inspires, with more musical elements eventually entering as the so-called "composer" sits for hours playing the piano or guitar, contemplating the sound. The great ones such as Mozart brought in vast quantities of musical "suggestions" in order to assemble orchestral extravaganzas. Mozart would hear all of the instrumental elements in his head and transcribe these onto sheet music, all prior to an amazed Viennese ensemble bringing the entire piece to life.

In my case, I can handle country, rock, and blues songs, but Mozart's IQ surely dwarfed mine, allowing him to assemble musical architecture of much greater scale then my simple tunes. The process is the same, but the "dudes" involved certainly differ.

For me, at least, I find the trance state very uncomfortable, something I would not put myself through, except for the deep *yearning* I have to get the entire inspiration *assembled*, just so I can familiarize myself with it. Once complete, I have little recollection of any songwriting moments, and I sincerely tell people I did not write the song, I merely assembled it. When inventors or artists no longer *hunger to discover and assemble*, they stop producing wonderful works, their glory days over.

But everyone has some ability to tap in. Everyone has "light bulb" moments. The difference comes in how much *hunger-to-understand motivation* the person holds, and how much *assembly expertise* they have to then assemble what "it" reveals.

I, for example, know music theory. I play keyboards, trumpet, and guitar and have studied American songwriting from the 1800's on. I have worked within bands for 50 years, and have made hundreds of recordings, and so, when a new musical structure hits my antenna, I recognize its nature, and know what to do with it.

Einstein worked years in the patent office understanding new discoveries, and his brother-in-law was a first-class mathematician who converted concepts into equations, so they, too, finely practiced and honed their craft, not unlike like a musical team such as Lennon & McCartney.

The good news for Homo Sapiens: with such an abundance of the above-mentioned faculties available in which to become proficient, plenty of space exists for anyone *willing to apply themselves.*

The ability to *tap into the world of ideas* has two tiers. First, everyone uses the world of ideas to quickly understand what others have figured out. Certainly, most of us grasped the idea of smartphones right away, though we did not invent them ourselves. Second, everyone yearns for the world of ideas once they badly need a solution, as in "necessity is the mother of invention." Some solely enter that pressure cooker when circumstances dictate, while others *voluntarily* enter this uncomfortable state to uncover new works … think Van Gogh.

But the larger point to all this follows: none of this *tapping in* occurred with the "standard-edition" Humans, the pure primate Humans who wandered out of Africa 70,000 years ago. They just kept on wandering until Alien genetic intervention enabled all the above. *Tapping in* is a specific genetic trait no species on earth previously possessed, way bigger than an odd mutation that causes something mundane, such as the rare appearance of an albino.

Once we got going with our new telepathic gift, impressive growth spurts and noted downturns in humankind's so-called teleological progression occurred. For instance, not much progress occurred during the Dark Ages. But the "discovery boat" took float once again, and as our base of know-how accumulated, the discovery process led to industrial, transportation, energy, and communication technologies, which in turn brought more and more people into the discovery game. What used to happen with the very few began to touch many.

For example, in the 1950's, a few thousand books were published each year. Now, just in the United States alone, 600,000 books come out yearly, mostly self-published. Everyone wants their say the way once only available to Darwin, Poe, Twain, Dickens, and the Bronte Sisters. Microsoft Word transformed Humankind, as once had Guttenberg's printing press.

And so, to lump Homo Sapiens and human hunter/gatherers together within the same species shows an embarrassing lack of understanding of who we are. But to defend this genetic equivalency with no evidence of it whatsoever requires one to close a blind eye to almost everything. Why would people of science obstinately maintain that we are the same as the pure primate humans who left Africa 70,000 years ago? We will soon see in *SUBJUGATED Volume III*.

But for the moment, if you will hypothetically accept that Homo Sapiens exist as a different species with different genes, do you still wonder about the Aliens and the likelihood of their role in why and how Homo Sapiens split from the human hunter/gatherers? Again, let's start from my personal reference point ...

You may find interesting my second admission—that of my very own UFO encounter—more interesting than my first (that I'm a songwriter). Well, let's hope..

At age 13, I had just moved to Connecticut. One night, my cousins and I decided to spend the night in sleeping bags behind my parents' house. Chatting while gazing up at the night sky, we kids see two luminous orbs rapidly approaching us. They do not slow, but suddenly halt 75 feet north of us, hovering a few feet above the tree line. They appear about a foot-and-a-half in diameter. Both float for mere seconds, when Orb #1 takes off on a 90-degree angle west. Orb #2 stays put for another few seconds, then descends directly south towards us. I duck into my sleeping bag, remembering nothing else until dawn. Likewise, my cousin Gail remembers everything up to, but nothing beyond the approach of Orb #2. So,

I guess, put us down for a "Close Encounter of the First Kind." Anti-alien types attribute it to "ball lightning," but never explain how this ball of energy knew when to stop ... and how to focus on us.

Although I don't argue in support of Alien intervention based upon this isolated encounter, it certainly keeps me from scoffing at the idea. The reasons laid out throughout this book drive the assertion: Alien intervention remains the most likely explanation accounting for both our sudden rise on Earth and the unearthly behavior we have shown ever since.

Again, Homo Sapiens do not live within nature. We kill our own. We lie. We deceive. We destroy. We dismiss. We ignore.

We clearly lay claim to the worst invasive species ever, worse than poison ivy, something—even with our more noble qualities vouched for here—that neither God nor evolution would ever foist upon a global biosphere seeking Gaia-like (self-balancing) harmony.

We remain the only species whose intelligence timeline matures *after* its reproductive timeline. Dog intelligence stands near complete within months, and Fido does not reproduce until much later. Human timelines thus appear strikingly unnatural.

Consider also the fact that natural species possess an elegant uniformity to their appearance (so, for example, all zebras look great), whereas humans all look, well, *different*. Because, for the most part, we humans do not live up to an ideal, whether that's "Barbie," "Ken," or whomever. The rare genetic specimens, e.g., the George Clooney's and the Angelina Jolie's, look, well, *marvelous*. How could the one-in-a-million editions enjoying good looks occur due to natural-selection situation if every Monarch Butterfly displays perfection?

So, let's assume destabilizing intervention exists, but ... so what? The answer—is coming up next in SUBJUGATED Volume II – "History Re-imagined"

But first a few examples of Humankind's great inventors using revelation:

*"When I am traveling in a carriage,or walking after a good meal, or during the night when I cannot sleep; it is on such occasions that ideas flow best and most abundantly."*

—WOLFGANG AMADEUS MOZART—

*"I think and think for months and years. Ninety-nine times, the conclusion is false. The hundredth time I am right."*

—ALBERT EINSTEIN—

## JOHN LENNON

The *Beatle* song, "Strawberry Fields", written by John Lennon, has two components that fit well within this *Plato* chapter. The first aspect shows John's telepathy into the world of ideas, the second aspect considers the song lyrics themselves.

To start, when on a vacation break in Spain from The Beatles, John took a bus from Madrid to visit the medieval city of Toledo. While drifting off to sleep on the bus, the melody and lyrics to *Strawberry Fields* came to him. Having no tape recorder, John struggled to keep the song's image intact in his mind until he returned to the Madrid hotel to sort it out. Finally, with guitar in hand, he reverse-engineers the chords that underpin the melody. The combination of intricate chord movements juxtaposed against the exotic vocal melody line appears beyond human possibilities. The whole structure was simply revealed from above and assembled by John.

Second, the lyrics themselves reflect the mentioned concept of Plato's cave allegory as follows: "Living is easy with eyes closed, misunderstanding all you see."

*Aye Johnny, the angels be talk'n ta you that day!*

# RICHIE HAVENS AT WOODSTOCK

Richie Havens was the first performer at Woodstock in 1969. All revved up, pounding his acoustic guitar—breaking strings—after performing for three hours, with a fresh guitar in hand, from the back of the stage he saunters towards the microphones until one finally hears the torrent of sound pouring out from him. Then Richie begins to sing:

*Freedom, Freedom, Freedom, Freedom*
*Freedom, Freedom, Freedom, Freedom*
*Sometimes I feel like a motherless child*
*Sometimes I feel like a motherless child*
*Sometimes I feel like a motherless child*
*A long way from my home, yeah*

*Sing*

*Freedom, Freedom, Freedom, Freedom*
*Freedom, Freedom, Freedom, Freedom*
*Sometimes I feel like I'm almost gone*
*Sometimes I feel like I'm almost gone*
*Sometimes I feel like I'm almost gone,*
*yeah A long, long, long way from my home,*
*yeah Clap your hands, Clap your hands*
*Clap your hands, Clap your hands*
*Clap your hands, Clap your hands*

*Clap your hands, yeah, Clap your hands*

*Hey, hey, hey, hey*
*Hey, yeah yeah yeah yeah*

*Hey, yeah, yeah, yeah*
*Hey, yeah yeah yeah yeah*

*I got a telephone in my bosom*
*And I can call him up from heart*
*I got a telephone in my bosom*
*And I can call him up from heart*

*When I need my brother / (Brother)*
*Brother / (Brother)*

*When I need my father / (Father)*
*Father, hey / (Father)*
*Mother / (Mother)*
*Mother, hey / (Mother)*

*Sister / (Sister)*
*Yeah / (Yeah)*

*When I need my brother / (Brother)*
*Brother, hey / (Brother)*

*Mother / (Father)*
*Mother / (Mother)*
*Mother / (Mother)*

*Hey, yeah, yeah, yeah*
*Yeah-yeah, yeah yeah*
*Hey, yeah, yeah, yeah*
*Hey, yeah, yeah, yeah*
*Hey, yeah, yeah, yeah*
*Hey, yeah, yeah, yeah*

The whole song came to him in real-time while on stage, pure telepathy and revelation.

Richie: "I think the word 'freedom' came out of my mouth because I saw it in front of me. I saw the freedom that we were looking for. And every person was sharing it, and so that word came out."

Notice as well, the revealed line: *I got a telephone in my bosom and I can call him up from heart.* This is the transceiver in our neuron system. For Richie, it was on fire that day.

## STEVE JOBS

The ability for people to tap into ideas uncovered by others is explained nicely here by Steve Jobs:

> *Japan's very interesting. Some people think it copies things. I don't think that anymore. I think what they do is reinvent things. They will get something that's already been invented and study it until they thoroughly understand it. In some cases, they understand it better than the original inventor.*

## EINSTEIN

Finally, another explanation of discovery by Einstein:

> *The intellect has little to do with the road to discovery. There comes a leap in consciousness, call it intuition or what you will, and the solution comes to you, and you don't know how or why.*
>
> —ALBERT EINSTEIN—

Plato was on the right track. Organic neuro-transceivers implanted into our gene bank 6,000 years ago explain how ideas are revealed and who we have become.

# EPOLOGUE

Hmm ...

*"It is true that liberty is precious; so precious
that it must be carefully rationed."*

—VLADIMIR LENIN—

**For those who have read this far I commend you.**

**You too wonder.**

For more, please read *Volume II – "History Re-imagined"*, up next, a
5 Season, 38 Episode series that proposes the more likely drama of
our Homo Sapient beginnings.

And please read the upcoming, *Volume III – "Genetics Drives Political
Preference"*, to see how our primate/alien genetic conflict explains
political conflict in the modern world.

*"What are we to do with ourselves?"*

SUBJUGATED Volume II is up next,
presenting a more likely rendition
of early Homo Sapient history.

# SUBJUGATED
## VOLUME II

*Primates & Aliens*

*"humanity re-imagined"*
The 5-Season, 38 Episode Series

*Zeus was real; they all were!*

# THE REVELATION

**Zeus was real; they all were!**

*Subjugated Volume II* is a five-season drama re-examining Adam and Eve, their Alien Overlords, plus their descendants ... Enoch, Noah, Gilgamesh and Ishtar, plus Satan, plus claims from the earliest writings of India, Egypt, China, the Mayans, and the Greek Olympians – Gaia, Cronos, Zeus and Heracles, along with the plights of ... Moses, Joshua and Goliath,... while also factoring in the American Bigfoot, Tennessee Little People and the Ohio Giants ... all of these luminaries stemming from the singular Homo Sapient launch back in 4,000 B.C. ... quite a launch, but one with unintended consequences!

Proof of historical events becomes daunting the further back in time one goes. The early Homo Sapient writings relied upon here in *Subjugated* have the additional problem of the ancient writers limited by the knowledge shortcomings of their era, easily misinterpreting what they saw.

Nevertheless, the words of the ancients represent *sincere accounts* of the past which we can then upgrade by applying today's improved level of scientific and historical awareness. This upgrade process yields a still imperfect, yet *more likely* explanation of Homo Sapient origins than do prior interpretations.

And so, with noted artistic license taken to weave this revised history together, *Primates & Aliens – "Humanity Re-imagined"* will now connect the dots.

# CONTENTS

# SEASON 1

## Noah

## Homo Sapiens & the Flood

"*Often it does seem such a pity that Noah and his party did not miss the boat.*"

—MARK TWAIN—

# THE ADMIRAL

## 4,100 B.C.

An "Alien" spacecraft from *Siros* approaches Earth, with *Admiral Xi* and his lieutenants *Michael, Gabriel, Uriel & Raphael* abord, on a mission to explore and mine Earth's mineral assets.

Upon setting up mining operations, the Aliens encounter a primate species who call themselves *Humans*, not too bright, with a slight vocabulary, an understanding of fire, possessing stone tools, accompanied by camp dogs, with an ability to construct pottery, but little more.

As mining operations progress, the Humans sit and watch, amused as primates would be, while Alien shipmates do the dirty work of mining.

Finally, one female Alien named *Eve* is severely hurt, and the crew stops working. A rebellion in the Alien ranks unfolds, as the free-spirited, space-travelling crewmen bristle against the work they suddenly are being made to carry out.

A worker spokesperson named *Satan* steps up to speak to the ship's four lieutenants. Satan proposes transforming the Humans into laborers rather than the crew members. Yes, the Humans appear too stupid to be effective, but they could be genetically upgraded by the ship's doctors, enabling them to be taught and directed.

Admiral Xi, seeing it a mistake to convert space travelers into mine workers, agrees to the proposal, but only if one of the Alien crew members agrees to be sacrificed for the genetic neuron materials needed for infusion into Human embryos.

A volunteer is found – Eve, the injured Alien already dying. Months later, two test-tube babies – Adam and *baby* Eve are born, bright and ambitious, with high IQs, able to amass knowledge and wisdom – proudly named by Xi himself as Homo Sapiens – "the wise ones", a hybrid of Primate and Alien genes.

Sure enough, the minds of the resulting Adam and Eve babies impress all, but at a big cost. Unlike the human parents that sired the Adam and Eve embryos – who both looked the way all animals of a kind appear, each identical, each uniformly beautiful – the genetically modified "Homo Sapiens" look different.

As would unfold, Homo Sapiens rarely possess beauty, they appear anxious, depressed, or worse, prone to lying and deception.

Admiral Xi, though, remains confident in the spirited ways of young Adam and Eve and instructs lieutenant Gabriel and GAIA, an alien woman, to care for them while XI is gone on other space missions.

The little family is transported from the mining camp to a protected enclave called Eden.

Episode I ends with Gabriel and the children looking on as Xi departs.

# EPISODE 2
# THE GARDEN
## 4,000 B.C.

The Aliens depart, leaving Gabriel and GAIA behind to foster the new Homo Sapient race. The ship would return shortly in space time, but because of time relativity, many Earth years would transpire before Admiral Xi's return.

The year is 4,020 B.C. and the Earth is mainly a vast ocean, with just one large continent called Pangea surrounded by endless water. Gabriel explains to Adam and Eve that Pangea was formed long ago when a meteor struck the water planet, breaking open the crust, resulting in materials that became the moon, and in a lava island that cooled forming Pangea.

Living in a garden paradise at the center of Pangea, Adam and Eve mature and begin to sire offspring.

The children are vigorous and competitive, but like their parents, prone to bouts of dissatisfaction, plagued by anxiety and occasional depression – an unintended consequence of the unnatural mix of primate and alien genes.

More, unlike the original primate humans who were obedient, controlled by virtue signaling and always in fear of their troop leader, the Homo Sapiens hold a need for personal independence, something akin to their Alien brethren who defy authority. After all, Homo Sapiens are part Primate troop-think and part Alien free-form-think.

A genetic tug of war exists.

Gabriel works to teach the budding Homo Sapiens, regularly holding class at the tree of knowledge. He explains they were given the gift of imagination, an ability to tap into the universe of ideas, housed in the spirit world.

But Gabriel warns that every idea is not automatically true, and that imagination can invent falsehoods. And so for now, they must abide by the instruction they are given. As a test, Gabriel forbids they eat an apple from one of the trees in the garden.

With this Eve grows intrigued, and one day gets Adam to pick an Apple for her. Gabriel becomes incensed, saying that unchecked rebellion like this will lead to misery. They are not ready to think on their own.

So far the Homo Sapient adventure has uncovered something much different than the control culture of the original primate humans. Homo Sapiens yearn for something they call freedom, even if this leads to mis-steps.

Soon afterwards, ignoring Gabriel's warning, their freedom-loving son Cain kills his own brother in a fit of anger.

Episode 2 ends with Gabriel banishing Cain to the world of *Nod*, the world outside of the garden.

# EPISODE 3
# THE NEPHILIM
## 3,200 B.C.

Many centuries go by, and Homo Sapiens number in the thousands. Finally, Admiral Xi's ship returns. Gabriel and GAIA are pleased to be with their own kind again.

Though a bit unruly and sometimes violent, as mining and agricultural workers, the Homo Sapiens prove useful to their overlords, who the Homo Sapiens now consider to be "the Sons of God". Already they use their imaginative power to invent explanations.

Because of the genetic incorporation of Alien genes, the Homo Sapient offspring appear close in image to their space-travelling relatives, so much so, that the Alien crew members become attracted to their earthly wards.

Admiral Xi sees this and imposes a strict restriction on fraternization.

But "boys will be boys", and crewman Satan, always wanting to lead, works on his fellow crew members, firing up their imaginations about the Homo Sapient women, and one day actually instigates unauthorized shore leave.

Under Satan's direction, 200 or so of these Sons of God "land", spread out, and wantonly begin taking Homo Sapient women, impregnating them by the thousands.

Full sexuality like this is not a simple neuron genetic transplant. Instead, the complex combination of Alien and Primate genes produces a disturbing consequence, a new species all together – something like a mule created by a horse and donkey.

Nine months later, the birth of many crossbred Nephilim babies transpires; huge babies, undoubtedly cut from their Homo Sapient mothers' bellies, who would mature into unstoppable sexual beasts, wanting to beget even more Nephilim babies.

Apparently, Admiral Xi – responsible for these 200 interlopers – came down hard on them and their mutinous behavior, and XI directs lieutenant Michael to transport the 200 to the *Hellion* penal colony for lifelong imprisonment.

Though punished for the crossbreeding, the horses had left the barn, so to speak, and the Homo Sapient gene pool now stood corrupted.

As a result, from then on, Homo Sapiens must live amongst these Nephilim giants who soon want to rule instead of the Aliens.

Episode 3 ends with a Nephilim killing an Alien chief, then declaring himself King. He is soon destroyed.

# EPISODE 4
# ENOCH & THE WATCHERS
## 3,000 B.C.

The Homo Sapiens and Nephilim populations somehow co-exist, but in just this tiny outcropping of Pangea.

It is 3,000 B.C. and a baby named Enoch is born. Enoch is the 7th descendent of Adam and Eve, and he lives amongst the brutality of Homo Sapiens trying to survive the onslaught of their giant Nephilim cousins.

The Aliens still come and go as they please. They are now called "the Watchers" by the Homo Sapiens, as it is clear that Aliens closely monitor their work in the mines and their educational progress. After all, though Homo Sapiens were given the power of imagination, able to accumulate knowledge, they started with nothing, an empty slate – with a long, long way to go.

Admiral Xi's lieutenants take a liking to Enoch's potential, and elevate him to acquire special know-how about the Earth and the cosmos.

Enoch is invited on board the Admiral's ship and travels as the understudy of Michael, Gabriel, Uriel and Raphael. They explain much, starting with the Nephilim disaster, and how Satan and the fallen crew members were punished by the Admiral.

Then he learns the breath of the earth.

Vast expanses of land found in distant territories of Pangea house exotic Animals that inhabit biospheres suited for their specie-specific attributes. To the west, giant dinosaurs dwell in what will become the Americas. Giant primate species are found to the east.

Great jungles and forests saturate the atmosphere with concentrations of oxygen. Living things imbued with high-potency metabolisms can live longer in this oxygen-rich environment than will be possible even a few thousand years hence.

It is 2,900 B.C., and Enoch's grandson Noah is born. Enoch has much to teach Noah, as Noah and his wife stand destined to become the next father and mother of the whole Homo Sapient race.

Noah is being prepared for what is to come: the flood and its aftermath. Enoch works to educate young Noah, writes "The Book of Enoch" for posterity, and then in 2,600 B.C., when Noah is already 300 years old, Enoch departs with the Aliens never to return.

Episode 4 ends with Enoch saying his goodbyes to his family before being transported up to the Alien ship named "The Ark".

# EPISODE 5
# THE ARK
## 2,400 B.C.


It is 2,400 B.C., Noah is now 600 years old, yet will live another 350 years.

The Nephilim horror has raged on for centuries, and one wonders why, after so many visits to Earth, that the Admiral has done nothing about it. After all, the wanton sexuality of his crew caused the whole debacle, plus, the admiral's prize project is his manufactured Homo Sapiens race.

Yet though he cherishes his Homo Sapiens, the original simple human primates still wander the Earth, as do the Nephilim. Too many adverse species compete. An idea to use a flood is put forward to clear out the others – no matter where they have roamed on Earth – and preserve the Homo Sapiens.

The dilemma? Some Homo Sapiens are contaminated with recessive Nephilim genes. Male and female Homo Sapiens who carry these genes can beget one of these giants, but luckily, like mules, two Nephilim cannot reproduce.

If Homo Sapiens are to be saved, only purebreds can be selected. The Aliens know that Noah and his wife come from unbroken Homo Sapient lines, and because of this – as well as Noah's education under Enoch – the decision is made to build the rescue plan around Noah.

The flood plan includes housing Noah's family on board the Alien space craft called the Ark, along with as many male and female embryos of various prized animal species as possible. Some species, though, are to be left behind, including the dinosaurs who live in Western Pangea. As the Admiral instructed "all corrupted flesh must be eliminated".

For years, Noah collects animals for the Ark, and Alien doctors freeze the embryos, keeping them on board. Finally, the day comes. Noah, his wife, his three sons, and his son's wives are brought up to the Ark to watch the flood unfold.

Lieutenant Raphael explains the scenario to Noah.

Pangea, though one land mass, has a giant fault line traveling the whole length of the continent through what today are the coasts of Europe and Africa touching the coasts of North and South America. It is this fault line that has kept the dinosaur population isolated in the west.

The Aliens will disrupt the fault using the same anti-gravity force that propels their ship. North and South America will slide away into the vast ocean causing tidal waves 30 miles high, which will cover the Earth.

Episode 5 ends with the anti-gravity beam cleaving Pangea along the fault line, with gigantic geysers shooting up as the land masses begin to separate.

# EPISODE 6
# THE FLOOD
## 2,400 B.C.

Once the Pangea fault line is broken open, Western Pangea starts to slide into the ocean at greater and greater speeds, a skimming stone over endless waters.

Immense waves are created on the far western side of Pangea as the ocean is pushed away, and a great hole opens up between the separating land masses.

All of this can be seen from the Ark, hovering hundreds of miles above the Earth's atmosphere.

Lieutenant Michael explains that the Earth has water trapped beneath its crust and points out where other areas of Pangea are becoming destabilized. All watch as India, a huge African land mass, breaks off, slides north, crashes into Asia thrusting up a mountain range 5 miles high – the Himalayas.

The same result occurs as a drifting Africa suddenly shifts north, forming the Alps.

As Western Pangea slides away at increasing speed, title waves grow larger and begin to sweep across the land masses, slowly penetrating with each larger wave extending further inland than the previous. Each wave deposits enormous amounts of silt, hundreds of feet thick.

On Western Pangea, after six of these waves, only a corridor of land is left. Lieutenant Uriel focuses the ship's optical sensors to reveal millions of dinosaurs running north towards Montana through the corridor seeking shelter. After seven of these waves, everything is covered by water.

Finally, the sliding continents hit a shelf under the ocean bringing them to a violent halt of almost infinite proportions. Like the Himalayas and Alps, massive mountains buckle up to become the Rockies in the north, and the Andes in the south.

Then, even these become submerged.

Episode 6 ends with no trace of land seen on Earth.

# EPISODE 7
# THE AFTERMATH
## 2,400 B.C.

Looking down from the Ark no land can be found. Noah and his family have been saved but now stand devastated.

Lieutenant Michael explains.

> *The land is still there, though now re-configured into separate continents, and the water that came from below the Earth's crust will gradually find its way back. And so, as the months go-by the higher elevations will show themselves and within a year a new normal will prevail.*
>
> *Many of the fish and even some insect species have survived the flood, and these will easily rebound.*
>
> *Though much of the vegetation lies buried in compressed graves to become vast store houses of oil someday, vegetation remnants on the surface will quickly reclaim the Earth's surface.*
>
> *The dinosaurs of Western Pangea are all dead, lying in mass graveyards along the final corridor from Colorado up through Montana.*
>
> *However, two things will change. First, the climate. Now that Pangea has been altered into multiple continents, greater dichotomies of hot and cold biospheres will take hold in different parts of the Earth. Second, though vegetation will rebound at a*

*dramatic pace, there will be less of it. This means less oxygen in the atmosphere.*

*At first it will be harder to breath, but bodies will adjust by taking many thousand breaths more each day. But even with this, looking into the future, with less oxygen, Homo Sapiens life spans will shorten, and they will accumulate genetic weaknesses that further impede long lives."*

Months of waiting go by and sure enough the continents present themselves, though great bodies of water remain trapped inland where sediment deposits block drainage.

The trapped water bodies start to find outlets. These turn into torrents that instantaneously carve great canyons through the fresh sediment layers. Exploding water a thousand feet deep and a mile wide sculpt the Earth. As the water finds open land, it still moves with a height of 100 feet 20 miles wide, goring the silt fields.

Thousands of years from now, compressed silt layers will turn to rock, but for now the sand and mud sediments remain soft, and hundreds of the Earth's canyons and wide river valleys are born. Episode 7 ends with the creation of the Grand Canyon, seen from the Ark.

# END OF SEASON 1

# SEASON 2

## *Satan*

## *The Scattering & Alien Warfare*

*" Like a good chess player,*
*Satan is always trying to maneuver you*
*into a position where you can save*
*your castle only by losing your bishop. "*

—C. S. LEWIS—

# EPISODE 1
# THE NURSERY
## 2,400 B.C.

The Earth stands barren, though plants, sea creatures and insects still have modest life-sustaining footings. But what about the frozen embryos held on the Alien ship, the Ark? How are these to be deployed, able to repopulate the Earth across continents?

Noah and his family are placed on fertile, dry ground on Mount Ararat, Turkey, told to work with lieutenant Raphael in constructing a nursery where young animals released by the Ark's doctors can mature.

Noah's three sons and their wives pitch in, building pens, growing and harvesting both plants and small animals to feed the conglomerate of animals. Raphael directs the sequencing of this elaborate food supply line. The animals prosper.

Many are released into the wild, and Noah ponders where they will go.

Raphael explains that each species instinctively moves out to new territory as their numbers grow, and through genetic switch options they vary their biological makeup to fit diverse biospheres. Adaptation takes place as generations are born, and because most species have yearly offspring, in a matter of just 100 years, a baseline species can spread and adapt to many locals.

For twenty years Noah and his family manage the release of young animals supplied to them from the Ark. At first, plant eating animals are released to give them a head start, carnivores later on.

And along the way, Noah's offspring have children of their own. Soon 16 grandsons and many granddaughters are in tow.

But something is happening. Due to volcanic pollution, the Earth cools, and a fast-moving ice sheet descends from the north. It smooths out the low-lying silt hills, but – and to this day – the high mountains are left stark, without signs of erosion.

Rather than returning to their mid-Africa home, Raphael decides to move Noah's family south, beyond the ice sheet to build a city called Babel, set in a warmer climate near the Persian Gulf. Here they are taught many aspects of basic civilization, like how to make bricks from clay and straw, and how to build irrigation ditches from the river, systems able to sustain their growing numbers.

Soon the 16 grandsons lead clans of their own, with Noah the patriarch of a few thousand souls and of many thousands of domesticated animals that Raphael taught them to breed from the wild stock.

Episode 1 ends with Noah, happy, sitting with Raphael, looking out at the humble city of Babel.

# EPISODE 2
# THE TOWER OF BABEL
## 2,200 B.C.

It is 2,200 B.C., two centuries after the flood. Noah is now 800 years old, destined to live 150 years more. The clans of his 16 grandsons have become too concentrated to stay in one place. Just like the animals released into the wild, instinct says to spread out.

But for now, everyone stays put, pre-occupied with building the Tower, mankind's first attempt to do anything on its own.

Until now, the Homo Sapiens have used mud and straw bricks to build simple huts and irrigation channels, but Noah's son *Ham* has an idea: *Why not build a tower so that the Homo Sapiens can reach the heavens just like the Admiral and his Aliens?*

A spiraling colossus is cooked up, and once one's daily chores are complete, one keenly puts in hours towards building the Tower. After all, it is theirs, the first thing *owned* by the Homo Sapient race.

Raphael is still in charge of the Homo Sapiens and expects the Admiral to return shortly with the next step in the colonization plan. Yet the Tower project soon takes on a feverous pitch and Raphael sees his grip slipping. Yes, the Homo Sapiens continue to work, stock piling mined goods for the return of the Ark, but for how long? When will the rebellion come?

Finally, Admiral Xi returns, along with a crop of young officers recently commissioned from the home planet of Siros. The Admiral is not pleased. The Tower is already 100 feet high, with its base built to eventually allow 300 feet, and the Homo Sapiens believe they alone are needed to achieve this.

Clearly, the Homo Sapient race must be broken up, prevented from operating as one. To break up the 16 clans Admiral Xi assigns each a young officer plus a contingent of Alien enforcers. This step precedes the "diaspora", the scattering of clans to different corners of the Earth.

Three things come of the diaspora. First, like all animals, each clan's physiology will change with new environments, they'll all look different. Second, the common language spoken amongst the 16 clans will morph into different languages, cutting off communication. Third, and most significantly, the Homo Sapiens will continue to be governed by the Aliens, not by themselves.

Colonization also calls for nurturing the primate side of the Homo Sapiens which accepts obedience. Homo Sapient intellect will be used, but free-wheeling Alien traits are to be suppressed, fostering a culture of "produce, consume, obey" subjugation.

And so the nations are born, with Noah's three sons and 16 grandsons sent off as described in the Hebrew bible:

| JAPHETH (Son) | HAM (Son) | SHEM (Son) |
|---|---|---|
| Gomer—Europe, | Cush—Ethiopia, | Arphaxad—Chaldea/ |
| Magog—Ukraine, | Mizraim—Egypt, | Hebrews, |
| Madai—Iran, | Phut—Libya, | Lud—West Turkey, |
| Javan—Greece, | Canaan—Palistine | Aram—Syria |
| Tubal—Georgia, | | |
| Meshech—Russia, | | |
| Tiras—China/Japan | | |

Episode 2 ends with the *Tiras* caravan headed east to the Yellow River in China with his Alien overlord "The Yellow Emperor" leading the way.

# EPISODE 3
# GILGAMESH
## 2,100 B.C

It's 2,100 B.C., 100 years since the diaspora of Babel. One of the clans, the *Chaldeans*, resides in the Tigress Euphrates valley under the watchful eyes of Alien overlords who continue to work the Homo Sapiens … as well as teach them.

Gilgamesh, a perfect Homo Sapient boy is born, some say made this perfect by Alien genetic doctors. Like Enoch hundreds of years prior, Gilgamesh is championed by the Aliens, taught the world's expanse and kingdoms, taught about engineering and how Alien aircraft work. More, he is taught how to write, using clay tablets imprinted by cuneiform markings.

Entering manhood, he appears a god to everyone, a warrior with supreme courage, intelligence, holding a deep belief in his destiny. He is so esteemed that when his Alien chief travels, Gilgamesh is allowed to govern in his place.

A beautiful Alien woman becomes enamored with Gilgamesh, her name Ishtar. But ever since Satan and the 200 caused the Nephilim crises, an Alien/Homo Sapient union stands unthinkable. Still Ishtar pursues him.

Gilgamesh rejects Ishtar, and declares himself co-King of his city *Uruk*. The implication? For the first time since the Flood, a Homo Sapient has dared to see himself equal to Aliens, a sacrilegious step of the highest order.

Ishtar and the Alien counsel send in a wild, ferocious Homo

Sapient to kill Gilgamesh. Gilgamesh defeats this adversary but rather than kill him, offers the assassin a job as his squire, and they become loyal partners. Next, a dangerous bull is unleashed on Gilgamesh, the beast slaughtered.

Feeling himself exalted through adversity, Gilgamesh declares himself King and tells the people of Uruk that he will journey out to meet the other regional Kings he has been told about. Also, hearing that at 900 years, Noah still lives, he wants to meet the patriarch of the Flood, his great, great, great grandfather.

Upon finding Noah, Gilgamesh asks for the secret of long life. Noah explains there is no secret, that rich air in the pre-flood era slowed aging. "Now we just breath faster to keep up." Noah tells Gilgamesh that The Admiral had mixed feelings about the Flood, and promised never to use this strategy again.

Noah also warns Gilgamesh that with 10,000 years to accumulate knowledge, Aliens hold the upper hand, and that by making himself the first Homo Sapient King, he will be destroyed.

Gilgamesh comes home to write the first Homo Sapient literary piece – *The Epic of Gilgamesh* – on clay tablets.

Episode 3 ends with Gilgamesh in bed, writing, then bitten by an Asp, a poisonous snake, supplied by Ishtar. Though still held down, Homo Sapient trajectory rises.

# EPISODE 4
# SATAN ESCAPES
## 1,900 B.C.

It is a big universe. Admiral Xi and planet Siros are not the only participants. Like all life forms, the Sirons – as they call themselves – long ago came to a point where they needed to expand.

Charged with finding suitable planets to colonize, the *Siros Space Force* identifies undeveloped worlds that cannot offer resistance.

One of the worlds – Hellion, a hot, volcanic planet – though technically viable for life, was not a place any Siron would tolerate. Instead, Hellion became the penal colony for the Siron community at large. Here, underground in the heat, they keep Satan and the other 200 fathers of the dreaded Nephilim.

But beware, the top prisoner "Satan of many talents" uses deceit and compelling acting skills to entrap targets. Once arrested on Earth, Satan immediately played the part of a fully defeated, pathetic retch, doing favors for guards, ridiculed by other prisoners, just bidding time until finally death would end his misery.

In reality he was plotting his rise to power, and not just his escape, but the acquisition of military assets. He would start with Hellion itself, recruit its prisoners and hijack the planet's three heavily pro-tected star cruisers.

Satan's focus? Earth, and the Aliens subjugating Homo Sapiens. After all, genetic subjugation was Satan's concept to begin with. As well, Satan wants to see the offspring of the so called "Satan 200 Violators", his Nephilim nieces and nephews.

To the shock of the whole Siros Empire, just like Napoleon escaping Elba in the deep future, Satan organizes the prisoners, tricks the prison officers, and overtakes the security forces.

Episode 4 ends with Satan in a space cruiser's command seat, ordering coordinates for a safe haven deep in space. He will bide his time, and then wreak havoc on Earth.

# EPISODE 5
# INDUS VALLEY WAR
## 1,800 B.C.

By 1,900 B.C. the 16 clans of Noah's grandsons have settled, usually along a major river, as rivers offer much as they do now.

The Indus River in India, a warm climate below the Himalaya ice sheet, becomes home to multiple advanced cities, headed by Aliens, populated by Homo Sapiens.

They invent their own language with 60 letters, very different than the cuneiform writing of Gilgamesh.

While Admiral Xi travels in gigantic space cruisers, smaller craft are used to get around locally. In common, the large and small ships of the fleet use anti-gravity energy to propel the vessels – technology that pushes and pulls against the gravitational mass of the stars and planets encountered along one's travel path.

Since migrating here 300 years ago, the Indus Valley Homo Sapiens proudly service the Alien transport vehicles, called *Vimamas*. These structures will not break, cannot be cut, will not catch fire, cannot be destroyed, and can hover motionless or become invisible.

Also, Vimamas, like Space Cruisers, are armed with atomic weapons.

Apparently, though a caste structure exists, the arrangement here between Aliens and Homo Sapiens is working, with Homo Sapiens the second caste. They live, something akin to what Japanese Colonel Shito said to his English prisoners in the movie *Bridge Over the River Kwai*, "Be happy in your work."

But tranquility is fleeting, once an outside force enters the equation. Satan – the outside force – and his warrior fleet choose the Indus as their first target.

Indus valley writings from those times describe the devastation. Whole cities evaporated in a single consumption, with Alien combat vessels blown from the sky. And to what purpose? Even in victory the attackers neither descend nor take possession of anything conquered.

Satan has one idea, the destruction of happiness, just as his happiness ended, and physical devastation is only the beginning.

Episode 5 ends with Satan and his fleet, now larger than just three space cruisers, flying off. Like Hitler in the future, Satan laughs; he is beside himself with the joy of successful audacity.

# EPISODE 6
# YELLOW RIVER WAR
## 1,800 B.C.

It is 1,800 B.C., a short time after the Indus Valley War, and Satan turns his attention to the Yellow River Colony in China.

After Babel, Noah's grandson *Tiras* and his Alien chief, the self-proclaimed *Yellow Emperor*, who dressed in gold, migrate across southern Asia, settling down in one of the longest river valleys on Earth. They name it *The Yellow River* after the Emperor. For the next three hundred years the Emperor fosters the wellbeing of his Homo Sapiens. He surely is a good and wonderful Wizard of Oz.

The Emperor's lessons include building shelters, taming animals, the five grains, carts, boats. clothing, music, mathematics, martial arts and medicine, including *acupuncture*, an art unlikely founded upon trial and error. An elaborate picture-based writing system is devised.

After exploring the region, Tiras and the Emperor discover a giant body of barricaded water left behind from the flood, a threat to every soul in the valley. A means to slowly release the water is devised. The Alien/Homo Sapient team works well.

And so, the colony thrives, but then it happens. Satan and his warships arrive, and not just the three star cruisers from Hellion, but others, as another race of Aliens, the *Pentons*, has formed an alliance with Satan against Siros.

The Emperor's pilots eliminate all of the warships but one, Satan's.

One against one, The Emperor himself fights Satan in nine engagements to no avail. The Emperor sends for help. A great Alien

warrior called the *Enigmatic Lady* arrives with new technology –
sound weaponry.

A low-frequency beam of anti-gravity directed at a target lowers
gravitational attraction amongst its atoms. Once weakened, a sonic
wave breaks the material down.

Until now direct military hits on *Vimamas* rarely occurred, as
only the best pilots could pull these off. But sonic weaponry goes
after the material itself.

The Enigmatic Lady focuses anti-gravity on Satan's ship and has
all of the Homo Sapiens hit hand-held drums at her signal. The ship
turns to dust.

As this happens Satan watches his last war ship destroyed.

Satan ducks into the forest to begin his escape. No longer will
he use overt force. Instead, he will use his acting talents to pit Aliens
against Aliens, with the Mayan colony his next target.

Episode 6 ends with The Emperor and his Alien subordinates board-
ing a Vimamas. A tired Yellow Emperor is retiring, going home to
Siros, but proclaims that going forward, rather than Aliens, Homo
Sapiens will fulfil the role of China's emperors.

# EPISODE 7
# MAYAN CITIES WAR
## 1,600 B.C.

Breaking up the Homo Sapiens at Babel to dilute their will cut both ways, as on their own, the clans would feel a new kind of independence that fed their Alien side. Not only did their look and their language digress from Babel, but their way of life, their choices and their moral codes did as well. Plus, the Aliens living with the Homo Sapiens would have no restraints, and would even war amongst themselves.

Genetically, being both primate and alien, even then, some Homo Sapiens preferred group obedience as the most comfortable way, something left over from the Human primate troops. But other members held Alien-like yearnings for what would someday be called liberty. Neither could understand, nor influence the other.

Tiras' son *Xel* was one such freedom lover. Of all the clans, the Chinese population was by far the largest, and had been so ever since the days of the Ark. Xel, then living in Mongolia, felt it time to move on, away from the obedience rules set upon him by the distant Chinese clan, and he was not alone.

A party of Homo Sapiens and like-minded younger Aliens left Mongolia, crossing to where dinosaurs once roamed – America. Moving south along the coastline, beyond the glaciers, and avoiding the western deserts and mountain ranges, they settled in tropical Central America to form their civilization, doing it their way.

Homo Sapient units paired off with Alien units, who spread out to build autonomous cities. With neither Homo Sapient chiefs nor senior Aliens around to say otherwise, a deep Homo Sapient/Alien partnership developed in each city.

Unbridled young Aliens want huge stone structures and use anti-gravity technology to move the stones, with the Homo Sapiens doing the detail work. The city dwellers take great pride in their achievements, simultaneously holding a lack of trust of the other cities.

Distrust would become the centerpiece of Satan's design to destroy all of these freedom lovers.

No longer possessing a military force, Satan now relies upon guile, telling the Mayans he lived a Sorion who had retired from active duty but decided to explore Earth rather than return to Siros. Charming, knowledgeable about faraway places and far away times, all the cities welcome Satan at their banquet tables.

His psychological warfare approach had each city fearing they could be taken over by the other. The only defense, a first strike offense. Never tipping his hand about exactly what he might have heard at the other banquets, it was implied that things were getting worse.

Finally one city had had enough and launched a first strike. Soon 30 Mayan cities were destroyed, with surrounding farmlands contaminated by radiation. Few survived and when the jungle finally grew back, it buried the city structures under forest carpets.

Episode VII ends with Satan on a hill watching the cities burn.

# END OF SEASON 2

# SEASON 3

## Heracles

### Escaping Greece's Nephilim Kingdom

" Heracles attained panhellenic (Greek wide)
status through a variety of opposing characteristics
– he is at once a man and a god (part alien),
a city-founder and city-sacker, a killer of monsters
and a monstrous killer, capable of both wicked and
heroic deeds, a slave and a hero – the antithesis
of the Greek maxim "nothing in excess". "

—PROFESSOR KRISTIN HEINMAN—

# EPISODE 1
# GAIA BEGETS THE TITANS
## 2,100 B.C.

After the flood of 2,400 B.C., besides Noah, numerous Aliens from Admiral Xi's command return to earth.

Like all free-wheeling Aliens, the more defiant ones, those particularly bored with the Homo Sapient experiment in Babylon, pine to relocate from the Tigris Euphrates valley to form colonies not directly under the thumb of Admiral Xi.

When in 2,200 B.C. Admiral Xi disperses the grandsons of Noah from Babylon, *Gaia*, a female Alien, and the most willful of those now stationed on earth, is assigned to oversee Noah's grandson *Javen*, who has been posted to Greece. Gaia is thrilled with the assignment.

Savoring her new found freedom, Gaia dangerously takes a Homo Sapient man *Uranus* as her spouse, breaking the "no fraternization" rule. With Javan's clan, her new beau Uranus and a contingent of other Homo Sapient slaves in tow, Gaia moves to Greece with a few other Aliens as support. There, through Uranus, Gaia gives birth to Nephilim children called the Titans. Gaia begins her Nephilim kingdom, calling it *Olympus*.

Like all Nephilim, the offspring of the alien Gaia and earthling Uranus are sometimes human looking, but just as often grotesque beings with vile desires and violent traits. The *Cyclops*, with only one eye, and others born with multiple arms and other genetic distortions, show the extreme results of Homo Sapient/Alien cross breeding.

216

The Cyclops, though, are interesting: huge, voracious creatures, with special abilities as engineers and craftsmen. Gaia appoints them guardians of Alien technology.

Uranus, the Homo Sapient father, disgusted by at least some of his Nephilim offspring, stands helpless under the power of Gaia. But eventually Uranus imprisons some of the most abhorrent of his children, including the one-eyed Cyclops. Aghast at this indiscretion against her children, Gaia steps in to finish off the disgruntled Uranus once and for all.

To get this done, Gaia arms her youngest son *Cronus* with a razor-sharp *Sycle*, and dutifully Cronus castrates Uranus. As Uranus lies bleeding out, he tells Cronos that Cronus too will die under his own child's hands.

With violence now at its center, Olympians from every caste fear the future, including the Homo Sapient slaves stuck within this Nephilim madness.

Episode 1 ends with Gaia sitting on the Olympian throne, son Cronus at her side, surrounded by her other surviving Titan children, who for now, rule the Nephilim colony of Greece. Though all Titans are her children, the alien Gaia keeps the valuable Cyclops imprisoned. This will prove her demise.

# EPISODE 2
# GAIA BEGETS THE GIANTS
## 1800 B.C.

After the murder of Uranus by Cronus, Gaia now takes her son Cronus, already possessing Nephilim genes, as her spouse, and begins to produce a compounded crop of Nephilim babies called *Giants*, perhaps 14 feet tall. On the surface, they appear somewhat human, though beastly, possessing Nephilim strength and ferocity, able to throw huge stones around like baseballs – as is their wont!

With no controlling authority above them, the Giants begin to rampage without restraint, and many Homo Sapient slaves die as collateral damage stemming from Gaia's unbridled sins. But, Gaia nevertheless provides cover for her precious Giant children.

But young Cronus, the father of the Giants, fears the Giants. The prophecy is always present, that a son of Cronus will murder Cronus, just as Cronus murdered Uranus. Cronus, a fairly grotesque Nephilim himself, begins to kill some of his offspring Giants, even eating them.

But unbeknownst to Cronus, while slowly killing off his and Gaia's breed of children, he sires a separate child named Zeus with the alien Rhea, another Olympian. Rhea hides baby Zeus – who looks human – away in distant Crete, but eventually sneaks him back into Greece, getting him the job as cupbearer (wine pourer) to Cronus.

Young Zeus harbors a deep resentment of Cronus, killer of children, but cannot, for now, take action.

At this time, around 1,700 B.C., two Sorion scouts of Admiral XI, Lieutenants *Poseidon and Hades*, visit Olympus Greece only to find a Nephilim nightmare far worse than the first one unfolded before the flood. These agents of Admiral Xi decide to cull the Nephilim population, starting with the worst of the lot, the Titans. For now, they trick the Giants into going against Cronus and the Titans, planning to address the Giants and Gaia in a separate phase.

Thus begins the war between the Olympians and the Titans, with Cronus and his brother Titans going against against GAIA and the Giants.

Imperial lieutenants Poseidon and Hades, are soon told by Rhea about Zeus, and about his proximity to Cronos. Stealthily, Zeus is recruited, given a *poison* by *Poseidon* to slip into Cronos' wine. Once Cronos dies, Zeus and his step-brothers *Prometheus and Themis* finish off the Titans.

Episode 2 ends with Sorion Lieutenant *Hades* imprisoning any surrendering Titans.

# EPISODE 3
# ZEUS THE GIANT KILLER
## 1,500 B.C.

Recall that while Cronus had killed some of his Giant children – fearing one would murder him – his son, Zeus, a humanoid-appearing Nephilim by the alien mother Rea, stayed hidden away in Crete. There, Zeus is raised by a nurse Amalthea, and when Amalthea dies, Zeus covers his shield with her dead skin believing that even in death Amalthea can protect him.

Young Zeus returns to Olympus and soon poisons Cronus fulfilling the patricide prophecy. With Cronus gone, Zeus lives indomitable, siring many children with many Alien and Homo Sapient women, and this extended family will play a role in the coming fight with his half-brothers, the Giants – the children of Gaia and Cronos..

Matriarch Gaia, the still living mother of the Giants, now fears Zeus. She organizes the Giants to vanquish the young upstart. It is said that like a Sumu wrestler, a Giant cannot be defeated while his feet are on the ground, and with secure footing, under Gaia's leadership, the Giants soon rain stones and burning tree trunks down upon Zeus and his followers all huddled within the walls of Olympus.

Desperate, Zeus frees the Cyclopes, still imprisoned by Gaia. It becomes an alliance of convenience, with the Titan Cyclopes' hating their Giant half-brothers as much as Zeus hates all of his ancestors.

Under the direction of Lieutenant Poseidon, using alien engineering blue prints, the Cyclopes build Zeus a cache of rockets that, with shock and awe, descend like lightning bolts upon the Giants. Once stunned, a troop of Homo Sapiens under their leader Heracles is sent in to finish off any injured Giant found off his feet.

Slowly the war against the Giants is being won. But it is essentially "all over" when mother Gaia, the alien Queen, now leading her children Giants, is herself killed in one of the rocket onslaughts. *Hera*, Zeus's wife, now claims the title of Queen of Olympus.

Following Gaia's death, as Lieutenants Poseidon and Hades depart to rejoin Admiral Xi on the star cruiser *The Ark*, they proclaim that Zeus, a Nephilim, has fought like an Alien brother, and accordingly, is to be placed on the throne of Olympus … a first for a Nephilim.

Though a Nephilim himself, Zeus is directed to finish the unnatural job of eliminating both the remaining Nephilim Titans and Nephilim Giants – his uncles, aunts and half-brothers. To do so, Zeus has one more advantage, Heracles, the leader of the Homo Sapient slaves.

Heracles has risen up from the ranks to become the *secret sauce* that will lead Zeus to finally defeat the Giants.

His birth name was Alcaeus, but during the war, Zeus re-names him Heracles – meaning "glory of Hera – after Heracles saves Queen Hera from a rampaging Giant.

Episode 3 ends with Zeus departing. The endless Olympian wars, first against the Titans and then the Giants, have taken a toll on Olympus. Zeus is returning to Crete, his birthplace. About to leave he tells Heracles "You have been like a son to me.", and from then on the people say: "Hercules Son of Zeus".

*Yuchtas Mount*, Crete – the burial place of Zeus.

# EPISODE 4
# HERACLES THE LIBERATOR
## 1,500 B.C.

History says, that in the war between Zeus and Gaia's Giants, that most of the Olympian Aliens cut and ran … to Egypt. This left Zeus abandoned, with only the Cyclopes, his wife Hera and the Homo Sapient slaves, led by Heracles, to finish the war.

One can almost claim Heracles the perfect Homo Sapient. Like other naturally-trained warriors of antiquity, Heracles – who slept in the open air – possessed massive physical strength, mind-boggling physical dexterity and most of all, a resourceful mind. With these abilities in combination with Cyclops-made rockets, the Giants would soon fall.

And the Giants do fall. But as soon as the Giant-killing carnage ends, both the Cyclopes and Heracles demand their prizes – freedom from Olympus. Zeus, like Pharoah years later with the Hebrews, has no choice but to let them go. And with these concessions, Zeus effectively begins to dismantles Nephilim Olympus.

The Cyclopes escape to Sicily, while the Homo Sapient slaves slowly settle Greek and Anatolia locations, like Athens and Troy, forming small "city state" communities where they attempt a free life of self-rule. Heracles, though, has a separate and singular fate.

Like Gilgamesh hundreds of years prior, Heracles stands a unique Homo Sapient, and with the world now his oyster, his coming adventures await, destined to be vast. But to tie up loose ends within the Olympian kingdom, Zeus grants Heracles complete freedom only upon completing 12 labors, as follows.

It has been 700 years since the flood, and Noah's animals have spread far and wide without interference from humankind. Now they are a vicious threat to expanding Homo Sapient populations. Indeed, in 1,700 B.C., Homo Sapiens still huddle around the foundation centers of the Nile, the Indus, the Tigress Euphrates, and the Yellow River sites. Elsewhere, natural danger awaits, needing push back.

Described here, Heracles's first labor:

*In one part of Olympus a lion has killed many, and its hide proves so thick that the arrows of local farmers bounced off it. Indeed, upon tracking the lion, even the arrows of Heracles cannot penetrate it, and so Heracles deduces a vulnerability; he will choke the lion to death and does so in its lair. After that, rather than plated amour, Heracles wears the lion's skin, using the lion's head for a helmet.*

Many other local creatures meet their death at the hands of Heracles, who through his labors liberates the Greeks from their savage environs just as he had liberated them from slavery in Olympus.

Next, a different kind of labor:

*Augeas, an ally of Zeus throughout the war, whose large herds had supplied Zeus's troops with a steady supply of meat, now wants the favor returned. He needs his vast stables cleaned out as they have become overrun with animal dung. Heracles is to achieve this in a day.*

Episode 4 ends with Heracles diverting a river, making it swirl through Augeas' stables, flushing them clean in a single move. Through the labors, the Homo Sapiens in Greece now stand independent of Gaia's Nephilim kingdom. What will they achieve?

# EPISODE 5
# JASON'S ARGONAUTS
## 1,400 B.C.

After a while, the former Greek Slaves become accustomed to their freedom, with freedom presenting open pathways to imagination. The ambitious ones wish to see the world, and an expedition led by one Jason is eyed by Heracles who gladly joins as a "common" crewman.

1,400 B.C. remains ancient by today's standards. At the time, the Hebrews, for example, have just migrated out of Egypt, and the Indus Valley war recently happen. Homo Sapiens in charge of their own fate, unencumbered by Aliens or Nephilim, stays a rarity. Yet here Jason stands.

Back then, "the world", for Jason, consists of shore line colonies founded above Greece in the Black Sea area, and Jason and the crew are keen for the trip. *Just as the Tower of Babel had been humanity's first solo project, the voyage of the Argo would prove its second step towards self-fulfillment.*

King Pelias of Thessaly, warned that a man with only one sandal will one day bring about his downfall, sees that *Jason* has recently lost a sandal. Pelias decides to send him on a suicidal task to bring back the mythical Golden Fleece from Colchis, a kingdom on the distant shores of the Black Sea, ruled by a warlord King.

Besides Heracles, 50 others, like Orpheus – all from the generation preceding those of the Trojan war – join the expedition seeking glory and the fleece as plunder. Jason wants the crew to elect a leader, and Heracles nominates Jason, recognizing that management trumps raw physical prowess in such a complex endeavor.

The first port of call is Lemnos, where the women have killed off all their menfolk. The self-made widows are keen that the crew of the Argo should stay with them. *Jason* soon moves into the Queen's palace, along with most of his fellow questers. Only *Heracles* remains unmoved, able to make *Jason* and the other Argonauts see sense and continue the journey.

After this, to rescue his personal squire, Heracles separates from the crew, going off on his own set of journeys, with the Homo Sapient crew now left fending for itself. Grit, innovation and negotiation become the evolving traits of the Argonauts as alone, they grapple with obstacles in their path.

Finally they reach Colchis, set on the Black Sea beneath the Caucus Mountains where, after the flood, Noah first settled. Medea, daughter of the king, a sorcerer of potions, falls in love with Jason. More, four young lords of Colchis sign on with the Argo. But the King holds onto his fleece.

Medea offers to use poison against the serpent guarding the fleece clearing a path for Jason to steal it, but in turn, Jason must marry her and make her famous throughout Greece.

As the Argo escapes, it is blown across the sea to the mouth of the Danube. With a Colchis armada in pursuit, Jason's crew retreats into Europe, and makes their way out only above Sardinia. From there they drift to Libya on the African coast, form a small settlement and finally make it back to Greece. Jason does marry Medea, but with trouble ahead.

Episode 5 ends with the Argonauts sitting at a banquet table, clear eyed, now comprehending the extent of the earth, with many open horizons remaining to be mastered by these evolving Homo Sapiens. Medea sits with them, esteemed, basking in her station as a key contributor to an evolving Greece.

# EPISODE 6
# THESEUS THE LAW GIVER
## 1,400 B.C.

Decades before the Voyage of the Argonauts, there had been a shorter voyage made under Heracles. One of his crew was a young man named *Theseus*, who would mature to lead Athens into its experiment with "democracy.

Back then, the Amazons, an all-female, war-loving kingdom, lived along the Black Sea, but much closer to Greece than the distant Colchis kingdom of the golden fleece. The ninth labor of Heracles required that he bring back a leather belt owned by the Amazon Queen. But it is obvious that this invented labor was just a pretext for a war Zeus wanted to remove Amazon's threat to Greece.

Heracles had no trouble in finding a crew of young men anxious to travel with him on this ninth labor mission. *Theseus of Athens* joined, as his hero was Heracles. Heracles, through the freeing of Homo Sapiens from Olympus and by eliminating the most dangerous creatures roaming the land, had already cleared a rough road for civilization. But there was still more to do, and Theseus would carry humankind a step further.

In Theseus' boyhood, when Athens was yet a small village in the Attica region, the recently freed Athenians were continually inundated with marauders and pirates. A maturing Theseus steps into this void, personally killing the worst offenders, and with these credentials earned a seat on Heracles' boat.

Once Heracles' team reaches Amazon, initial talks break down, just as designed by Zeus. A slaughter erupts, with many Amazonians killed, and the Queen's belt taken. More, upon their exit, Theseus abducts the Queen's sister, bringing her back to Athens, though once there, he does not stay long. Emboldened by the preemptive strike against the Amazons, another adventure awaits Theseus in Crete.

At some point, the Greeks had killed the King of Crete's son, and rather than costly warfare, Zeus agreed to send 14 young Athenians each year to Crete to be killed by the Minitour, a bizarre 12-foot Nephilim monster with – what looked to be – boney hoofs for feet, wearing a bull's head for a helmet. Victims would be placed in a maze to be hunted down by this absurd monster. Theseus volunteered to be one of the 14, keen to kill the Minitour. He succeeds, returning to Athens in glory.

But while Theseus is away, Jason's Argonauts complete their voyage, and once they return, the political sands of Athens shift. Assuming Theseus dead, Medea, Jason's wife of ten years, "trades up", to marry Theseus's father, the King of Athens. Together they have a child, and Medea, always the schemer, expects her baby son to become king.

When Theseus returns, Medea, surprised by Theseus, prepares a poison to kill him. But the King – knowing Medea's propensity for poisons – bats the cup away saving his son, finally exiling Medea back to Colchis.

Episode 6 ends with Theseus being Attica's elder. Theseus who holds the alien trait craving independence, implements democratic self-rule in Athens. Now, at least for a brief moment in time, Homo Sapiens are no longer subjugated by either Aliens or Nephilim. Would this formula last and become humankind's way, or would primate traits for troop order and obedience lead humanity into a subservient life under Kings, Emperors and Dictators.

# EPISODE 7
# TROY ENDS OLYMPUS
## 1,200 B.C.

Zeus built his empire by eliminating older siblings and replacing them with children sired through his wife Hera and many other Alien and Homo Sapient woman. From Olympus, across 300 years, Zeus' extended family rule over their Homo Sapient underlings.

Being aliens from Siros, the Olympians prove a willful lot, doing as they please and defying Zeus himself. These young Olympians want their own projects and amorous conquests, and though Zeus tries to keep order, he must let them pursue their ambitions. It's a Sorian right.

Zeus's son Apollo claims Troy as his playground, and builds a giant walled city for Troy's Homo Sapient residents. Using anti-gravity, a massive stone wall is amassed to ring the city, and over the years, Troy becomes a dominant powerhouse, sitting between Greece and the other alien kingdoms further east.

But then there is Paris, son of the Trojan king Priam. Females adore Paris, and the Trojan war will be ignited in Olympus by Zeus' females, with Paris the spark.

Hera, Zeus' wife, with Athene and Aphrodite, Zeus' daughters, each believe they are the fairest females of the Olympian kingdom, and to decide the winner, they appeal to Paris. Hera offers Paris a place in Olympus, Athene offers protection in military situations and Aphrodite offers him the power to attract any woman on earth.

Paris choses the latter, making Aphrodite the winner, and from then on, making her a solid supporter of Troy. The rest is history, as

Paris uses his new charms on Helen.

And as the Greeks prepare to launch a thousand ships and Troy readies its defenses, Zeus explodes at his family's audacity to create havoc in his kingdom. Yet spoiled Apollo, Aphrodite and Athene go even further. Apollo and Aphrodite side with Troy and Athene sides with the Greeks, no matter how loud Zeus yells.

Odysseus, one of the Greek kings being recruited for the expedition, speaks out against this "petty" alien "god" madness. To any who might listen, he complains that Homo Sapiens are being used and abused by matters not of Homo Sapient making. Nevertheless, the cynic Odysseus reluctantly joins his fellow Greeks and journeys over to Troy.

The war becomes a stale mate, and this drives the respective alien backers crazy. Olympians on both sides begin to join their favorites out on the battle field … but in stealth. Unlike the Homo Sapiens, the Siron aliens can hide themselves in an adjacent time bucket, still there, but not seen. And through this stealth, boost military prowess out on the battle field. The carnage builds, with Odysseus becoming more despondent with the selfish, manipulative Olympians.

After ten years of war, Odysseus concocts the wooden horse device, a way to get into Troy and finish the war. It succeeds, but the further carnage caused is almost incomprehensible. Many of the great Homo Sapiens on both sides have died over the course of the war, and Odysseus preaches that it is time to abandon the Olympians, time for the Homo Sapiens to be on their own,

Up on Olympus, Zeus' family disintegrates, with many abandoning Greece to return to Siros. Basically Zeus only has Athene as his supporter, but she also stands devoted to Odysseus, though Odysseus rails against the gods.

Other holdout gods want to destroy Odysseus because of the anti-god mind set he is spreading to other Homo Sapiens. Athene, however, respects the true nobility of Odysseus, seeing him equal to any alien god. She will stay in his corner.

Episode 7 ends with Odysseus out at sea headed home from the war.

# EPISODE 8
# ODYSSEUS CYCLOPS KILLER
## 1,250 B.C.

1,250 B.C., and the Greek Nephilim era nears its end. Zeus will soon retire to Crete, with Admiral Xi directing his aliens to return to Siros. Do other renegade Nephilim colonies flourish elsewhere?

A lot has transpired in the 800 years since the alien Queen Gaia established Olympus, her blasphemes Nephilim kingdom. It would corrupt Greece for centuries. But ever since Zeus freed Heracles and the Homo Sapient slaves, many Greek villages have grown into city states, now run by Homo Sapient kings. Athens stands "democratically" free allowing noble Homo Sapiens a say in how their city's business takes shape.

Over on the Turkish coast, *Troy*, founded in Zeus's time by his son Apollo and once visited by Heracles before the war, has been destroyed. It was the guile of Odysseus, the quick-thinking Greek warrior who implemented the *Trojan Horse* tactic, that brought Troy to its knees.

But as the saying goes, "no good deed goes unpunished". And so, in returning home, Odysseus's ship is blown west, by Poseidon, Zeus's brother, beyond Italy, towards the last outposts of the original Greek Nephilim – the Cyclopes. Here, hundreds of years after the War of the Titans, Odysseus will finish the Titan extermination, wanting to or not.

Throughout his ten-year journey, no matter what the remaining Olympians throw at him, Odysseus will not capitulate into obedience. They are not gods, they have become alien obstacles to the Homo Sapient race.

Passing an island, Odysseus' crew hear sheep bleating and they all go ashore seeking food. Finding a cave full of cheese they are soon trapped inside when the last fertile female Cyclops on earth enters, blocking the cave door with a bolder.

Like other Titans, she sees Homo Sapiens as a delicacy and each night devours one of the crew. She asks Odysseus his name to which Odysseus responds "Nobody".

The crew offers her strong wine that has not been watered down and soon she dozes off. Once asleep, a sharpened pole is thrust into her eye. Screaming, the older Cyclops on the island come running asking "who did this". Her response "nobody".

The elders say it serves her right for being careless. She is to wait for her husband to return. The next morning as she lets her sheep out, Odysseus and his crew hold themselves underneath the sheep, as each sheep passes through the fingers of the now blind Cyclops.

Her husband returns, but his wife soon dies of her wound, leaving no Cyclops able to bear children. All die in the decades to come.

Episode 8 ends with her husband crying in despair. The Greek Nephilim are gone forever. Zeus, at 300 years old, after enduring three wars, and after losing his family, has had enough, and retires to his birth place Crete, where he lies buried today.

# End of season 3

# SEASON 4

## Moses

## *Return of the Nephilim*

*" Behold, I say unto you that the law is fulfilled that was given unto Moses. "*

—JESUS—

# EPISODE 1
# TUTA MOSES THE GENERAL
## 1,500 B.C.

In 1,700 B.C., 70 Hebrews, a people of Chaldean stock through Noah's grandson Arphaxad, and the offspring of Abraham, arrive in Egypt. As described in *The Exodus* of the Hebrew bible, they live along the Nile River for 225 years until led out of Egypt by 80-year-old Moses.

In those days, the Pharaoh ruling Egypt was an Alien from Siros.

In 1,550 B.C. the Pharaoh's sister adopts a Hebrew baby hidden in river reeds naming him Tuta Moses.

Though Homo Sapient, Tuta Moses is brought up a court prince. One day, Moses' adoptive uncle the Pharaoh calls on Moses – then 26 years old – to lead an army south against attacking forces from The Sudan.

*General Moses* crushes the enemy, and sets up ASWAN a garrison city for Egypt's protection thereafter, today the site of the Aswan Dam. All of Egypt sings his praises but one, Pharaoh, as this mere Homo Sapient suddenly stands too exalted. Exiled, Moses flees to the Persian Gulf, marrying an African Cushite girl named Zipporah, where he lives happily until age 80 when a new Pharaoh takes the throne allowing Moses' safe return to court.

Admiral Xi, though, has other ideas. He has chosen the 80-year old General to lead the Hebrews east, where Moses is to kill the descendants from one of Noah's other 16 grandsons, Canaan. A new crop of Nephilim giants somehow evolved from the Canaan line.

Unbeknownst at the time of the Ark, Canaan's mother was not pure, but carried *recessive* Nephilim genes. Her descendants therefore would have a chance of producing Nephilim babies, and a sure chance of passing recessive genes along. And though the people stood re-infected, a second world-wide flood was out of the question.

Lieutenant Uriel was not pleased when the Admiral ordered him to recruit Moses, to spend the next 40 years turning the Hebrews into an unstoppable special ops unit with the ability – and more importantly the will – to destroy all living beings across 32 Canaanite cities.

It was a bad assignment, but not all bad, as the might of the Siros empire would stand behind Uriel, including the *land Ark*, which housed the anti-gravity weaponry developed by the Enigmatic Lady during the China campaign.

There was no saying "no". The die was cast, as the Admiral had failed with the flood, and had even tried nuclear weapons, evaporating the most-depraved Nephilim strong holds, Sodom and Gomorrah. But the Siros high command no longer wanted these options, so it would be hand-to-hand, under Uriel – their version of Lt. General George Armstrong Custer.

Episode 1 ends with Noah and Noah's older brother Aaron listening in shock to Lord Uriel, called thereafter by all "the Lord".

# EPISODE 2
# LORD URIEL
## 1,500 B.C.

Lord Uriel is not a "nice guy", he is the best ground op's officer in the Siros ranks. As such, it is his way or the highway, and this often-meant execution of anyone crossing him.

"The Lord", as he demanded to be called, was not going to accept much "bunk" from his fellow Alien the Pharaoh, though like all Aliens, Pharaoh would likely resist authority coming from the higher ups. Moses, who grew up with these "live free or die" guys, could not see the new Pharaoh letting the Hebrews go, no matter the agenda coming down from Siros.

Like the Mayans, the Egyptian Pharaohs were proud builders of stone structures and communication beacons. They too used anti-gravity technology to do the heavy lifting with the Hebrews around for finishing jobs. At the time, a major Pyramid was going up, and without the 5,000 Hebrew laborers on hand, progress would grind to a halt.

Moses did not want to do it, but Lord Uriel made Moses go to Pharaoh's palace demanding the Hebrews be allowed to leave. It took all of Moses' diplomatic experience in court to calmly pitch this outrageous proposition. Like the Wizard of Oz, Pharaoh blew the doors off as Moses was escorted out.

Lord Uriel concluded "Ok, no more mister nice guy" and had the *Land Ark* readied. The absence of gravity can really get frogs and locusts going, and the assault continued. Finally, anti-gravity was used against Egyptian newborns, many dying of dis-equilibrium.

The Hebrews, 5,000 men, 20,000 woman and children and domesticated flocks of thousands march towards the Red Sea where the *Land Ark* uses gravitational push to divide the waters. The Hebrews make it across, but Pharaoh's chariots – sent out to fetch them back – get swallowed up.

The Hebrews are now in the Sinai dessert, and Pharaoh has lost his army. Soon, The Sudan desert peoples – called the Shepard's – will attack a defenseless Egypt, killing Pharaoh and his Alien family line. Lord Uriel, yet another Alien, though, is in business. Because, in the Sorian world, everyone is on their own.

Episode 2 ends with Uriel feeding the Hebrews, using gravity from the Land Ark to drive birds from the marshes into the desert.

# EPISODE 3
# SINAI & THE ADMIRAL
## 1,450 B.C.

Moses and his brother Aaron are in charge of the Hebrew horde, as Lord Uriel wants no contact with them whatsoever. Still, it would help to know the plan, as the 25,000 Hebrews sitting in the desert are already complaining. Little do they know that they will not go into battle for another 40 years.

But that's the point, Uriel does not want the current lineup of "stone masons" for the job of killing giants, he wants the next generation, the ones he can turn into steel from scratch.

But first, Lord Uriel wants things his way. He wants a tent where he can meet privately with Moses; he wants meals brought to him prepared just so. When food is not prepared properly, someone dies. Uriel actually lives in a *Vimamas* hovering high above the tent, and he rides a gravity field down to communicate with Moses.

He dictates all kinds of rules kept in books – possibly papaya paper with Sumerian cuneiform writing, as Egyptian writing consists of only 900 decorative pictures, whereas cuneiform is an actual articulate language.

Some Hebrews get too close to his tent, and Uriel uses anti-gravity to have them swallowed by the desert. Aaron's sons do something wrong and are incinerated. All of these things – and more – are told in the first books of the Hebrew bible.

Military training is one thing, but unwavering will power is something more, and the Admiral fears that rather than despise the

Nephilim, that Hebrew men may join the rampant sexuality practiced in that society. The Admiral comes down from his star cruiser, the Ark, to Mount Sinai.

Until then, Homo Sapiens were taught practical things like "the wheel", but the Admiral wants Moses to learn wrong from right, with Nephilim practices recognized as being as wrong as can be. To get Moses started, the Admiral hands him ten basic tenants of good behavior, etched in stone, and lets Moses and Uriel return down to the desert.

Here the worst happens, as while away, the Hebrews began worshipping a gold cow, an actual Nephilim god, and heads roll.

Next, Lord Uriel orders a scouting mission into Nephilim territory. Joshua is selected as captain, and out they go. He is to report on "the land of milk and honey", the land promised to the Hebrews for their participation against the Nephilim. When back, Joshua endorses the bounty of those fertile lands and says "though we appear as grasshoppers next to the giants", that he, Joshua believes they can be beaten.

With that, Uriel has finally found his military rock.

Episode 3 ends with Joshua speaking to everyone amongst camp fires, with the worried faces of the people visible in the night.

# EPISODE 4
# JORDANIAN NEPHILIM
## 1,400 B.C.

After the Babel diaspora, Canaan's "genetically infected" people settle both sides of the Dead Sea. By 1,400 B. C., one thousand years have gone by since the flood, and occasionally, Nephilim babies pop out. You see, much of Canaan's population hold recessive Nephilim genes, but at conception, only should both parents deliver a recessive Nephilim gene, will a giant be created. After that, typically, no one gets in a giant's way, and so Nephilim giants rule their cities.

In 1,400 B.C. there are approximately 32 such Nephilim strongholds in the region, with dominant family clans like the Jebusites ruling Jerusalem.

After 40 years, Lord Uriel is finally ready to move against the Nephilim, but first a few adjustments.

Number one, Uriel wants a personal staff to move his tent, to tend to sacred rites, and to cook his meals. There are 12 Hebrew tribes, and Uriel decrees that the Levites will be attached to him as full-time valets. The other 11 tribes will pay a tax to support the Levites so that Uriel is fully served.

Second, though Moses will stay with the horde while attacking the first two Nephilim kings on the Jordanian side of the Dead Sea, at 120 years old he will retire, and the top military commander for the full 32-city campaign will be Joshua.

It starts with Kings Sihon and Og on the Jordanian side of the Dead Sea, true Nephilim giants. Og, for example, stands some 13 feet tall, has lived for more than 1,000 years, and upon his death by the Hebrews, his 16-foot bed is taken with them and held in Jerusalem for another thousand years.

Along the way, the *Land Ark* knocks down city walls and drives ground hornets into the eyes of the Nephilim. The Hebrew special op fighters move in for all the rest.

After killing *all* on the east side of the Dead Sea, the Hebrew horde sits across the Jordan river in front of Jericho, their first true "milk and honey" target, and it represents the end of the road for one of the great figures of Homo Sapient history: MOSES.

He dies on the Jordan side of the river, buried on a mountain top.

Episode 4 ends with Joshua starring across the Jordan River at the lights of Jericho.

# JERICHO TUMBLES

## 1,400 B.C.

Upon the death of Moses at age 120, Joshua, probably 80 years of age himself, works directly with "the Lord" to exterminate the "crossbred" Nephilim giants still living in Canaan. Across the River Jordan, the Nephilim people of Jericho cower in fear, with reports of the feats of the Hebrew horde.

Joshua claims an army of 40,000 fighters hardened by the Sinai desert waiting to cross the Jordan River. Lord Uriel orders the Land Ark brought up, warns all not to look at it, and suddenly the river stops flowing. The army crosses, parking itself on the broad plain in front of the walls of Jericho.

Next, with terrified Nephilim citizens huddled inside the city, Uriel resets the Ark and has it *quietly* marched around the city seven times. Upon his signal every Hebrew shouts and stomps, and all the bricks, the walls and buildings come tumbling down.

40,000 Hebrews pick through the rubble finishing the annihilation.

From Jericho, many other events transpire as 32 kingdoms are to fall, but the common denominator of the campaign bares the complete destruction of entire populations. For example, read Joshua's report on the city of Ai, which fell following Jericho:

*When Israel had finished killing all the men of Ai in the fields and in the wilderness where they had chased them, and when every one of them had been put to the sword, all the Israelites returned to Ai and killed those who were in it. Twelve thousand men and women fell that day—all the people of Ai.*

In many locations, the local king reigned a giant, a Nephilim byproduct of insemination by the Watchers in the time of Enoch 1,500 years back. And now, via the army of the Exodus, these genetic bloodlines are finally about to end.

But the mystery remains ... why does Joshua stop at 30 kingdoms when two more remain, those of Jerusalem and the Philistine? The Philistine territory stood south, between Canaan and Egypt, a known Nephilim society. And some 400 years later David would have to fight the nine-and-one-half-foot-tall Philistine Goliath, and Goliath had brothers of this same stature, so ... what gives?

Did the army have enough of warfare? The Book of Joshua concludes with bickering over parcels of land being handed out to the 12 tribes.

Episode 5 ends with a distant image of Joshua in debate with Lord Uriel .

# EPISODE 6
# SATAN'S SABOTAGE
## 1,400 B.C.

Satan's Nephilim "children" are being slaughtered by the Exodus army. He needs to do something.

Satan is, most of all, flexible! He has done what damage he can both militarily and through the poisoning of minds, but at this juncture new tactics are needed.

Because Satan learns from experience, he respects the kernel of the Enigmatic Lady's achievement. Rather than attack the object, weaken the object's basic material.

Siros itself must be weakened.

Satan contacts his old ally, *The Pentons*, and works them over, saying that Siros is weak, on the edge of collapse, overextended and vulnerable. The time for a first strike is now!

And this predictable dream takes hold. Penton attacks Siros right at the end of the Exodus campaign. With Siros engaged in inter-galactic war, Lord Uriel is called back as the Nephilim issue on Earth pales in comparison.

Uriel, though, upon his final departure, takes the anti-gravity device from the Land Ark, leaving only the stone tablets given to Moses by the Admiral many years back.

Joshua suddenly must work alone, and without anti-gravity weaponry. He adopts a policy of not being bogged down by long sieges, and so decides to go around fortified Jerusalem, leaving its Nephilim rulers be, and forgoing an attack on the Philistines.

And then, when two Hebrew tribes desert Joshua to take possession of the former Jordanian kingdoms of Og and Sihon, the Exodus car finally runs out of gas, and the other tribes too clamor for their prizes.

Joshua has done what he can with the cards dealt. Israel, left with an unfinished campaign, will have to wait for the other Nephilim shoe to drop.

Episode 6 ends with an exhausted Joshua standing next to an empty Ark, looking to the heavens.

# EPISODE 7
# EGYPT FALLS
## 1,400 B.C.

Pharaoh stands devastated. Losing the Hebrews appears an inconvenience compared to having lost most of his army in the Red Sea. His southern border with Sudan, once sealed off by the young General Moses, appears an open door enticing the jealous Homo Sapiens living further south, people who have been subjugated for centuries by the Alien dynasty of Pharaohs.

Pharaoh, at first, hateful of Lord Uriel, his fellow alien, finally accepts that in defying Uriel, he defied the Admiral, empowering Uriel to unleash the anti-gravity weaponry held in the land Ark.

Lacking man power, an idea surfaces. Engineers suggest converting the electrical might of the pyramid system into a defensive weapon deployed against enemy ships coming up the Nile from the south from the Sudan.

The pyramids already operate as a self-charging batteries. Electric energy from the earth builds up within the quartz stone held deep inside the pyramid, and the pyramid's limestone covering acts as a sheath, holding the accumulated charge in place until needed.

The white limestone plates appear as mirrors, making the pyramids visible from space as alien ships approach.

Building upon their electrical infrastructure, voltage guns are set up along the river, and the expected assault begins.

Just like the Egyptians had judged the Hebrews, the attacking Sudanese forces are called Shepard's by Pharaoh, due to their desert livestock way of life and their practice of eating animal flesh, something abhorrent to the Egyptians.

Know that Moses had once explained to Pharaoh that Hebrews sacrificing to their God inside of Egypt is not possible, as in doing so the Hebrews would be stoned by the Egyptians.

And so, Pharaoh both fears and despises the Sudanese Sheppard's.

The invading army soon shows itself up river. Getting closer it appears as a large flotilla of small boats. But unbeknownst to the Egyptians, only two Sudanese crew members operate each boat, though dummies are carefully planted to present a full contingent.

One-by-one the small ships are hit and effectively incinerated, but there are thousands of them, and Pharaoh becomes incensed, shouting at the gunners to take better aim, though the soldiers have had no other experience to build upon.

Amongst all of this consternation, the real Sudanese army, who had recently ridden on the boats before disembarking, where they disappeared into the desert, now arise out of nowhere on both sides of the river. Pharoah and his remaining army are crushed.

The Sheppard leader, a mere Homo Sapient, proclaims himself Pharaoh. Eight hundred years of Alien rule in Egypt has ended.

Episode 7 ends with the Shepard hoard marching inside the palace walls.

# EPISODE 8
# GOLIATH
## 1,000 B.C.

1,000 B.C., and four hundred years have gone by since Joshua's time. Israel – a land of milk and honey no longer *overrun* by Nephilim – is occupied by the 12 Hebrew tribes. Still, even now, two Nephilim societies prevail.

A Philistine stronghold lies south of Israel in the area of today's Gaza strip, with five royal cities, *Gath* the capitol. As well, the Jebusites' city-state of Jerusalem still stands inside its walls.

Through these remaining descendants of Canaan, recessive Nephilim genes float about. Because recessive, over time they will disappear from the species, but this could take thousands of years. Meanwhile, should two parents with recessive genes find each other, a giant can result. This is the case with Goliath, who has three brothers of similar make up.

Things start badly once Goliath's army defeats Israeli King Saul, captures the now symbolic Land Ark, and carries it off to the Philistine temple of *Dagon*. The next morning, however, Nephilim priests find the statue of the god Dagon face down before the Ark.

Philistines near the temple become infected with radiation tumors, and like a hot potato, send the Land Ark to the next Philistine city with the same result. Finally, loaded on a farm cart together with gifts, the Land Ark is returned to Israel.

Still, the Israeli/Philistine war continues as twice daily for 40 days Goliath challenges the Israelites to send out a champion for *single combat*. Saul, himself afraid, allows shepherd David to accept the challenge. David takes only his staff, sling and five stones from a brook.

As a shepherd boy, David had spent all day, every day flinging stones at targets with mindboggling, even long-distant accuracy.

David's first stone hits Goliath in the forehead, and like the statue of Dagon, Goliath falls on his face at David's feet. Using Goliath's giant sword, David cuts off the head, and the escaping Philistines are hunted down "as far as *Gath*". David becomes King and eventually mops up the Jerusalem Nephilim as well.

So one ponders, after all of this, are the Nephilim – Satan's nephews and nieces – finally kaput, or did some escape, and if so to where?

Regardless, Homo Sapiens still hold Alien genes from the original neuron implant. Mostly primate and partially Alien, we find ourselves anxious, different, wanting to control nature, wanting to control each other, some wanting to impose obedience, while others defy overlords, insisting upon fierce independence.

Since then, the obedience versus liberty camps live – alone together – in full conflict, and neither God, Aliens nor Evolution can save us.

# END OF SEASON 4

# SEASON 5

## *Renegade Children*

### Escaping to America

*" Come, let us choose us wives from among the children of men and beget us children "*

—ENOCH—

# EPISODE 1
# SASQUATCH –
# THE "BIGFOOT" FREEDOM FIGHTER
## 2,000 B.C.

His name: **Sasquatch**, leader of a great ape breed genetically upgraded by aliens ... just like we were. You see, Aliens experimented with other primates, not just Humans.

Upon settling China's Yellow River valley in 2,200 B.C., the *Yellow Emperor* of the planet *Sorios* (the lead Alien who escorted Tiras and the Homo Sapiens out of Babel to China) was allowed to operate autonomously, as is the right of all Sorions. This meant that the alien "Emperor" ran his territory with no restraint by the higher ups back at the home planet of Sorios, as genetically, Sorions stood ultra-libertarian.

Besides fostering his Chinese colony, the Emperor was keen to understand the numerous great ape species then multiplying in south east Asia, and in particular, an ape whose bones today are called *Gigantopithecus.*

The Yellow Emperor instructed his doctors to upgrade the ape and to include an alien ability to slightly shift time, allowing one to momentarily "disappear" through an energy alteration. Today we call this flexible property of energy quantum physics.

Within the laws of quantum physics, energy operates differently than matter. Energy particles – like electrons and light photons – have no weight. Each energy packet exists as a spread-out wave – like ripples in a pond. This is why one cannot pin point the location of an electron. Potentially the electron resides simultaneously in many locations across the span of the wave form. *Quantum physics* – the physics of energy and time.

The Yellow Emperor of China decided to try this "time shimmying" faculty out on the Gigantopithecus primates and accordingly, male and female Gigantopithecus embryos were manipulated. Out of this came the first enlightened Bigfoot male and, the first female … Sasquatch and Sasha – the Bigfoot versions of Adam and Eve.

And it worked, except for one problem. Once the Bigfoot offspring mastered this time shimmying ability, they decided to use it to hide from their overlords, an unintended consequence of bestowing the ability within the primate line. What is more, the hybrid Bigfoot species also inherited the independent streak that aliens are known for. Yes, libertarian Bigfoots were afoot!

And so, as the brood multiplied, like all liberty lovers, Sasquatch wanted to separate from both the Emperor and the Emperor's Homo Sapient slaves.

As the escaped plan unfolded, *Yeti* – Sasquatch's son – fled into the Himalaya mountains – becoming today's abominable snowmen. But most of the Bigfoot clan crossed the Asia/Alaska land bridge into North America.

Here they live today, known as Bigfoots, though American Indian legend calls them Sasquatches. Even now, a Bigfoot clan leader is called Sasquatch.

At first, the small clan settles in the Pacific Northwest, where they easily multiply and spread out across the continent. Existing alone for centuries, eventually American Mongolians coming in from Asia, moving east from the Pacific coast, and later Europeans moving west from the Atlantic coast, encroach Bigfoot's world.

Recently Bigfoot voices have been recorded – jesting with those who dare invade their wilderness domains – with footprints sometimes found. But it is their ability to disappear in time with that slight energy shift which keeps them isolated, safe from the Homo Sapient race.

Through biological stealth, Bigfoots can live in many North American regions. Tempestuous creatures who can lash out at and intimidate invaders, and even take Homo Sapient wives, revered as preservers of nature, and sometimes connected to UFO sightings, … they accumulate knowledge and history which they employ for their well-being, in their own way.

Today, their instinct for danger is so refined that in using time they can evade bullets the way their alien ancestors evaded missiles.

Episode 1 ends with a Bigfoot clan of 20 camped along a wilderness lake somewhere in Oregon.

# EPISODE 2
# THE MONGOLIAN TRIBES
## 1,000 B.C.

Episode 2 follows a Sasquatch troop leader in Northern California as he tests *Tanta*, a Homo Sapient tribal chief migrating from Mongolia down the Pacific coast.

For the Bigfoot people, many centuries of peaceful living transpire in North America, as no other sapient peoples invade their world. And indeed they are to be considered people, as like ourselves, they stand part primate and part alien.

All along, Mongolian tribes had been migrating from Asia across the Alaskan land bridge. But once in North America, the Homo Sapient immigrants keep to the coast, moving south into Central and South America, with the Rocky Mountains and the endless western deserts representing barriers to these wandering Homo Sapiens.

But one Mongolian chief, *Tanta*, has the ambition to peek over the hill – sort of speak – and does so in what today is northern California. He travels with just three others, leaving the tribe on the coast.

In deep timberland they camp, and at night the forest seems to speak to them. At around 2 a.m. they all hear a high-pitched scream. Then silence, then some stomping around, and then they hear the scream again, longer this time, and all agree it not a human scream or that of any animal they know of. Next, a few rocks fly out of the woods landing near Tanta, but not striking him.

So Tanta's men answer back, placing some food in the perimeter just beyond the fire light.

The local Sasquatch chief directs his Bigfoot lieutenants to grab the food, which they consume, staying out of sight. Then the Bigfoots resume their calls, which Tanta's people again respond to in kind. Alone, Tanta walks towards the perimeter, hands open, inviting an encounter.

Moments later, Sasquatch, at 9 feet tall and 800 pounds, shows himself. Tanta sits on a fallen tree. Thirty feet away Sasquatch squats to the ground, and they quietly stare at each other, two mature primate/aliens, unafraid, taking stock.

Sasquatch knew of the legends. Generations ago his Bigfoot ancestors had escaped these Homo Sapiens in China, but now here they stood, camped in his forest.

Sasquatch decides to make a point. Shifting his energy center, he slightly moves in time and disappears. Tanta is amazed. A moment later Sasquatch re-appears,. He laughs at this playful joke, and the hidden Bigfoot troop behind him laughs as well from the darkness.

It is a message – be careful with us! Stay away.

Episode 2 ends with both sides backing away.

# EPISODE 3
# ALIEN ALLIES –
# COPING WITH HUMANKIND
## A.D. 1950

In Episode 3, *Alien Allies*, a modern Bigfoot clan is visited by aliens, who try to help the Bigfoots survive the expanding Homo Sapiens.

People always wonder: are Aliens still here on Earth? The evidence, of course, is overwhelming. Modern UFO experiences are legion.

But if so why are they here?

In earlier times, Admiral Xi and Soros put all of their will into fostering the Homo Sapiens. But ever since Cain killed Able, they realized that a troublesome species was on the loose. But ever since World War II with our nuclear capabilities in place, with our taking over of the planet and with the extermination of many other species … us, their wayward children, have finally become a net negative.

And it's not simply our impact on Earth. It is our impact on each other. The conflict between obedience-loving primates and liberty-loving aliens seems unreconcilable, and it grows worse over time. Both the Socialist and the Libertarian Homo Sapiens defend their way of life to the hilt, taking no prisoners. Amongst all of this Homo Sapient chaos, the Bigfoot race clings to survival.

And so, out of thousands of Big Foot reports, some claim that UFOs shine a light to which the Bigfoot steps into to be brought on board. But consider:

Other UFO sagas featuring Homo Sapiens claim the same.

And recall, Enoch, Noah's grandfather claimed the same.

Perhaps we should consider these to be "sincere accounts".

Still, Bigfoot is just one renegade species surviving Homo Sapiens. Other cross-bred species – including the Ohio "Nephilim" giants and Tennessee's 3-foot Little People – have tried survival, also in North America, only to be squeezed out by migrating Mongolian Indians moving east, and English settlers moving west.

# EPISODE 4
# THE LITTLE PEOPLE –
# THE ISLAND OF PAN
## 1,700 B.C.

*Episode 4* covers the migration of the Little People to Ireland as they flee the Homo Sapient expansion in the Mediterranean/Black Sea basin.

The *Little People* are not some sort of Homo Sapient mutation – like dwarfs with mis-proportioned heads – they are a separate, elegant race trying to survive alongside the Homo Sapiens.

Years prior to Adam and Eve, Admiral Xi ran an experiment on the island of **Pan**, which before the flood, once sat as part of **Pan**gea, off the coast of modern day Ja**pan**. He was trying to genetically engineer a species suited for working the mines, until then operated by his rebellious Sorion workers. It was the first attempt by the Sorions to breed a working class species on Earth, but later they would conduct a second experiment that resulted in us, the Homo Sapiens, and then a third creating the Bigfoots.

The Little People bred on Pan were only 2 to 3 feet tall, perfect for the mining jobs all taking place in the tunnels.

When the decision came down to unleash the flood, just like Noah and his clan, Tye, along with his extended family living in Pan, was transported up to Admiral Xi's Star Cruiser *The Ark*.

Once the flood waters receded, the Little People, who were mainly vegetarians, spread out on Earth during the two hundred years that Noah's offspring occupied Babel. Eventually the Little People and the Homo Sapiens would come in contact in the Black Sea area and elsewhere, but the Little People generally lived in isolation, doing their own thing.

Aristotle said that in an outlying mountain region on the Black Sea, in springtime, their entire band – mounted on the backs of rams and she-goats, armed with arrows, went in a body down to the sea to eat cranes' eggs and chicks, and that this outing occupies three months.

But by 1,700 B.C., the Greeks begin to push north into Scythia, Little People territory, and a very old Tye decides to move his clans west, to the uninhabited reaches of Europe. Back then, sea levels remained low due to the remnant ice packs amassed at the poles, and what is now the British Isles stayed connected to mainland Europe across a deep valley called Doggerland. Tye and his people cross this valley and settle in. As the years go by, and sea levels rise, they become cut off, but protected.

In isolation they no longer work the mines, yet they retain their abilities to work the ground, and they build earth and stone struc-tures aligned with the heavens throughout the British Isles, the most famous Stone Henge.

The "Little People" as called by their Homo Sapient cousins, remain on the islands for centuries, tiny, human-looking, red-haired beings just two-to-three feet tall, living in caves, mainly vegetarian, with squinty eyes, generally operating at night.

Episode 4 ends with a small group of these "leprechauns" sitting on a rocky mountain ridge.

# EPISODE 5
# ESCAPE TO AMERICA –
# THE CELTIC INVASION OF BRITAIN
## 700 B.C.

In episode 5 – *Escape to America*, the Little People form an alliance with Nephilim giants fleeing the Middle East.

Arriving west around 1,700 B.C., the Little People live in isolation. Years later their world is shaken by the Hebrew assault against the Nephilim, as this disruption spills onto the British Isles.

Recall, Joshua does not exterminate every Nephilim, many escape. And in 1,400 B.C., with sea levels lower than today, a band of Nephilim Giants sail west along uninhabited coastlines and makes it across the then shallow North Sea waters into Britain.

Upon encountering each other, the Little People feel a kinship with these giants as both races dread the ever-violent Homo Sapiens. More, they can be of use to each other. Little People are natural builders, and the Nephilim know much about agriculture and in navigating the sea.

At first both races stay put on the islands, but the Nephilim gradually take their boats further north and west, past Iceland and Greenland, finding the Saint Lawrence Seaway in North America, making it as far as the Great Lakes. There they discover a copper source so rich, that huge chunks of the metal sit in the soil. Each spring, a few boats carrying Nephilim captains and Little People workers cross the Atlantic to work the Great Lake mines, returning to the British Isles by early fall.

It is estimated that half a billion pounds of copper were mined in tens of thousands of pits on Isle Royale set off the Keweenaw Peninsula of Michigan, mined by these ancient mariners over a period of a thousand years, ending only in A.D. 1,200.

Did the annual sea excursions go on for that length of time? No, something else took place.

After living cooperatively on the British Islands from 1,400 B.C. onward, in 700 B.C., the Little People/Giant partnership was finally threatened by Celtic Homo Sapiens who made it west, and invaded the islands. All Nephilim families and many Little People families sailed away, resettling in North America.

The Nephilim set roots in the Ohio River basin, and the Little People settled further south along the smoky mountains of Tennessee where they could better construct their underground homes. Still, every spring, some of the Little People travelled north to meet up with their Giant compatriots, and head up the Michigan peninsular for another season of mining.

This tradition continued for another 1,900 years, with copper sold west to the Vikings, and south to the Indian races of Central and South America.

"Michigan copper" has unique properties with district impurities that sets it apart from European and Eastern sources. Some relics turning up in Europe are of Michigan copper.

What caused all of this commerce to end? How did the Giants and the Little People cease to be? Episode 5 ends with a scene from the Michigan mining pits, showing the Little People at work, directed by giants.

# EPISODE 6
# THE OHIO MOUND BUILDERS –
# THE IROQUOIS &
# THE CHEROKEE MONGOLIANS
## A.D. 1000

*Episode 6 – The Ohio Mound Builders*, reveals the backstory behind the more than 10,000 mound formations built from the Great Lakes, south to Natchez Mississippi.

Today, in modern times, there are only a handful, and maybe only 3 people on Earth that stand 8 feet tall. No nine footers exist. And yet, within the thousands of mounds dug up in Ohio and further south, thousands of eight and nine foot skeletons have been discovered in the A.D. 1,800 onward time period.

These Giants had reddish and blond hair, and tradition has it that they once crossed the Atlantic to settle in North America, this happening 1,500 years before Eric the Red of Norway found Greenland. Our story picks up from this time perspective.

Once permanently in America around 700 B.C., besides copper mining, the Nephilim giants took stock of the land in the Ohio and Mississippi valleys, and with their Little People partners, slowly cleared it for agriculture, and for the building of cities.

And they built mounds and henges galore, mounds used as foundations for village complexes and for burial of the Nephilim chiefs, whereas henges were aligned with the heavens, used for religious purposes, just as the henges of old were built back in the British Isles. Their gods remain unknown, though we know that the Sun is featured.

Eventually, great agricultural works engulfed these lowland valley structures, the farmlands providing food for both the Nephilim and for the Little People.

We find the Little People commuting between Tennessee and the Ohio in the good weather, bringing their labor north for ground-building projects and for mining, lugging food provisions back with them south, to sustain the Little People families dwelling underground along the Appellation highlands.

Because the Nephilim gene is recessive, most Nephilim were five-to-six feet in height. But the "royal" members of the population with double Nephilim gene switches – the princes and princesses – married each other, keeping the seven-to-nine foot specimens in place, able to dominate society for centuries. Even the females stood seven feet!

Some Nephilim skeletons show double rows of teeth and six fingers and toes, indicating that royalty stood as a separate caste.

For 2,000 years – from 700 B.C. to A.D. 1,300 – this societal arrangement kept its equilibrium, unchallenged. The American Mongol tribes remained west and the Spanish, French and English, who eventually would come in from the east, were not yet even in existence.

And so the years went by.

Back in time, when the original Nephilim lived in Israel and Jordan, their political model was one of city states. Nephilim kings generally kept to themselves, as these beings were heavily weighted with the Alien trait of libertarianism. Each city stayed clear of the others.

Once in America, the same genetic behavior was replicated. Various Nephilim city states spread across the land, each with royal giants, common citizens, and loyal Little People workers. Conflict was avoided.

But in avoiding conflict, no experience in defense or in warfare was honed. Any invader would have the upper hand. And so, when the American Mongol tribes – fierce Homo Sapiens – crossed the Mississippi, the Nephilim were doomed.

Episode 6 ends atop the grand Nephilim city on the Mississippi (just east of Saint Louis), with Nephilim royalty looking west into the sunset.

# EPISODE 7
# THE TRAIL OF TEARS – THE DEMISE
## AD 1830

*In Episode 7 – Trail of Tears*, we consider the verbal traditions of the American Mongolian tribes, describing the move east across the Mississippi around A.D. 1200, encountering both the Ohio Giants and the Little People.

Why did it take so long for the races to encounter each other?

Mongolian Homo Sapiens had been in the Americas for close to 3,000 years before pushing away from the Pacific into the continental interior. Ultimately many of these wandering tribes reached the Atlantic, settling all the land from Canada down through Florida.

The Iroquois came across north, through the Ohio valley, ending in the New York forests. The path taken first brought them head to head with the Nephilim Giants of Ohio.

At the same time, the Cherokees were moving east leaving Texas and Oklahoma, travelling a more southern route. The Cherokees entered Little People territory near Sparta, Tennessee, just west of the Cumberland Gap.

Up north, history was repeating itself. Just as Joshua and the Hebrews annihilated the Nephilim Giants of Israel and Jordan, the Iroquois quickly took down the American Nephilim who after 2,000 years of isolation had no meaningful defense concept or ability.

Though the slaughter took time, as there were many Nephilim city states scattered throughout the upper mid-west, everything quickly ground to a halt, including the habits of the Little People, who, after 2,000 years of symbiotic dependency on their Nephilim overlords, suddenly found themselves abandoned with no economy or way of life.

But the Little People – by temperament and deep experience – knew how to survive amongst larger species, and somehow they made a pact with the Cherokees. In doing so, they hung on with their new partners for five more centuries – A.D. 1300 to A.D. 1800.

Not so for the Nephilim. The Iroquois closed the net. Legend has it that the extermination of the final Nephilim clan took place on Sand Island, on the Ohio River, near the Ohio falls. Centuries later bones from the slaughter fields still covered the area.

As said by the Iroquois, the fallen Nephilim chief stood 9 foot tall, brandishing reddish yellow hair. As in the days of Joshua, no man, woman of child was spared.

And the Little People, though mainly centered in Tennessee, would spread out, like they once did in Europe and Asia, looking for safe American places to set up homesteads. Consider these traditions:

> The Mohegans describe small people who lived below Mohegan Hill in Connecticut. They were not to be spoken about during the summer when they were active, and not to be stared at; otherwise, they would freeze you and steal your things. In return for the food and respect, they taught how to grow corn and use healing plants.

> The Eskasoni in Canada say that little people lived on a hill in Nova Scotia. Children were told not to go near it, lest they be stolen.

> The Shoshone tribe in the Rocky Mountains tell of little people who used bows and poisoned arrows to keep trespassers away.

> The Choctaw called them Kwanikosha, who supposedly kidnapped boys to test them and figure out their nature.

The Cherokee tribe believed in three different types of Little People: the Laurels, the Rocks, and the Dogwoods. They ranged from being good and helpful to being purely **malicious**.

Said to remain invisible most of the time, they watched humans from afar, inhabiting the most remote mountain peaks and darkest caves. Known to appear to the Cherokee during times of need, fiercely protective of the tribe, they would rally together with forces of invisible warriors to drive away enemies.

They constructed elaborate townhouses underground or within mountains. Humans who were lost or injured often told of being brought to these subterranean homes to be nursed back to health, and some Cherokee were said to even go off to live with them permanently.

The Little People were capable of doing good deeds for people who treated them with respect. However, to look upon one was bad luck, potentially resulting in premature death. Usually, those who encountered the Little People were warned by them not to tell others. It is also considered bad luck to even speak of the Little People.

When humans built homes near the Little People, it was important to leave food for them and not to block any of their paths. If the little beings were pleased, they did chores at night, like plowing fields and harvesting crops, as the Little People once did in Ireland. Sometimes the people in the house heard the work being done, but knew not to look outside.

When the Cherokees were driven out of the Cumberland area in the 1830s – during the dreadful *Trail of Tears* clearances – it is said that a few Little People families went with them to Oklahoma, but most were left behind. Since that time, no attempt by the Little

People to partner with the incoming English colonists has ever been reported.

It seems that in isolation, the Little People all died out – everywhere! And now, other than the hidden Bigfoot people, it is just us, the Homo Sapiens, all 8 billion of us.

# End of season 5

NOTE: The key historical findings and conceptual breakthroughs that underpin this five season dramatic series are presented in the previous section of this three-volume set, titled:

*SUBJUGATED Volume I – RESEARCH – "A More Likely Explanation"*

# SUBJUGATED
## VOLUME III

*Genetics Drives*

*Political Preference*

"PRIMATE-Socialists

Versus

ALIEN-Libertarians"

*"Primate/Alien Conflict Today"*

# THE REVELATION

## Genetics Drives Political Preference

Subjugated describes us, the Homo Sapiens, a primate/alien hybrid genetically-engineered for intelligence, but with unintended consequences.

We exist a volatile, unbalanced species, acting against both nature and ourselves ... prone to both genetic mental illnesses and to trauma caused by violence, rape, and neglected children.

And it goes deeper. Primate/alien duality drives today's political strife.

Politics is *not* "the debate of ideas" that it proports to be, but a genetic battle between primate-socialist cravings for managed societies and alien-libertarian impulses for unencumbered liberty.

In this battle, socialist disparage libertarians saying: they only put forth their labor to achieve selfish "private property" ends, and libertarians disparage socialists for using victimhood propaganda to sabotage personal responsibility.

How can we be so different?

Why? Because of one's genetic pull – which tugs you either more primate-socialist or more alien-libertarian. Genetics determines your *political* orientation just as strongly as it draws *sexual* orientation. We cannot repress political desire, and use all aspects of "ideology" to justify our innate political preferences.

We can easily recognize the polarized drivers sitting inside of our Homo Sapient *Jekyll & Hyde* species. Primate-socialists want strict troop control over the un-woke "deplorables", and the alien-libertarians see the primate-socialists as unabashed money-takers and enslavers.

But still, one wonders, what person born into America's liberty-based society would want to install government control over a free people?

The answer: The genetically-driven, obedience-obsessed primate-socialists, who despise the free-living, dangerous, prejudiced and racist cabal of untamed Americans.

Libertarians ponder: but surely the socialists realize that they make everyone but a few insiders poor!

Socialist conclude: it's time to get back to our primate roots, with troop discipline paramount and no tolerance for uppity apes, with a modest existence rationed for most as liberty is carefully doled out to the elite leaders.

Each side's explanation to justify their genetically-determined politics is presented herein ... both quite elaborate!

# CONTENTS

# AUTHOR'S NOTE

*" The marvel of all history is the patience with which men and women submit to burdens unnecessarily laid upon them by their governments "*

—GEORGE WASHINGTON—

I was born in 1952, right smack in the middle of what is called "the American century". In 1976, the first time I traveled overseas, to Spain, General Franco, the Fascist dictator, had just died. The sight of soldiers stationed at key buildings around Madrid shook me – soldiers with automatic weaponry in their hands, eyeing me. I lowered my eyes.

But it could never happen in America. We had too much legacy for this kind of misery, and anyway, what person born into a liberty-based society would ever want to install government control over a free people?

Though most baby boomers shunned authority, later I found this anti-authoritarianism trait sitting in two opposing camps. My libertarian camp wanted flexibility to carve out our destinies, freed from the old school institutional forces then in play. The socialist camp wanted to eliminate both the old institutions and us the libertarians, as socialist wanted a new phenomenon, a giant bee hive that would embrace them for their loyalty and protect them from those not inclined for bee hive living.

But we are not bees, and eventually it dawned on me. These socialist operate as one big *primate troop* with everybody protected so long as members fall in line, obedient to the elite apes. Yup, my baby boomer kin actually craved troop obedience over a life of liberty. How could this be?

Years went by. And as I took stock of the world, I eventually realized that almost all of humankind had lived and still lives subjugated by some form of elite overlords. Why? Could it be that Primate-socialism stands the preference, with free-living Americans like me outliers? And this got me thinking … because no species likes outliers, given the chance, would socialist Homo Sapiens want to shut down us American libertarians?

Though time proved me right, I had no expectation of the ferocity that would come from the socialist side of American society.

But once the onslaught arrived, inductively, with no other apparent explanation available, I envisioned *political genetics* as the driver behind the degree of systemic *intra-species* conflict. This intuitive starting point – political genetics – led to the research and development of the Subjugated Trilogy series.

Not pleased as to what I found. But it is what it is.

# INTRODUCTION

*" Man is not truly one but truly two. "*

–ROBERT LOUIS STEPHENSON–

This is volume III of the Subjugated trilogy. I invite you to read through volumes I and II as well.

Volumes I & II make the case that Homo Sapiens are a blend of primate and alien genes. The crossbreeding took place around 4,000 B.C., with:

A *Primate-socialist* genetic instinct causing one *to prefer* a more ordered, obedient society – as found in primate troop behavior, and with

An A*lien-libertarian* genetic pull *causing* one to crave liberty and independence, as found in America's original pioneer stock.

Volume III examines how this deep genetic variance plays out today.

Within the genetic polarity, some operate at the extremes, while others have less pronounced political cravings. Nevertheless, one's political choices stem *solely* from this genetic driver, and any political arguments or narratives proffered simply self-justify one's desired political configuration. Few *mature* minds are ever changed, though one may come of age later in life (e.g. Ronald Reagan), switching from one's youth-based political start.

For the most part, billions of our predecessors have lived under some form of subjugation – at first by Aliens, and then by Homo Sapient emperors, kings, priests, slave owners and dictators ... the United States the only society to break from this construct.

Why America? Because after 1620, those Europeans with alien-libertarian genetic leanings flocked to America wanting to escape subjugation. Later, other ethnic groups joined. And as America's core alien-libertarian base grew, America's self-image became the land of the free, home of the brave.

But after hundreds of years, America's genetic pool began to morph as increasingly children were born with primate-socialist leanings. Why? Because genetically, the *primate-socialist* trait is *dominate*, the *alien-libertarian recessive*. At conception, should just one genetic switch come from a primate-socialist parent, a socialist child will result. For a child to turn libertarian, both parents need to supply recessive alien gene switches.

And so, due to this basic dominant/recessive law of genetics, American *primate-socialist* numbers will continue to grow, and as these socialists gain members, they will look to assert their preferred "pyramid of control" operating model upon American society. Pyramid obedience, their comfort zone, will be instated even in America, the last alien-libertarian holdout on Earth.

Like all mammals, primates band together to mate, to nurture their young, to defend against enemies and to feed and provision themselves. A mammal's existence mainly involves engagement with other members of its species, governed by a harmonious set of accepted behavioral mores.

With Homo Sapiens – being two species – mores collide. The primate-socialist side wants stricter troop control over the "deplorables", with enforced autocratic mores corralling "selfish" behavior. The alien-libertarian side, always wary of authority, seeks individuality, and sees the overbearing demands made by the primate-socialists as unabashed money-taking scams and liberty enslavement ploys. These opposites do no attract, and this *unnatural* hybrid duality has Homo Sapiens uniquely craving competing comfort zones, a phenomenon not present in *natural* species.

As a result, today's democracy-led systems attract members by offering constituents their preferred comfort zones – be they obedience-centric or anti-authoritarian in nature. *Volume III – Genetics Determines Political Preference* – examines the deep, unmovable rationales developed since the late 1700's by both sides of the Homo Sapient spectrum to justify their respective, unreconcilable, political orientations.

# POLITICAL GENETICS

*" People do not really want freedom,*
*because freedom involves responsibility and*
*most people are frightened of responsibility. "*

—SIGMUND FREUD—

Lucky us, our bipolar primate/alien genetic makeup stands conflicted, and as with all genetics, one side surely represents a dominant trait, the other recessive. Which is which? How do we express the Primate-socialist versus Alien-libertarian traits in day-to-day life?

Quite simply, one yearns for either socialism or libertarianism *as one's preferred social order.* Primate-socialists seek discipline and obedience within the troop, effectively transforming individual pro-ductivity into collective group output. Alternatively, Alien-libertarians encourage personal liberty, with individuals trading their productivity with the bounty of others to generate "laissez faire" group output.

SUBJUGATED's mission untangles these contrary drivers, but, for now, envision the following: one's political orientation is, say, 80 percent genetic and 20 percent conditioned. Conditioning simply provides justifications. One is not conditioned into socialism; one emerges from the womb a socialist— and the same applies to the libertarians.

As a result, political conflict proves an all-out battle of genet-ics. *And if the primate trait seeking socialism dominates,* then those switched with Alien-libertarian preferences face a real survival challenge, not unlike "redheads" (red hair a recessive trait).

SUBJUGATED, therefore, finds today's political strife *not* "the debate of ideas" it proports to be, but a survival standoff, pitting socialist conformity against libertarian independence.

How does each side operate?

For decades, we have watched Socialist forces corralling and even inventing various interest groups, with each constituency making an agreement with the "primate" leaders to obtain benefits and protections in exchange for absolute loyalty.

Conversely, Libertarians are all about abstract ideology, the principles of liberty, "live free or die," and so on. Libertarians never fathom that socialists have no true ideology, just staged virtue signaling and firm alliances.

And as Libertarians "spin their wheels," sidetracked by arguments spewed out daily by socialists, the socialist leaders faithfully provision their loyalty partnerships within the primate troop, ever aspiring to build membership. Socialists keep Libertarians sidetracked in faux debate over the next invented "red meat" topic – abortion, race, equity, CRT, global warming, pronoun rules, etc...

Within the pyramid, the Socialist troop comprises both "little" people merely seeking their basic needs, and the elites, those who deliver the goods and get to live large—think Bill Clinton, think Vladimir Putin.

Libertarians stand more homogeneous, big and little guys respecting each other when either shows grit and independent capabilities—the type of achievement secondary to the journey— think Robert Kraft and John Bon Jovi sharing the owner's box at Patriots football games.

But after hundreds of years of tedious coexistence, this deadlock between American Libertarians and American Socialists stands in the final stages of resolution. And should the remaining, *almost-cornered* Libertarians continue to think it a mere debate of principles, *open to suggestion*—as most conservative radio and TV pundits habitually project—then Libertarians will go down as tricked animals.

Socialists only care about their respective interest group side-deals and their status within the pyramid. They pine to end the libertarian way of life, removing any obstacle, such as a libertarian Trump.

And while awaiting sentencing, the "slow-to-catch-on Libertarians" will continue to preach that socialism doesn't work. They ask, "Why can't the Socialists see this?" not realizing that Socialists don't care if wealth is compromised and liberty shackled, as long as each member fits into the pyramid hierarchy *without* a lot of fuss, where each gets their promised side-deal and rewarded level of privilege – think China, think welfare recipients, think American suburbanites, all wanting the status quo.

Unvarnished as it has become today, socialism reveals itself a pure genocidal play, not a debate, and the so-called liberals—the "kind" socialists standing right behind the dominant apes—enable the ultimate primate victory by loyally supporting top-ape politicians to the hilt.

Today's kind liberals may not appear the uncouth "brown shirts" of Hitler's yesteryear, but they vote for America's version of a National Socialist Party each cycle, no matter what – e.g. voting *en masse* for a clearly diminished Joe Biden. (National Socialism covered later).

And the party bosses the troop empowers—the top-troop leaders— want no opposition – e.g. recall both Hillary and Biden boxing out Sanders across two election cycles. Good-hearted liberals need not get their hands dirty in all this, they just need to vote in step with the party's choice and *not* protest the extermination run against the now-isolated libertarian stock of deplorables. In return – with continued good behavior – they receive a modest perch within the societal pyramid, absent any threat.

Consider these 13 subjugation tactics by American socialists:

*Fear*—Preach global warming, victimization & abortion

*Indoctrination*—Broadcast coordinated press-and-university-dominated attack inventions – e.g. Russian collusion.

*Historical Distortion*—Deface monuments & rewrite events – e.g. Slavery being ignored as a Democrat Party phenomenon.

*Alienation*— Teach White Privilege, Transgenderism & CRT to children.

*Intolerance*—Disparage anything "right" – e.g. Jan 6th, and show full tolerance for everything "left" – e.g. the BLM/Antifa riots.

*Weaponization*—Staff the Deep State to attack the unwanted – e.g. Tea Party audits & parents deemed terrorists.

*Judicial Corruption*—Finance activist DAs and judges who will ignore the law & selectively prosecute – e.g. no bail – no sentences.

*Representation*—Allow Blue states to freeze out minority voices – e.g. Connecticut having no Republican presence at the federal level.

*Taxation*—Siphon off Middle Class wealth via taxation and inflation, turning them into dependents – e.g. municipal home and vehicle taxes levied *without legislative authority*.

*Inflation*—Orchestrate runaway national debt and money printing to cause *inflation*, diluting accumulated personal wealth, edging people towards dependency.

*Immigration*—Conditioning the offspring of illegals to vote socialist for free resources, thereby ending assimilation & upward mobility.

*Elitism*—Lionize the "One Percent" who back Socialism – e.g. Zuckerberg paying $450 million to harvest inner city votes, funding 2,000 door-to-door "Biden ballot mules".

*Genocide*—Holdout resisters are imprisoned or eliminated.

Wait a minute! The first 12 tactics might be happening to tamper selfish libertarians, but liberals would certainly object to the last "unlucky 13" prophecy, after all, Jan 6th imprisonment yes, but genocide … it's simply not American.

But realize this, once in full control, *all* socialist dictatorships end absolute, from Stalin to Mussolini to Hitler to Mao to Castro to Pol Pot to Hussein to Putin to the Ayatollah, to the new permanent dictator in China, to the Rocket Man in Korea, and to the bus driver who just ruined Venezuela.

*Extermination* of rivals remains an inevitable outcome of socialism no matter the country. Socialists want obedience (not wealth distribution). Effectively, "kind" Liberals are used temporarily by the extremists to attain absolute power. Then the worst is unleashed.

Socialist rulers want their primate troops strictly controlled by sanctioned elites, with the layers of lower-ranking members falling in line. Ultimately everyone gets sucked into the vortex. Why would American socialists prove any different given the chance? Stop pretending, as they are already at stage 12 1/2 (above) out of 13.

So, as things stand, today's American socialists believe the deck stacked in favor of a permanent primate takeover, using indoctrination, immigration, wealth-transfer and vote harvesting schemes to consolidate power. More and more, strident radicals like Soros, Biden, Pelosi, Sanders, Warren, Harris, Clinton, Obama, Schumer, Newsom and AOC display their true colors, no longer feigning a debate of ideas, just seeking a permanent underclass with endless need, one that through its sheer numbers can drown out the remaining Alien-libertarians.

Napoleon, Lenin, Mao, and Hitler each only possessed a handful of confederates, so why not a try in America with the right guy or gal fronting a one-party system? And meanwhile, while feigning endless debate waiting for the right dictator to arrive, the socialist machine patiently readies socialist matrices at federal, state, municipal and deep state levels, while at every opportunity marginalizing the deplorables—those *not* of the pyramid.

As mentioned, the *Subjugated Volumes I & II* outline the degree to which "alien-sourced Libertarians" and "primate-sourced Socialists" diametrically oppose one another. And yet the Homo Sapient – presumably a single species – carries both political orientations within its DNA.

It appears that genetics draws people to their *political* orientations just as strongly as genetics draws humankind to its *sexual* orientations, neither of which have anything to do with logic. Similar to sexuality, we cannot arrest, alter, or repress political orientation. Genetics determine political choices, and Homo Sapiens use all aspects of rationalization to remain comfortable within their inherited political alignment.

That is the thesis.

Next, before digging into socialism's elaborate logic, we look at the equally-elaborate libertarian belief system, the system socialism wants to snuff out.

# 1

# THE ROOTS OF LIBERTARIANISM

*" The policy of American government is to leave its citizens free, neither restraining them nor aiding them in their pursuits. "*

—THOMAS JEFFERSON—

Jefferson, a libertarian of Anglo-Saxon heritage sounds heartless, doesn't he?

As outlined in "Subjugated Volume I – RESEARCH", ever since the Homo Sapient was "assembled" via implants of alien neuron matter into primitive Human embryos, *certain* Homo Sapiens born with *alien-libertarian* leanings have roamed the Earth, and though a minority, they still do.

But against the sheer numbers of world-wide primate-socialist, the libertarians are genetic outliers. Even though libertarians can rise in the ranks of their predominantly obedience-based socialist populations, only one culture – *the Anglo Saxons* – ever embraced every common man as a truly free citizen. In old England these commoners were called "Freemen".

The Anglo Saxons – originally from Denmark and northern Germany – ran an extreme libertarian operation. Over time, their mindset would be imported into Britain circa A.D. 400, when the Romans left and the Anglo's moved in, and later into America when the Anglo-English colonized it from A.D. 1620 onward. Yes, the "freemen" gene travelled far!

There's more.

According to Anglo/Saxon common law (the basis of American law), each commoner stood a "freeman", not obligated to others without mutual consent. This included one's relationship to the chief, who could not tax a Freeman's property, nor press him into military service. The Freeman joined the Chief to protect the Freeman's own family and/or for direct pay or for open-ended plunder. Anglo/Saxon personal property was deemed "Alodial". Allodial title meant absolute ownership without obligation to anyone else or to any government. These were Thomas Jefferson's role models.

Allodial libertarianism like this stayed intact throughout England from A.D. 400 up to A.D. 1066, when William of Normandy (the Conqueror) defeated England, replacing libertarianism with feudalism, a mid-ages form of socialism. At the Battle of Hastings in south-east England, with swords to their throats, the English lords ceded their Allodial deeds to William, who now claimed absolute Allodial title to many of the best estates in England.

To smooth things out, William granted Feudal titles back to the surviving conquered lords. Feudal titles, however, came with on-going tax and military obligations owed by the defeated subject to William and to William's successors. The English "bit their tongues" and learned to live with it, but the libertarian gene stayed in their blood line, waiting to break out.

A century later Norman-English *King John* became grotesquely oppressive, both against the native English population, and even with his Norman relatives, then living in castles throughout England, Wales, Scotland and Ireland. No one liked him! For his unbridled bad behavior, King John was forced to sign a 30-page contract called the

Magna Carta. This arrangement clawed back some of the common law "natural rights" lost more than a century ago. Even the common man was recognized.

> *"No free man shall be seized or imprisoned, or stripped of his rights or possessions, or outlawed or exiled. Nor will we proceed with force against him except by the lawful judgement of his equals or by the law of the land. To no one will we sell, to no one deny or delay right or justice"*
>
> —MAGNA CARTA—

I write about Hastings and the Magna Carta, not just to describe the famous battle between English Lords and the invading French Norman knights, but to relate how England's defeat, and the subsequent transfer of English land deeds to William the Conqueror, triggered an ongoing "primate/alien" property right struggle between the Norman overlords (the primate-socialists) and the subjugated English (the defeated alien-libertarians). The English would patiently fight back to regain the "natural rights" taken from them.

The more pivotal aspect of this history, as will soon be explained, is that this English/Norman freedom struggle ultimately fed the ideals sitting behind the "alien" American Revolution.

And so, to understand America, one first needs to meet the 1688 English-alien thought leader John Locke, as Locke influenced all of America's founders.

Stay tuned for the ultimate libertarian … John Locke!

# 2

## JOHN LOCKE

*" Men being, as has been said, by nature, all free, equal and
independent, no one can be put out of this estate, and subjected
to the political power of another, without his own consent. "*

–JOHN LOCKE–

We next explore the intellectual reasoning behind the libertarian way
of life by unbundling the 1688 writings of Englishman John Locke,
hero of the American founders, the ones who implemented Locke's
vision a hundred years later in 1776. As indicated by Locke's quote
– above – the ability to own property "free and clear" is essential
towards achieving lasting freedom, a sentiment reflecting the Anglo/
Saxon libertarian/allodial mindset to the hilt.

Let's dig in.

Other than the protest of the tea tax, most Americans know little
about the original thinking and philosophical views of the founders— ideas that fueled the American Revolution and made America
unique—an exception of human history.

Everyone considers Washington the Father of America (and that's because he was), the place where, if you wanted to, you could make something of yourself. It was up to you, and no one was necessarily expected to help you. Some perhaps would, but no one had to. It was up to you. This wasn't for everybody, but in the early years those who were game—such as the Yankee separatists—did whatever it took to come here and try.

But few people know who *John Locke* was, even though Locke, an Englishman, served as the dominant intellectual influence for all of the founding fathers, including Washington.

Key founders, you recall, include:

*George Washington* — the "Father", he won the war, and presided over the young country;

*Benjamin Franklin* — the Role Model, he created and embodied the idea and character of what it is to be an American;

*Thomas Jefferson* — the Artist, he painted the dream of America in words;

*John Adams* — the Dealmaker, behind the scenes everywhere, including in Paris when the English signed papers giving up claim to the colonies;

*Alexander Hamilton* — the Operations Visionary, knowing what worked in the day-to-day running of a country;

*John Jay*—the Lawyer, and first Chief Justice;

*Sam Adams*—the Activist, infusing rebellion amongst the people;

*Patrick Henry*—the Orator, giving voice to the movement, "Give me liberty or give me death";

*Thomas Paine*—the "Pamphleteer," keeping the people engaged;

*John Hancock*—the Financier, organizing and funding resistance against Britain;

*Roger Sherman*—the Observer, sitting on every committee to spot the missed point, the unintended consequence; and

*James Madison*—the Architect, the one who formulated the very structure of the United States by drafting the U.S. Constitution.

They were all Locke guys. They were all libertarians.

John Locke lived from 1632-1704, long before the founders, and published his now not-so-famous, yet earth-shattering work, *Two Treatises of Government*.

Locke explains to the world how humanity has evolved until then, what it all meant so far, and what humans should do next if they are to fulfill their God-given potential for liberty.

Locke charts out the relationship of property and ownership to human freedom. In a nutshell, his late 1600's vision:

> Similar to Descartes, Locke begins with the premise that humans exist as extensions of God, endowed with divine spirit. Our only true superior, therefore, is God as our spirit is an extension of His spirit, and so, any impingement of one person by another is inherently against the deepest desire of God's divine will. God did not create us, each personally, just to have us enslave, lord over, or bully each other.
>
> As Washington said: "We don't need masters."
>
> When God gave man His spirit, he included certain spiritually fueled faculties. These human faculties sit way above the purely mental abilities possessed by other animal species on the planet.
>
> Whereas other animals only live in the moment within nature, and even then in specific biospheres that sustain

them, humans use their special faculties to operate within time and to transform natural resources into things useful toward supporting their lives—no matter upon which corner of the earth we decide to dwell.

Only humans possess faculties for language, history, mathematics, physics, chemistry, biology, art, music, literature, philosophy, religion, architecture, engineering, agriculture, the transformation of basic foods into cuisine, knowledge accumulation and breakthroughs, fabrication of tools and the physical dexterity to use them, and other faculties, including warfare and the ability to breed other species – plus many others.

These faculties, which exist nowhere else in nature, therefore did not result from a micro-Darwinian mutation of some pre-human ape. According to the American founders, the faculty to understand things, comes from the fact that humans are endowed with spirit, allowing us to tap into the divine mind of God.

Humans possess an even higher trait called labor, something that allows humans to blend and apply all of these special faculties together toward one's survival, and more so, toward one's moral and temporal well-being.

For example, 10 acres of virgin forest represents only so much raw survival potential—a couple of squirrels, maybe. But through labor, we can transform this land into an agricultural resource that can feed and sustain many. Human labor, Locke argues, has so leveraged the bounty of nature that $99^{1/2}$ percent of what humans hold as valuable comes from the infusion of human labor into nature, and only one-half of one percent comes from raw nature itself.

And so, regardless of the proportions, we humans labor to improve our lot in life. But different people, cultures, and nations all choose different degrees of labor they are willing to infuse, because with labor comes "the pain of labor."

Property, according to Locke, stems from the above, consisting of the three things you inherently own: your life (no one can own you, you come from God), your material goods and land (no one should take the fruits of your labor, the result of the pain you were willing to infuse), and your liberties (no one should limit your choices for disposing of your life, land, or goods).

Property, in the broadest sense, when owned absolutely, is freedom itself. Most of Locke's writing then qualifies this by explaining how all of the freedom/property stuff sits inside a body of laws, but even here he speaks of a narrow set of laws prohibiting one from compromising another's property.

Now who could object to Locke's framework? Many.

And so, before getting to Thomas Jefferson, who would carry Locke's ideas forward, let's first look into the thoughts of the founders of socialism – the "anti-Locke's".

# 3

# SOCIALISM'S FOUNDERS

*" We're going to take things away from you
on behalf of the common good. "*

—HILLARY CLINTON—

That's her boiled-down definition of socialism.

Here's my definition:

*Socialism first became a distinct political movement during the
Social Revolution Era, from the late 1700s to the mid-1800's.
Socialism calls for public rather than private control of property
and natural resources—through the authority of government
to own, aggressively tax, and regulate— with individuals not
existing individually, but living in a cooperative system.*

*Socialism considers everything people produce a social product,
with everyone in that society entitled to share in it. Society as
a whole, through a pyramid of command, controls individuals*

*and property for the benefit of all its members. Government can compromise the individual to achieve these goals.*

Who were the thought leaders behind this, the ones who invented the perfect "pyramid of control" society, today able to govern billions?

## The Early Socialist Thought Leaders

*The bee is more honored than other animals,*
*not because she labors, but because she labors for others…*

−JOHN CHRYSOSTOM−
ARCHBISHOP OF CONSTANTINOPLE, 347 AD

Though many socialist streaks run through the words of Jesus Christ and the Christian church, most 1700's Enlightenment intellectuals were strict atheists who believed humanity an inherently selfish animal requiring taming at the hands of strong government.

This atheist/materialist/empiricist camp, the precursor socialists, believed that due to our tricky senses, we understand nothing in absolute terms, including right and wrong. We cannot be trusted, so we need heavy-handed management. And most certainly, no God or spiritual dimension exists that one can tap into to steer our moral ship. Socialism grew from this atheistic "fear-of-humanity and security-over-humanity" corners. Let's get to know the thought leaders.

## Kant

In the 1700's, Immanuel Kant asserted that our quirky human minds subjectively categorize things to make order of the chaos our senses perceive, and that what we consider reality merely exists as our *preferred* interpretation of this chaos.

In contrast to Descartes, who introduced the Scientific Method to uncover the rules in which nature repeats itself, Kant claimed that our sciences and our moral systems stood as nothing more than our *species determined, prejudiced preferences* bolstering the Homo Sapient comfort zone.

> *Note: My political genetics thesis takes Kant's "species determined" framework one layer deeper, proposing that within the singular Homo Sapient species, genetic switches driving political choice are set at conception, either Primate-socialist or Alien-libertarian, each orientation causing overwhelmingly-craved political preferences.*

Kant's broad conclusion? Humans create human ideas and morals. God bestows nothing; people and society do it themselves based upon the ways of the human mind. Accordingly, the elite leaders of any new, "people-based" society should enjoy the flexibility to envision "enlightened" morality and impose this morality via strong pyramid of control over the selfish excesses of the ignorant individual.

## Shaw

As Bernard Shaw put it in the 1900's:

> *When you are asked, "Where is God? Who is God?" stand up and say, "I am God and here is God, not as yet completed, but sill advancing toward completion, just in so much as I am working for the purpose of the universe, working for the good of the whole society and the whole world, instead of merely looking after my personal ends."*

Bernard Shaw's socialist genes clearly ran deep. When I read his biography and personal letters, it was through him that I began to understand the genetic pull of political orientation, for it never pulled stronger than with Shaw (Socialist) and perhaps with Daniel Boone (Libertarian). Read their histories for political genetic role models.

In the A.D. 1,800's, the majority of "enlightened" philosophers believed in rechanneling individuals away from selfish excess towards a yearning to participate in the will of the masses. In other words, the need to abandon the freedom *to do* one's will—something that wealth provides—and embrace freedom *from* violence, hunger, isolation, and responsibility—something that troop allegiance provides.

This "freedom-from" mentality – conjuring a 1930's Norman Rockwell painting – would get everyone on the same page, allowing leaders such as Franklin D. Roosevelt, for example, to more simply chart the direction of society as a whole, no criticism encouraged.

## Rousseau

Jean-Jacques Rousseau (d. 1778) proved a key articulator of how to channel individuals into submission and tamed behavior. He published his book *The Social Contract* in 1763, and it served as the blueprint for primate troop living, the antithesis of everything John Locke espoused in his *Second Treatise of Government.*

Rousseau:

*Each of us puts his person and all his power in common under the supreme direction of the general will and in a body we receive each member as an indivisible part of the whole.*

Interpretation: through such submission, people are *forced to be free* from their selfishness. With this, the Socialists finally emerged to offset Locke's selfish liberties, and so began the war between Right- and Left-Wing rationalizations. The modern era had arrived: the people suddenly mattered, and many stood available for the taking.

Rousseau, by the way, who hated the so-called "arrogant excesses" stemming from owning private property, sired five illegitimate children whom he abandoned to orphanages. Similar to many on the Left to follow, he hated the excesses tied to property ownership, but did not hold his personal excesses open to criticism, for after all, we create our own morality. But as soon as someone wanted property and refused to join the troop, Rousseau labeled that person "an Egotist."

And, because the people don't know their "real will" (as suggested by Schopenhauer and Freud, who claimed our subconscious minds rule us) we therefore need elite leaders to operate the levers of government.

Wasn't Rousseau wonderful? Apparently so, as Totalitarian and Socialist elites have pretty much followed his lead, ruling a willing subjugated world ever since. Today, a good chunk of Americans yearn for the same top-down elitist government, rather than the bottom-up `individualist engine espoused by Locke. "Please rule us, shield us from the rich "go getter" Egotist!" cries the tamed primate.

Hmmm ... but how to implement this elitist, atheist policy?

## Hegel

Enter Hegel (1770-1831). Hegel, the great primate strategist, living precisely when all of the "people-based" revolutions took place, witnessing the new competitive dynamics between political parties fighting for the vote of the common citizen.

He noticed that the common citizen hated conflict and accepted compromise (troop order) rather easily, and that one could capitalize upon this compromise-friendly trait to govern the masses and to move them in the preferred direction. Hegel preferred to move the masses left toward full submission to the state.

> *Once the state has been founded, there can no longer be any heroes. They come on the scene only in uncivilized conditions.*
>
> —HEGEL—

> *When liberty is mentioned, we must always be careful to observe whether it is not really the assertion of private interests which is thereby designated.*
>
> —HEGEL—

Hegel gave his historical theory a fancy name: "Dialectic." He derived the term from Plato's use of *dialogue* (discussions between Socrates and others) to uncover Truth. Dialogue is not debate, where one endeavors to win the other party over. Dialogue produces a process wherein ideas on each side intertwine toward finding a higher truth. The dialectic process, when applied to politics, uses the compromise inclination of democracy to resolve Right/Left conflict to slowly move obedience-for-entitlement side deals left.

With dialectic tactics, no rush exists, no need for revolution or overt battling. Absorb the past as a series of back-and-forth steps of discussion, which, through minor compromise along the way, inevitably lead to reduced liberties (freedom to *do*) for the individual, and fuller dependency by most people upon the state (freedoms from the bad stuff already mentioned).

Thanks Hegel. What's next? This:

*Man owes his existence to man.*

–KARL MARX–
FROM THE 1844 MANUSCRIPT

Karl, let's take a look…

## Karl Marx

Karl Marx – an extremely upset ape – incorporated dialectic concepts into political tactics. He renamed it Dialectic Materialism, still unsure of what he meant.

I found his *1844 Manuscript* the most convoluted piece of writing, worse than Kant or Sartre, that I encountered in the 1970's when paying socialist professors to proselytize socialist philosophy to me at Trinity College in Hartford, Connecticut. Witness the first utterance of Marx's manuscript:

*I have already announced in the Deutsch-Franzosische
JahrbUcher the critique of jurisprudence and political
science in the form of a critique of the Hegelian philosophy
of law. While preparing it for publication, the intermingling
of criticism directed only against speculation with criticism
of the various subjects themselves proved utterly unsuitable,
hampering the development of the argument and rendering
comprehension difficult. Moreover, the wealth and diversity
of the subjects to be treated could have been compressed
into one work only in a purely aphoristic style; whilst an
aphoristic presentation of this kind, for its part, would
have given the impression of arbitrary systematism.*

—THE 1844 MANUSCRIPT—

Somewhere amidst all of this long, unintelligible writing lives the main thrust: that private property exists as the cause of evil. That's because private property can create alienation, a sad combination of separation, isolation, estrangement, loneliness, anger, and despair.

After existing in the presence and under the thumb of these propertied ones, you will feel all of your humanity and all of your wellbeing stripped away. You will exist with no freedoms "To Do," as well as no freedoms "From…" No freedoms whatsoever, a slave of the society in which you live.

It became obvious that some ape needed to restore humankind's natural world order, and Marx would go on to advocate Hegel's back-and-forth method to create the ultimate primate pyramid—Communism—and, gosh darn it, once it got going, it worked! Soon, they tell us, China will be the best place ever!

Four years after publishing his 1844 paper, Marx, with his partner and financier Engels (a factory owner, no less) and other radicals, met in London and published *The Communist Manifesto*, an eminently more readable volume then Marx's 1844 rant, but still over-the-top primate speech for the most part:

307

*The "dangerous class," the social scum, that passively rotting
mass thrown off by the lowest layers of the old society, may,
here and there, be swept into the movement by a proletarian
revolution; its conditions of life, however, prepare it far
more for the part of a bribed tool of reactionary intrigue.*

−THE COMMUNIST MANIFESTO−

Some declarations, though, proved very straightforward:

*The distinguishing feature of Communism is not the abolition
of property generally, but the abolition of bourgeois property.*

*In this sense, the theory of the Communists may be summed
up in the single sentence: Abolition of private property.*

*We Communists have been reproached with the desire of
abolishing the right of personally acquiring property as the
fruit of a man's own labor, which property is alleged to be the
groundwork of all personal freedom, activity and independence.*

*You are horrified at our intending to do away with
private property. But in your existing society, private
property is already done away with for nine-tenths of
the population; its existence for the few is solely due to
its nonexistence in the hands of those nine-tenths. You
reproach us; therefore, with intending to do away with
any property for the immense majority of society.*

*In one word, you reproach us with intending to do away
with your property. Precisely so; that is just what we intend.*

−THE COMMUNIST MANIFESTO−

These primate-socialists really hated selfish, right-winged bourgeois creeps who, over a lifetime of hard work and innovation, could

carve out something as ugly as, say, home ownership. And I am not waxing sarcastic. Socialists really hate a decent-looking home if it means that some smug, selfish Egoist taker lives comfortably inside, with no concern for anyone else in the troop. Socialists do not care that the homeowner achieved that status through personal labor, *because the individual only put forth the labor to achieve selfish "private property" ends.*

Labor only achieves nobility when applied to societal troop property ends, such as municipal soccer fields in U.S. suburbs, or *everything* in Russia, Iran, North Korea, Venezuela and China. All of the pollen gathered by the noble worker bees belongs to the Hive.

But to really understand the logic of the Left—that the troop *owns* your productivity you must accept their premise that one's productivity exists not a function of an individual's isolated bit of labor but as a function of Society. Socialists despise entrepreneurs because the entrepreneur champions just the opposite. *"In spite of everything the human race could throw at me, I found a way to succeed."*

"What?" screams Elizabeth Warren. "No one ever got rich on their own!" And so, Warren rationalizes:

> *You—the factory owner crying about paying taxes—yes, you, the one bringing your goods to market on the roads we built; you, using the labor we educated; you, the one protected from marauding bandits by the police force we provide ... Yes, you... Do you get it? Society, it's ours. it belongs to all the people; and so, we own your productivity, and we can tax and regulate you however we want.*

Besides, anyway, the Socialist continues...

> *Those profits that you grab with your grubby hands are the surplus monies skimmed off of the indecent wages you pay your labor. You intimidate workers, making them feel grateful for their jobs so that they accept low wages. You are a bully and a thief who pockets surplus labor profits that don't belong to you in the first place.*

Thus emerged the famous "Surplus Theory of Labor" brainchild of Karl Marx. Anyway, once you see things in this manner, all you want to do is neutralize Egoist Libertarians before they get away with further selfish and damaging behavior that threatens troop living.

In particular, entrepreneurial behavior such as inventing products and services, and running companies—orchestrating the people, facilities, supply-chain arrangements, production and quality assurance systems, marketing, sales and competition face-offs, financing, and endless business continuity measures, so that everything works in concert toward achieving ongoing results—well, this behavior performed for personal gain ... deserves punishment.

In all of this, the Socialist never mentions the endless sweat equity invested by the individual entrepreneur, because the Socialist views the alien entrepreneur as solely out for himself, rather than the troop.

*You're using our roads!* Yeah, right... It's genetic!

So, while all of these socialist rationales were being formulated over in Europe pining for state power, the Americans were counterpunching for the individual, and America had a heavyweight puncher in the ring, one Thomas Jefferson – next!

# 4

## THOMAS JEFFERSON

*" I'm a greater believer in luck,*
*and I find the harder I work the more I have of it. "*

—THOMAS JEFFERSON—

Ok, so through John Locke, we better understand "free and clear" property's role in achieving liberty. But does one, even after exerting painful labor into the creation of property, hold absolute rights to this property? According to the English feudal Kings, the answer … a solid "no." And so we need a special person, say a Thomas Jefferson, to unravel the rope.

Jefferson's dissertation follows. He focuses on what we call "Common Law," the unwritten law that English people lived by for centuries. Even today in America, should no constitutional or statutory directive exist on a topic, we cite old Common Law.

Jefferson points out that in old England, before William the Conqueror took over in 1066 and introduced "French" feudal arrangements to property, that the property rights held under Anglo Saxon Common Law stood absolute, allodial (no feudal duties owed to any other person).

Moreover, when the Conqueror decreed feudal claims to English land, he did not claim all lands, as many estates not involved at Hastings still remained with the Anglo Saxon lords under the old Common Law system of allodial rights. Jefferson's words:

*That we shall at this time also take notice of an error in the nature of our landholdings, which crept in at a very early period of our settlement. The introduction of the feudal tenures (land controlled by a monarch) into the kingdom of England, though ancient, is well enough understood to set this matter in its proper light.*

*In the earlier ages of the Saxon settlement feudal holdings were certainly altogether unknown, and very few, if any, had been introduced at the time of the Norman conquest.*

*Our Saxon ancestors (prior to 1066) held their lands, as they did their personal property, in absolute dominion, disencumbered with any superior.*

*William the Conqueror first introduced that system [feudalism] generally.*

*The lands which had belonged to those who fell at the battle of Hastings, and in the subsequent insurrections of his reign, formed a considerable proportion of the lands of the whole kingdom. These he granted out, subject to feudal duties, as did he also those of a great number of his new subjects, who by persuasions or threats were induced to surrender then for that purpose. But still much of the land was left in the hands of his Saxon subjects, held of no superior, and not subject to feudal conditions.*

*A general principle indeed was introduced that "all lands in England were held either mediately or immediately of the crown": but thus was borrowed from those holdings which were truly feudal, and applied to others for the purposes of illustration.*

*Feudal holdings were therefore but exceptions out of the Saxon laws of possession, under which all lands were held in absolute right. These therefore still form the basis of the common law, to prevail whenever the exceptions have not taken place.*

***America was not conquered by William the Norman, nor its lands surrendered to him or any of his successors. Possessions are undoubtedly (still) of the absolute disencumbered nature.***

*Our ancestors however, were laborers, not lawyers. The fictitious principle that all lands belong originally to the king, that they were early persuaded to believe real, and accordingly took grants of their own lands from the crown. And while the crown continued to grant for small sums and on reasonable rents, there was no inducement to arrest the error.*

Boy oh boy, Jefferson could really figure stuff out! The King made it all up; he never had an allodial claim on American soil, as we never surrendered our land to him.

But through the Hasting's surrender, a *myth* slowly took hold, a con, called the Divine Right of Kings, claiming that all rights, liberties, and properties across the land belonged to the king. The king alone had allodial title; he merely permitted subjects to use his possessions with feudal strings attached.

Locke and Jefferson debunked this audacity.

## English Common Law & the American "Law of the Land"

Of note: Jefferson's statement that *"Our Saxon ancestors held their lands, as they did their personal property, in absolute dominion, disencumbered with any superior,"* would soon be echoed in the Declaration of Independence, the U.S. Constitution and the Bill of Rights, its sentiment part of America's *Law of the Land.*

The Saxon Law of the Land embraced vast natural rights. Winston Churchill, in his *History of the English-Speaking Peoples* describes the "freeman" rights of the Engle, Saxon, and Jute tribes who moved into England when Rome departed around 400 A.D. as follows.

*Within this society of "freemen," each person together*
*with their fixed and movable property, controls himself,*
*with no obligation to the chief. One's allegiance*
*to the chief stays voluntary, primarily concerned*
*with defense of the community and nothing else.*
*The Saxon Freemen's right to allodial autonomy—*
*encompassing one's property—becomes the foundation*
*of English Common Law, law still in effect in both*
*the United Kingdom and the United States today.*

−CHURCHILL−

The English Freemen carried on in this allodial manner up until 1066, when the French Normans took over and instilled feudal arrangements across the land. The old English allodial guard would eventually push back against feudalism, starting in 1215 with the Magna Carta, then through the English Civil War in the 1600's, reaching equilibrium during the Glorious Revolution of 1688, when Parliament gained many powers against the monarch.

The United States, by its adoption of old English Common law, shares in this legacy of natural, absolute rights to property.

To be thorough, again, let's peer into the English Magna Carta of 1215. Besides giving the lesser nobles rights under the King, it reaches back into English Common Law for the little guys, too. Consider:

*No freeman shall be taken or imprisoned or diseased,*
*or exiled or in any way destroyed, nor will we go upon*
*him or send upon him, except by the lawful judgment*
*of his peers or the Law of the Land ... from the*

−MAGNA CARTA−

This *Law of the Land* does not refer to written laws. It refers to one's natural rights sitting separate and above the reach of government. As you will soon read, Common Law rights, some of them set forth in the Magna Carta, are preserved in our Bill of Rights.

## The Declaration of Independence

This "Declaration", written by Jefferson, tweaked by Adams and Franklin, and signed by the colonial representatives about to endure seven years of warfare with England... merges Locke's philosophies and Jefferson's ability to blend philosophy with historical context.

The first part of the Declaration is pure Locke:

> *We hold these truths to be self-evident, that all men are created equal, that they are endowed by their Creator with certain unalienable Rights, that among these are Life, Liberty and the pursuit of Happiness.—That to secure these rights, Governments are instituted among Men, deriving their just powers from the consent of the governed...*

Next comes the long and exhaustive list of grievances, spelled out by Jefferson, so that mankind can understand the course of action the colonies will undertake:

> *...a decent respect to the opinions of mankind requires that they should declare the causes which impel them to the separation.*

Once the unfathomable list of grievances concludes, Jefferson closes:

> *We, therefore, the Representatives of the United States of America, in General Congress, Assembled, appealing to the Supreme Judge of the world for the rectitude of our intentions,*

*do, in the Name, and by Authority of the good People of these Colonies, solemnly publish and declare,*

*That these united Colonies are, and of Right ought to be Free and Independent States, that they are Absolved from all Allegiance to the British Crown, and that all political connection between them and the State of Great Britain, is and ought to be totally dissolved; and that as Free and Independent States, they have full Power to levy War, conclude Peace, contract Alliances, establish Commerce, and to do all other Acts and Things which Independent States may of right do.—And for the support of this Declaration, with a firm reliance on the protection of Divine Providence, we mutually pledge to each other our Lives, our Fortunes, and our sacred Honor.*

Next, state by state, come the famous signatures.

None of these high-quality patriots accepted the coming terrors of war with the idea that the new American government created in England's place should someday reinstate the very oppression they sought to escape. Government control of ourselves and our extended selves—our property— would be shut down for good. Life, Liberty, and Property would stand as the new *Law of the Land...* or so they thought.

To counter the founders, modern socialist would up the game, wanting to carve out a new Law of the Land exterminating the alien-libertarian Americans. But before examining the many socialist counter-attacks, let's first look at the U.S. Constitution and its Bill of Rights, designed to protect the individual and his or her property from government encroachment and mob rule, "natural rights" now under full attack by the American primate-socialists.

# 5

# THE BILL OF RIGHTS

*" The beauty of our country is that when it was founded that they took some time to lay out civil liberties in the first 10 Amendments – the Bill of Rights. I'm a firm believer in those civil liberties and the ability to have your own opinion. "*

−AARON RODGERS−

The Constitution was not written overnight. Out of the amazing list of founding fathers mentioned earlier, three nuts-and-bolts guys took the lead, largely Madison, as supported by Hamilton and Jay. Published dialogue amongst the three became known as the *Federalist Papers*, with Hamilton the most outspoken.

The Federalist Papers crafted the essential features for assembling a federal government that kept the states as independent as possible. With this the goal, the debate centered on where to draw the line between federal and state authority.

Before the U.S. Constitution, the states, during the Revolution years, operated under The Articles of Confederation. This arrangement left the central government weak. States could "opt out" of things like paying money toward the war.

During the war, Hamilton, a battlefield commander and member of Washington's personal staff, experienced the small-minded stinginess of the states that allowed the military to starve at Valley Forge. And so, he argued heavily for central governmental power over the states.

Yet no one questioned that once the central (federal) government was provisioned properly, all other matters should remain with the states... except for the following:

*The highest ideal for American government remained that the government should serve the people and not the opposite.*

To solve this, the interplay between the states and the federal government needed one more safety measure: *The Bill of Rights*, designed to protect the individual from overreach and abuse of power by *either* state or federal authorities. The key protections include the Due Process clause which reaches back to the Magna Carta, claiming natural rights separate and above written law.

In addition to certain famous rights – such as Freedom of Speech (again, opinion part of your property) – and Freedom of Religion (belief also part of your property), much of the Bill of Rights deals with protecting *any* form of physical property from said abuse. The people demanded these protections in writing as amendments to the originally proposed Constitution draft. Ten amendments surfaced; six, besides Speech and Religion, also relate to property as follows:

*The 3rd Amendment—No soldier shall in times of peace be quartered in any house, without consent of the owner, nor in times of war, but in a manner prescribed by law.*

*The 4th Amendment—The rights of people to be secure in their persons, houses, and effects against unreasonable searches and seizures shall not be violated and no warrants shall issue, but upon probable cause…*

*The 5th Amendment—Nor shall [anyone] be deprived of life, liberty, or property without due process of law; Nor shall private property be taken for public use without just compensation.*

The 7th, 9th, and 10th Amendments preserve "absolute" Common Law property rights for the individual for any subjects not specifically delegated to the government:

*The 7th Amendment—No fact tried by a jury, shall be otherwise re- examined in any court of the United States than according to common law.*

*The 9th Amendment— The enumeration (listing) of certain rights, shall not be construed to deny or disparage others retained by the people.*

*The 10th Amendment—The powers not delegated to the United States by the Constitution, nor prohibited by it to the states are reserved to the states and the people.*

And so… due to Common Law property rights, backed by due process guarantees, backed by absolute common law rights cemented by the Bill of Rights … in the first decades of the United States, clearly until the Civil War, individuals owned property in absolute terms, the *Law of the Land.*

As in Anglo/Saxon times, the hall marks of alien independence prevailed again, but more so, they were now codified into written law.

And so how did the American primate-socialist erode the purity of this founding?

Step by step. Next.

# 6

# JOHN BROWN AND THE
# TRANCENDENTALISTS
# ABOLITION 1840 – 1860

*" When I appoint a nigger to the bench,*
*I want everybody to know he's a nigger. "*

–DEMOCRAT PRESIDENT LYNDON JOHNSON–
ON APPOINTING THURGOOD MARSHALL
TO THE U.S. SUPREME COURT

Sorry to remind the reader about Lyndon B. Johnson (above), but he was a slavery connoisseur, and slavery would still be perpetuated through his institutional welfare system created in the 1960's. The details of LBJ's sins are covered in a later chapter, but we start here by looking back at related events taking place before and after the Civil War.

Most who fled England and Scotland to settle America in the 1600's were Puritans of various faiths. They wanted privacy in communicating with God ... meaning they did not need organized religion as the "middle man". Throughout most of the 1,600's, believers of this persuasion were being persecuted by both the English king and the Church of England.

The people had become estranged from their earthly authorities and were now only thinking about their intimate friend, God. Many fled to the American colonies. Inadvertently, the English Civil war of the mid-1600's had diverted England, allowing these Puritan migrants to become used to day-to-day religious liberty in faraway America.

But as previously presented, the founders of the American republic were "Deists", not Puritans. The difference? Though Deists believed in the spirit world and usually in a God entity, they did not claim to know the mind of God, and hence they rejected religious dogma which arrogantly proclaimed knowing the thoughts and wants of the deity.

The 1770 – 1820 Deists envisioned a new ultra-libertarian "alien" system of representative government that provided absolute protection from both church and state over one's personal property, as follows:

> Property ... protecting what's yours ... your pursuit of happiness, your land, your home, your moveable goods, your savings, your opinions, your speech and beliefs ... all of this, your "property", became a fundamental American right.

Of course, what was most notable about this bunch of libertarians, was the acceptance of slavery, a topic the next generation of Americans would grapple with.

Abolition started with the next generation of elite American thinkers born in the early 1800's. They would craft a new world view called *Transcendentalism*. Transcendentalism celebrated humans as individuals both endowed and directed by God to live moral lives *within nature*. Slavery was inherently a human violation of God's natural world, a phenomenon non-existent elsewhere in nature.

Who were these transcendentalists?

Ralph Waldo Emerson, Henry David Thoreau, Walt Wittman, Fredric Douglas, Oliver Wendall Homes, Mark Twain, Harriet Beecher Stow, Luisa May Alcott, Nathanial Hawthorn, Henry Wadsworth Longfellow and even Lincoln (though first a Deist) all espoused transcendentalism and the need to abolish slavery. The big debate centered on how to achieve this – via peaceful means (by example) or through war (by force).

By 1850, the whole northern transcendental/abolition movement had embraced pacifism, believing the South could be fixed by a show of piety coming down from the North. But upon hearing this kind of parlor talk, the southern states – deeply immersed in slavery for 200 years, "owning" 4 million slaves – despised these northerners as "goody two shoe" types not to be taken seriously. *Who are these whiny northerners to tell us anything?*

More, not only were the southerners never going to be converted by flowery transcendental talk about living in nature "on Walden's Pond", but the south wanted to expand slavery into the territories, and to turn these territories into slave states and not free states. In 1790, there were 700,000 American slaves; in 1860, 4 million. Slavery was on the march and the abolitionist stood perplexed.

This stalemate of opposing *North versus South* slavery ambitions lasted for over 30 years. And then, one John Brown entered the ring showing everyone the way. Brown, the ethical yet violent abolitionist warrior was willing to take on the depraved, devil-like enslavement fiends of the South.

But to understand Brown, in the 1,800's, we need to take a glance over at Englishman Oliver Cromwell, from the 1,600's, John Brown's historical hero.

The daring to defy entrenched power started way back in 1534 when Henry VIII broke from the "all powerful" Catholic popes to create the Church of England.

Then, a hundred years later, in 1620, English King Charles the 1st wanted to further tighten royal control by asserting his will over the property and rights claimed by the freemen of England. Charles next doubled down by moving from property oppression to religious oppression. For speaking against the Church of England, Puritan advocates had their ears cut off by royal enforcers.

The king's distain for both landed freemen and common religious worshipers, resulted in the ascendency of the mentioned role model, Oliver Cromwell, an aristocratic Puritan who led parliamentary forces in the English Civil War against the King. Cromwell who operated from 1642– 1658, took the title *"Lord Protector of England, Scotland, and Ireland"*.

Combined, the English civil wars and Cromwell's subsequent assault on Ireland resulted in one million deaths.

In the 1800's, Calvinist John Brown, a devout student of English bloodshed in God's name, was keen to apply Cromwell's tactic to America's abolition drama.

Here's what happened.

In the late 1850's the Kansas "Indian" territory was up for grabs. *Pro-slavery* people moved into Kansas to swing the vote their way, and northern *free-state* settlers did the same. The free-state people, however, found themselves terrorized and murdered by the pro-slavery camp. It was a wild-west setting with no controlling legal authorities, and the northern pacifists stood helpless.

And so John Brown and his sons went to Kansas and murdered five pro-slavery people (with swords). Due to the absence of law and order, Brown was not arrested. After that, the "pro-slavery crowd" in Kansas continued to murder many of the New Englander "free state" colonists. So, according to Brown, he had been justified in taking off the gloves.

Returning north after the five killings, Brown was lionized by the transcendentalists who helped raise money for Brown's failed raid on Virginia's Harpers Ferry armory, where Brown had hoped to amass weapons for a slave rebellion.

The Federal government sent in Colonel Robert E. Lee to arrest delusional Brown, who at Harpers Ferry saw himself as America's *Cromwell*. When Brown was tried and hung, the North rang church bells, and the South suddenly learned to fear the North. Just in time!

Once Republican Lincoln was elected, the Democrat South immediately split to cloister their world of 4 million slaves from the "goody two shoe" northerners. Robert E. Lee then sided with Virginia and the south, rather than with the northern federal government, and the rest is history.

## How It All Played Out – "Separate but Equal"

The dismantling of the Democrat South's ownership of the black race did not end with the Civil War. Democrat forces soon formed the KKK as a terrorist force (think Antifa) and used Jim Crow state laws to keep the former slaves in place. Jim Crow laws accepted Blacks as equals, while keeping Black's separate in day-to-day circumstances … the so called "separate but equal" doctrine of the Democrat party, still in play today via urban ghettos.

We will pick up the story later in the coming *Malcom X & Martin Luther King* chapter, featuring racist Lyndon B. Johnson as a manipulator of history. But first, what of the original Transcendentalists – Let's not forget them!

Today, the sentiments of the 1800's *Republican* Transcendentalists have flipped, becoming the hallmarks of the *Democrats*. Rather than seeking liberty for Black slaves, Democrats now require open-ended welfare to prop up former slave victims, and to use the arrangement to hold this voting group tight. And, rather than respecting nature's call for unfettered individual liberty, Democrats now demand citizen-wide obedience across many aspects of private life, especially in the domain of environmental dictates.

And so, while everything looks to have changed since 1860, the genetically-driven battle between the libertarians and socialists stands. Time has simply re-arranged the chairs on the Titanic.

## A Note on Fredrick Douglas

Douglass, mentioned above as a staunch abolitionist, was a close ally of John Brown.

325

In the 1830's Douglas escaped slavery in Maryland, where he had been whipped, where he slept on dirt floors, where he secretly learned to read and write. Once north (he never revealed how he escaped, fearing reprisals against supporters), Douglas became the darling of the Transcendentalists. John Brown wrote his manifesto while staying in Douglas's upstate N.Y. home, and it was Douglas who leaned on Lincoln to re-state the war mission as the end of slavery, and not solely an attempt to hold the Union together.

After the war Douglas begged the whites to "Just leave us alone". They did not.

Read Douglas's autobiographical "Narrative of the Life of Frederick Douglass", where he explains how slavery debased both the slave and the overlord whites from achieving the full potential of the Homo Sapient species.

# 7

# AMERICAN SOCIALISM
# A.D. 1880 – 1900

*" We are fast approaching the stage of the ultimate inversion: the stage where the government is free to do anything it pleases, while the citizens may act only by permission; which is the stage of the darkest periods of human history, the stage of rule by brute force. "*

−AYN RAND, 1900'S−

The American Left grew slowly, and certainly not with Jefferson, founder of the Democrat Party. The determined attack on private property took place later, once immigration accelerated, after the American Civil War, and the attack continues through today. Overall, "property right" erosion became a major weapon within the Socialist arsenal – especially in the use of home taxation to fund government/union controlled schools.

The American migration towards socialism, therefore, starts around A.D. 1880, with the industrial revolution and the onslaught of Irish, Italian, German and Jewish immigrants descending upon America. This onslaught would be used to install permanent constructs that moved people away from personal responsibility towards dependency life styles. In this and subsequent chapters we cover these migrations in succession.

It always starts so innocently, a U.S. President trying to solve a problem, and then things get heavy.

## The Early 1800s

They say that **Adam Smith, 1776,** stands the first modern economist, "modern" meaning in the era of the people. Before this, economic structures certainly existed, but in Smith's time a fundamentally new economic dynamic suddenly surfaced centered on people interacting democratically with each other, both politically and economically.

Here are some of the key sentences from Smith's *The Wealth of Nations*...

> *As every individual endeavors as much as he can to employ his capital in the support of domestic industry, he neither intends to promote the public interest, nor knows how much he is promoting it. He intends only his own gain, and is led by an invisible hand to promote an end, which was no part of his intention.*

**Noam Chomsky**, a 21st century professor at MIT, placed his well-spoken critique of Smith as follows:

> *He's pre-capitalist, a figure of the Enlightenment. What we would call capitalism he despised. People read snippets of Adam Smith, the few phrases they teach in school. But not many people get to the point hundreds of pages later, where he says that division of labor will turn people into creatures as stupid and ignorant as it is possible for a human being to be.*

*And therefore in any civilized society the government is going to have to take some measures to prevent division of labor from proceeding to its limits.*

This view, of course, stands correct. Noam's view is called "Liberalism". We could not tolerate unchecked industrial barons while millions suffered shackled to factory posts all across America's industrial revolution mill towns. That was not a Citizen's Economy. Something had to give to provide individuals a way to pull themselves up.

But, mind you, nothing really gave for a long time. Since Adam Smith in 1776, the American economy remained *laissez faire (unencumbered)* for more than a century.

No one taxed your income or your property other than the brief time during the Civil War. Instead the government raised money through import taxes. Law concerned itself with murder, runaway slaves, and bank robberies, with regulation and code dictates nowhere in sight. Government agents such as the Earp Brothers, never burst onto someone's property with commercial building code manuals blazing.

Government exercised day-to-day law enforcement at most. It remained *unconcerned* with business and it did not touch the economy: the people's domain. Keep in mind that the federal income tax only began in 1913 under Woodrow Wilson. Until then, our society breathed unfettered and alive.

Change, however, loomed large… Let's look at the coming pre-and-post World War II chapters to understand our transformation towards primate-socialism. The next chapters cover much forgotten detail, with each political move trending away from libertarianism.

# 8

# PRE-WORLD WAR II

*" The things that will destroy America are prosperity-at-any-price, peace-at-any-price, safety-first instead of duty-first, the love of soft living, and the get-rich-quick theory of life. "*

−TEDDY ROOSEVELT−

By 1900, three forces came together: Immigrants, Industry, and Oil. The big boys who could play at this level enjoyed a field day. **John D. Rockefeller**, for example, cornered 96 percent of the world's known oil supply with a company called Standard Oil.

**J.P. Morgan**, the towering financier, used capital to buy and merge sister companies to create behemoths including the likes of General Electric, U.S. Steel, and at least 100 others. These men proved the ultimate industrial fighting machines.

Their workers, many of them immigrants, suffered brutal treatment.

And in the other corner stood an ultimate fighter named **Teddy Roosevelt** – *"The Man in the Arena"* (his words). Teddy, President 1901-1909, would go all out – as a Republican – to break these giants up, promising to give the people a *"Square Deal"* (his words again).

Teddy used his bully pulpit and big government stick, including Supreme Court appointments, to legally block the monopolies. They called Teddy a "progressive," a term later adopted by the Left.

Today many say that Teddy proved the first Leftist. I see it differently. Yes, he went after Standard Oil and others, but to foster competition, which would enhance the overall economic *opportunity* of the individual. Similar to any Leftist, though, Teddy expanded the power and role of government, but never for the purpose of wealth transfer – a Socialist objective – but only to foster competition and establish certain operating standards – a classic Liberal objective.

For example, Teddy created the Food and Drug Administration, but mainly in response to **Upton Sinclair's** novel *The Jungle*, which tells the tale of a meat packer getting caught in assembly line machinery and unwittingly contributing a little "added flavoring" to the ground beef.

## Woodrow Wilson

The next economic transformer, Democrat college professor Woodrow Wilson, arrived soon after Teddy, ready to further Teddy's "instinct" for what was to be called "Liberalism", i.e., the need for government to play a role in protecting the common man against the forces of history and against the naturally able – "unstoppable" – elite members of society.

On his watch, to provision the government in its new role, Wilson, President 1913–1921, created the Federal Reserve and the Federal Income Tax, giving the government full control over American money. (He also created the League of Nations after World War I, insisting that no nation should judge another – just be kind).

Now the government could raise all the money it wanted either through taxation or simply by printing more. **Ron Paul** put it this way:

*Strictly speaking, it probably is not "necessary" for the federal government to tax anyone directly; it could simply print the money it needs. However, that would be too bold a stroke, for it would then be obvious to all what kind of counterfeiting operation the government is running. The present system combining taxation and inflation is akin to watering the milk; too much water and the people catch on.*

But even with Woodrow's systemic shift, the government did not seek to transfer wealth *a la* a Socialist. But still, with his "bleeding heart", Woodrow was abandoning a founding principle of America, saying things like:

> *Some citizens of this country have never got beyond*
> *the Declaration of Independence ... The Declaration*
> *of Independence did not mention the questions*
> *of our day. It is of no consequence to us.*
>
> −WOODROW WILSON...−

Somewhat like throwing the baby out with the bath water.

Wilson, following up on Teddy's start, and during his two terms in office, bolstered the unions to create some parity between companies and their workers. Yet the government did not yet seek the role of middleman, taking money from one to bribe another.

Yet by going all out to solve the goals of Liberalism, Wilson, the first powerful Liberal in America – and not quite a Socialist – nevertheless did not know where to draw the line between Liberalism and Socialism. He was the first U.S. President to dismiss how precious the rights of owning private property are to those who have climbed up the latter and acquired property and independence, saying:

> *In fundamental theory socialism and democracy are*
> *almost if not quite one and the same. They both rest*

*at bottom upon the absolute right of the community to*
*determine its own destiny and that of its members. Men*
*as communities are supreme over men as individuals*

—WILSON—

## Franklin Roosevelt

Then came the Roaring 20s and finally The Depression, with our next economic evolution personified by **John Maynard Keynes** and **FDR**.

In 1932 the country elected FDR to the White House and he soon launched the government-spending agencies that continued into World War II, intended to bolster employment.

In 1935, Keynes wrote his book – the one I read back in school – titled, *The General Theory of Employment, Interest, and Money.*

Keynes proposed the breakthrough idea that a government could borrow money to stimulate the economy. Governments had borrowed money before this, but only to go to war. After the war, those governments mopped up the debt ASAP. But why not extend the concept to other issues such as unemployment?

So, when Keynes published his book in 1936, it dovetailed with the borrowing scheme already funding FDR's government dole. After all, another pillar of Keynes' theory stood that when people did not buy enough at the retail level, recessions occurred. Handing out jobs would fix this, as people would start to spend again at the level needed to sustain the civilization.

I admit, Keynes possessed a great imagination to come up with this, and were I his contemporary, I would have wanted to try it as well. Others back then, with FDR at the helm, *did* try it out, and called it "The New Deal."

Keynes and FDR, certainly meaning well and expecting people to gain employment, proved the first quasi-Socialists, using government to redistribute wealth in the guise of fixing problems.

Most of what FDR and Keynes cobbled together back then still exists today. Here, though, Keynes reveals himself:

*The love of money as a possession as distinguished from the love of money as a means to the enjoyments and realities of life will be recognized for what it is, a somewhat disgusting morbidity, one of those semi-criminal, semi-pathological propensities which one hands over with a shudder to the specialists in mental disease ... But beware! The time for all this is not yet. For at least another hundred years we must pretend to ourselves and to everyone that fair is foul and foul is fair; for foul is useful and fair is not.*

−KEYNES−
THE ETHICS OF CAPITALISM

Keynes mistrusted a Citizen Economy where people made money, which made them wealthy, which made them independent, which made them mean-spirited, which made them foul, a danger to all. He was, quite simply, a government guy – a true primate socialist.

FDR hired an interesting fellow named **Henry Morgenthau** as his secretary of the Treasury. Henry, a Conservative, agreed to work with Roosevelt, believing that he could temper the massive introduction of Keynesian spending that Roosevelt sought to initiate, and Roosevelt went with Henry, believing him eminently competent to coordinate the sprawling programs.

First, I present a list of 23 New Deal programs for your consideration:

- *Reconstruction Finance Corporation (RFC)*
- *Civilian Conservation Corps (CCC)*
- *Homeowners Loan Corporation (HOLC)*
- *Tennessee Valley Authority (TVA)*
- *Agricultural Adjustment Act (AAA)*
- *National Industrial Recovery Act (NIRA)*
- *Public Works Administration (PWA)*

- *Federal Deposit Insurance Corporation (FDIC)*
- *Glass–Steagall Act*
- *Securities Act of 1933, created the Securities and Exchange Commission (SEC)*
- *FERA camp for unemployed black women*
- *Civil Works Administration (CWA)*
- *Indian Reorganization Act*
- *Social Security Act (SSA)*
- *Works Progress Administration (WPA)*
- *National Labor Relations Act (NLRA)*
- *Judicial Reorganization Bill, 1937: gave the president power to appoint a new Supreme Court judge for every judge 70 years or older; failed to pass Congress*
- *Federal Crop Insurance Corporation (FCIC)*
- *Surplus Commodities Program, the Food Stamp Program*
- *Fair Labor Standards Act*
- *Rural Electrification Administration (REA)*
- *Resettlement Administration (RA)*
- *Farm Security Administration (FSA)*

Surprisingly, with all of the above, unemployment silently hovered at 18 percent through the 1930s, as the national debt as a percentage of the overall GDP grew to 40 percent during the New Deal years.

Note: In comparison, in 2012, Obama brought the national debt to 100 percent of GDP and as with FDR, real unemployment did not budge. Issuing debt to cure unemployment starts to look like "pushing on a rope." As an aside, in 2012, Australia's debt was only 20 percent of its GDP.

Yet, with all said and done, Morgenthau offered the following about the results:

*We have tried spending money. We are spending more than we have ever spent before and it does not work. And I have just one interest, and now if I am wrong somebody else can have my job. I want to see this country prosper. I want to see people get a job. I want to see people get enough to eat. We have never made good on our promises. I say after eight years of this administration, we have just as much unemployment as when we started. And enormous debt to boot*

—MORGENTHAU—

Morgenthau missed the point. Even if the Roosevelt Administration intended the New Deal to restore employment, it became bribery. By handing out jobs and money, FDR and the Democrats won over the Italian, German, Irish, and Jewish immigrants then flooding America – plus most of the newly emancipated women. These voting blocks, even after many attained parity with the male WASPs, would never, thereafter, let the Democrats down.

Yet under FDR, no plan yet surfaced to bring Blacks into the Democratic corral. At the time, Democrats still derided their old slave population. LBJ would eventually sort this out.

An important note, however, is that the monies that FDR doled out were mostly tied to invented work, where the recipient had to contribute their labor in order to earn a stipend. Roosevelt wanted to keep some element of the work ethic alive.

In modern times this has clearly morphed into unabashed handouts.

But "luckily" the Japanese bombed Pearl Harbor, and FDR finally got everyone a real job. No tongue-in-cheek comment this: in 1942, unemployment dropped to two percent.

FDR had jumped out of the unemployment frying pan and into the war fire. And he died at the bitter end of this last fight. While I am sure that he gave his all in trying to find solutions to this rotten era of American history, the solutions he chose led the way to political manipulation of the poor through federal and state handouts.

# 9

# POST-WORLD WAR II

*" Only Americans can hurt America "*

−EISENHOWER−

## Eisenhower Versus Nixon

During World War II, the U.S. borrowed all kinds of money to pay for the war, more than 100 percent of GDP for years.

But afterward, something wonderful happened. The U.S. economy took off for four straight decades, more than doubling every 10 years, *tripling* (that's 300 percent) in the 1950s.

With massive growth, and a top tax rate of 90 percent, the government inhaled huge tax revenues, easily paying off the FDR war bonds, plus it simultaneously invested in gigantic infrastructure projects like **Eisenhower**'s national interstate highway system.

At the same time personal wealth climbed, and life just got better and better for more and more people, hence the slogan a very few of us still remember: "I like Ike" (Eisenhower).

Whereas during the New Deal years 50 percent of the population lived below the poverty level, by 1970, that number had shriveled to 15 percent. People were tapping into the free enterprise, citizen economy – designed for the individual – and had climbed out of poverty.

Post Eisenhower in 1960, we will cover LBJ, MLK and the *Great Society* in the next chapter. But first, as a contrast to the Eisenhower prosperity of the 1950's, we next consider the reverse, an assault on individual self-determination through the introduction of "perpetual inflation" ushered in by Richard Nixon in the early 1970's.

## 1970s Nixon's "Open Bar" – Eroding Savings, Independence

*When the President does it that means that it is not illegal*

—NIXON—

Most people do not know that FDR made the use of gold illegal during his New Deal years. Before doing this, in the early 1930's, depositors "ran" on the banks because they wanted to get gold instead of paper monies. Ten years prior, Germany's paper money lost all its value due to those in power printing it at will. Americans dreaded the same outcome.

FDR took action to stem this and got his Democrat-controlled Congress to pass laws to back him up.

First, citizens could not hold gold, and *had* to sell it to the government for $22 an ounce.

Second, once FDR confiscated everyone's gold at $22, he suddenly declared gold to be worth $35 an ounce, which meant that he could print more dollars and still claim to enforce some sort of gold standard.

Third, FDR used the new money for his social, vote-fetching programs.

By 1968, when America elected Nixon, gold still stood at $35 an ounce. By then, Americans were making big money, but with an Asian war, an ambitious space program, and huge social expenditures, the debt level had crept up to 36 percent of GDP, only four percent lower than FDR.

By 1971, the third year of Richard Nixon's presidency, LBJ's two blunders – the Vietnam War (a temporary phenomenon) and The Great Society program (a systemic phenomenon) – still carried strong and for political reasons, Nixon did not rush to end either money pit.

On the heels of this, the country began to flirt with recession (the economy bottomed out in '73). With tax dollars suddenly scarce, and not wanting to borrow more with debt already standing at 36 percent of GDP, Nixon decided to print more greenbacks.

The problem? Our gold standard pledge remained steady at $35 per ounce, and if you added up all the gold at Fort Knox and in the various Federal Reserve basements, Nixon could not print any more money and stand by the gold standard commitment.

Moreover, other countries, such as France, unhappy with the U.S. debt situation, wanted their gold removed from Fort Knox and shipped to Europe.

Nixon saw an easy fix, and he appeared on TV to announce to the world the "temporary" suspension of the dollar's convertibility into gold.

In effect, Nixon declared an open bar: go ahead, have as many drinks as you like, for there will be no tab. Print all the money you want. After all, it only would spill out a few years later in the form of double-digit inflation under **Jimmy Carter** – who got blamed for the effect. Nixon surely was "Tricky Dick".

From that day forward succeeding presidents bellied up to Nixon's bar, except perhaps Clinton, who had so much tax money coming in that he enjoyed a surplus.

Forget gold at $35 an ounce. The price of gold would climb with every newly printed U.S. Dollar. And as I write this in 2023, gold sells for more than $1,900 per ounce, meaning the price of gold against the dollar has increased 50-fold in 50 years. That's a lot of money printing. That's a lot of inflation. That's a lot of watering down the milk – your savings.

Of course primates say that savings should be tapped … it's for the troop! And let's boost taxes as much as possible to impinge those "selfish" alien-libertarians. Primate-socialist needs come first, let the alien-libertarian horses pull the wagon.

A footnote on Nixon: his great legacy was in "opening up" China. Perhaps he woke a sleeping dog…

Now let's return to the 1960's and size up LBJ's *Great Society.*

# 10

# MALCOM X AND DR. MARTIN LUTHER KING JR.

*" I cannot swallow whole the view of Lincoln as the Great Emancipator. "*

—OBAMA—

## 1950 – 1970 Separatism Versus Socialism

My black American heroes are Fredrick Douglas and Malcom X. Plus ... Martin Luther King (MLK) and Muhammad Ali receive honorable mention for demonstrating pure courage. How do these luminaries stack up in the context of SUBJUGATED? To find out, let's look back.

Fredrick Douglas in the 1800's was previously mentioned for his role in both the slavery abolition movement and in his attempts to influence Lincoln during the Civil War. After the war, other black leaders rose, particularly Booker T. Washington (1856 – 1915), who advocated black incorporation into the American system through generational advances in education, skills and productivity. Booker's trajectory was in place despite Democrat head winds designed to stymie blacks through Democrat party mechanisms like the KKK and Jim Crow laws.

Booker's vision did not last.

In 1906, a new doctrine of victimization and inevitable failure was introduced by one W.E.B. Du Bois (1868 – 1963), the black, Harvard educated son of professional-class parents living in Great Barrington, Massachusetts. This new doctrine of no assimilation would lead to the Nation of Islam, founded in the 1930's by Elijah Muhammed of Chicago, and carried forward in the 1950's and 1960's by Elijah's agent Malcom X.

As will be seen, during this era, contemporaries Malcom X and MLK would advocate different paths for black advancement: Malcom X preached liberaltarianism, and MLK succumbed to socialism. How dare I reach this conclusion?

Alex Haley's "The Autobiography of Malcom X" explains the great mind of Malcom X (1926 – 1965), as he fights off the worst aspects of a shattered childhood and a criminal early adulthood. He finally finds his libertarian voice under the guidance of his mentor Elijah Muhammed (1897 – 1975).

Like the Puritan separatist who settled New England, starting with the 1620 Mayflower colony at Plymouth Massachusetts, the Nation of Islam advocated complete separation from society if blacks were ever to achieve self-determination.

The Puritan separatists, escaping hard persecution (ears cut off) in England for their religious belief in practicing direct communion with God, felt that any participation with the Monarchy, with the Church of England and even with the economy of Europe would result in a corruption of their chosen ways. So they escaped into the forests of New England and built their 1600's society right when England was consumed by civil war. The separatists were left alone for generations.

In the 1930's Elijah Muhammad created the Nation of Islam in the same vein. Not only should blacks separate themselves from the abuse of white society, but Blacks needed to separate themselves from the whole Judeo-Christian world, by embracing Islam and taking on Islamic names.

This movement would only flourished when Elijah Muhammad found young Malcom, then wasting away for 6 ½ years in a Massachusetts's prison. During this time, Elijah corresponded regularly with Malcom, and invited Malcom into the fold upon his release from prison in 1952.

Malcom travelled America setting up mosques in many cities, preaching that black families had to build themselves up, generation-by-generation, until they could compete properly with whites. Malcom's centerpiece was the family unit – a dedicated mother and father nurturing the nobility and readiness of their offspring children.

And so, years later, when Malcom discovered that Elijah was having children out of wed lock, Malcom split from the program. For this audacity, in 1965 he was assassinated in Washington Heights New York City by multiple Nation of Islam gun men.

Unlike the Puritan separatists who in the 1600's were left alone to evolve their society, the Black separatists lived exposed to the vast, unaccommodating society surrounding them. But worse, with Malcom's death, the libertarian voice of black America was silenced.

Of note, it needs saying: to fill the void of Malcom X's demise, one Louis Farrakhan, a Nation of Islam heavy weight, rose in prominence, finally taking over the whole movement after Elijah's death in 1975. Some in Malcom's family believe Farrakhan an orchestrator of Malcom's assassination.

Farrakhan, a staunch Islamist, took the Nation down an antisemite path, accusing Jews of controlling the media, government, and global economy, along with being behind the slave trade, Jim Crow laws, and black oppression in general. He regularly called Jews "Satanic" and praised *Adolf Hitler* as a "very great man".

Ok, so much for Malcom X's interrupted vision. But what of MLK's vision?

Martin Luther King (1929 – 1968) operated concurrently with Malcom. Martin advocated assimilation rather than separatism. He too was assassinated, but not until he inadvertently damaged the fate of black America. This conclusion is manifest, though it has been covered up by ongoing propaganda and hero worship ever since. Here are the historical facts.

Too bad for Martin Luther King Jr. (MLK) – a positive man – that Lyndon Baines Johnson (LBJ) – a purely evil man – so badly corrupted his destiny. Why do I say so?

In my youth during the 1960s, I grew up in a rural Connecticut town that grew tobacco. I worked on those tobacco farms from age 13 through age 15. As it happened, in the 1940's, MLK, then a boy, twice resided in my town, living in farm dormitories during the summer.

One day my father and I visited the historical society to view old letters Martin wrote to his mother explaining how Northerners treated him – compared to the severity Martin grew up with down South. In the letters, Martin explains to his mother how he could do whatever he wanted… go on the bus to Hartford to see a movie without any of that "back of the bus" stuff happening…

His message? "Mom, we could live like this!" Us 13-year old's in the tobacco fields felt quite proud to literally be walking in Dr. King's footsteps.

And so I know that at the start of his maturation, Martin's intentions emerged pure, his wanting to eliminate conflict, not feed it. Yet quite the opposite occurred once he rose to the big leagues.

His secret arrangements with LBJ inadvertently – but clearly – made racial matters worse, leading to today's pattern of pitting welfare recipients against taxpayers, all pawns of the Socialist Left. Let's look at what MLK's capitulation to the Democrats did to everyone…

Never stated anywhere, the Kings (Martin's parents) stood Republican, as did many Blacks in the early 1900s. After all, it was

Republican Lincoln and then Grant (who crushed the KKK) that had derailed slavery. Hence many Blacks were Republicans.

Recall, that after the Civil War, Democrats sought workarounds to one's natural rights by inventing the notorious Jim Crow Laws, passed by Democrat controlled state legislatures.

Using a *separate-but-equal argument*, Jim Crow Laws finessed the assertion that all men are created equal by asserting that one can still be separated even if equal – like chickens, all equal, placed in different coops.

Protection of Life, Liberty and Property – our Due Process rights – could be segregated.

In 1954, the core of the Jim Crow Laws, i.e., segregation, was shuttered via a U.S. Supreme Court ruling, but many other aspects of individual rights remained, such as discrimination in the hiring process.

Enter Lyndon Johnson (Mr. Evil) and Martin Luther King, Jr (Mr. Goodness).

In 1964, the country watched the drama taking place over the passage of the Civil Rights Act, a cornerstone piece of legislation designed to retire remnants of the Jim Crow era. Eighty percent of the Republicans supported the bill, with 18 Democrat Senators in opposition.

The main Democrat who stood with the Blacks? Bobby Kennedy, who hated LBJ and planned to wrest the 1968 Democrat primary away from Johnson.

Things got a bit dicey, but LBJ experienced a political epiphany; he would flip history in a way that would get the Blacks behind him, while simultaneously taking the wind out of Bobby's sails.

LBJ's plan?

Johnson would co-opt the Black community through financial bribes, calling it the *Great Society* program. He would cut the deal with four civil rights leaders and did so over a 90-minute meeting in the White House, January 18th, 1964.

Johnson solicited Dr. King and three of King's allies – *Roy Wilkins*, executive director of the National Association for the

Advancement of Colored People, National Urban League Executive Director *Whitney Young,* and Congress of Racial Equality National Director *James Farmer.*

Though the 90-minute meeting was not open to the press, *The Chicago Daily Defender* published the four activists' comments to the media outside the White House in an article headlined *"LBJ Meets with Negro Leaders; All Five Worry About Poverty."*

For sure, LBJ proved the devil incarnate, and his satanic river of welfare money formed an offer King couldn't refuse. The civil rights leaders said the discussion with the president revolved around how to address the fact that poverty afflicted blacks far more than whites. Johnson would raise the money to fix this, and as a show of good faith, get the Civil Rights bill through the Senate. He did this by arm-twisting his old Democrat cronies.

Of course in return for Great Society largesse, the Negro down-trodden would have to abandon the Republicans, who had defended them since Lincoln. Yes, now the Blacks must cast their votes for the Democrats (but not Bobby...).

Months later, to witness the signing of the Civil Rights Act, Johnson invited the four activists back to the White House. They accepted. On July 2 1964, in the East Room of the White House, Johnson signed the provision into law, fewer than six months after the January meeting. LBJ could move mountains.

The president gave King the pen used to sign the bill. King described it as one of his *"...most cherished possessions."*

Suddenly the world forgot the previous 200 years, that the Democrat Party fostered black enslavement, wanted to spread it west, that the Democrats led The South into war to preserve enslavement, that the Democrats held the Blacks back by concocting "Jim Crow" segregation laws, and that Democrats tried to torpedo Civil Rights!

Guess what? LBJ's tactic worked, the world forgot... everything!

Following the assassination of King during LBJ's presidency, ML King pretenders, e.g., Jesse Jackson, Al Sharpton, The Reverend Wright, would each step into King's power vacuum, using hate speech to condition Blacks into permanent dependency, unable to tap into and compete within society, a permanent underclass whose only salvation sat with the Democrats.

When LBJ took over, the rate of illegitimate births in the Black community ran at eight percent. Today, that statistic tallies 70 percent, a 9X increase – imposed dependency by eliminating the need for the family unit.

How LBJ brokered this deal with King remains amazing; it documents the manipulative capacity of the dominant primate Johnson, and the gullibility of Reverend King.

And so, with excellent propaganda everywhere, after 60 years of the Great Society, it's no wonder that 19 out of 20 Blacks still vote Democrat, as they believe that the Democrats "...got their backs." LBJ and his naive partner MLK rendered more long-term harm than anyone to everyone. Their contrived alliance successfully covered up the stain of *Democrats against-Blacks* by blaming all Whites, entrapping most Blacks.

Do you know what a "bellwether sheep" is? It is the special sheep working in league with the shepherd. It wears a bell, and as it walks to the slaughter pen all the other sheep follow it in to their deaths. This is the unintended legacy of Martin Luther King Jr. He might have begun and died with a pure heart, but he sold himself and his followers to the socialist devil.

King's words regarding con artist Johnson:

> *I have no doubt that we may continue to differ concerning the tempo and the tactical design required to combat the impending crisis. But I do not doubt that the President is approaching the solution with sincerity, realism and, thus far, with wisdom. I hope his course will be straight and true. I will do everything in my power to make it so, by outspoken agreement whenever proper, and determined opposition whenever necessary.*

> –KING–

Like many in the 1960's, MLK fell in way over his head thinking he could trust LBJ, not foreseeing that the monies came with heavy, permanent chains attached. But modern Democrats have no excuses for perpetuating the consequences of welfare, and instead wantonly double down on the whole socialist paradigm no matter the horror, simply to hold onto the dependency voters that welfare incubates.

*They're gonna put y'all back in chains.* **Biden.**

No Joe, you guys did. And now a whole race of people, told they are being protected, find themselves trapped in a primate-socialist pyramid of control, operated by party elites.

# 11

## BILL CLINTON

*" It depends on what the meaning of the word 'is' is. If the—if he—if 'is' means is and never has been, that is not—that is one thing. If it means there is none, that was a completely true statement. … Now, if someone had asked me on that day, are you having any kind of sexual relations with Ms. Lewinsky, that is, asked me a question in the present tense, I would have said no. And it would have been completely true. "*

—BILL CLINTON—

## 1990 – 1998 Socialism's Slippery Slope

Other than reminding the reader of the above ridiculous dodge attempted by Bill to disguise his "picadillo" with Monica, this chapter examines the real damage he did to the American economy and to the wellbeing of most American taxpayers.

Since World War II, the gravy train kept chugging, surviving the likes of the Jimmy Carter presidency, itself hobbled by Nixon's inflation policy.

Each decade found a new phenomenon enabling America to expand while masking our waste. But the main driver proved the entrepreneur, who created small, medium, and large businesses. The vast U.S. stock market further propelled these businesses in combination with the private equity firms that infused capital into compelling concerns.

This capitalist formula for fostering companies existed at this scale only in the USA. The Citizen Economy had grown more sophisticated, but individuals still ran it, just as **Woodrow Wilson** understood decades earlier:

> *No country can afford to have its prosperity originated by a small controlling class. The treasury of America lies in those ambitions, those energies that cannot be restricted to a special favored class. It depends upon the inventions of unknown men, upon the originations of unknown men, upon the ambitions of unknown men. Every country is renewed out of the ranks of the unknown, not out of the ranks of those already famous and powerful and in control.*

To keep things humming, the 1990s gave America two key gifts: an explosion in computing technology, and a global expansion of U.S. companies into the "other" 100 + countries around the world.

Plus, new American companies formed and sales multiplied everywhere. Bill Clinton raised taxes, but for sure, he wanted people to make money, and he set a winning tone.

When all is said and done, Americans either work for a company or an institution started by themselves or someone else, or they collect money from the government.

If we aspire as a nation to remain prosperous, we require motivated entrepreneurs who will run until they drop. As we have heard repeatedly, small business creates the vast majority of new jobs.

But also, while still in the 1990s, something bizarre occurred that permanently injured working class Americans in a self-inflicted-wound manner.

## NAFTA – Giving Away Jobs

The North American Free Trade Agreement, signed by Democrat **Bill Clinton**, started the systemic demise of manufacturing jobs in the USA., and Bill, being a naturally-driven primate-socialist, stubbornly chose this destructive path even after going to Yale and then to Oxford!

From the 1990s onward, America lost tens of millions of manufacturing jobs to overseas entities, especially to China who today hires hundreds of millions of its own instead. And now the USA finds itself in the precarious position of making hardly anything, nor able to create skills-oriented jobs for the working class. Consider the following information published by the Federal Labor Department.

Let's add it up using 2012 statistics. In 2012, including illegal's, there were 333 million "Americans". (In 2023, I hear it's almost 350 million).

The 2012 stats:

- *100 million are stay-at-home housewives/husbands, pre-school children, or seniors.*
- *80 million are students.*
- *20 million more are home wishing they could work but they are not looking.*
- *20 million more receive unemployment benefits.*
- *20 million serve in the military or supply the military.*
- *7 million work for federal, state & local government.*
- *20 million work in healthcare.*
- *13 million work in education.*

- *10 million work in financial services.*
- *12 million work in leisure & hospitality.*
- *5 million are in retail.*
- *7 million work in transportation.*
- *6 million are "professionals," e.g., attorneys, CPAs, etc.*

That's 320 million who don't make anything, leaving…

… get this … 13 million who actually make cars, food, clothing, electricity, fuel, and homes…. Obviously, this is not good.

Why on Earth Bill Clinton signed the NAFTA Agreement escapes me. I suppose the winners were the multinationals who seem to support both Democrats and Republicans.

I remember Bill's campaign: *Training* -- We will re-train America to pick up the slack of the lost jobs that we expected to drift overseas (that *Giant sucking sound* to which **Ross Perrot** loved to refer).

Training? How do we train millions of working class Americans to perform new age jobs, such as financial services, when each person – due to either temperament, drive, aptitude or education – could never exist in that sphere under any circumstance? What were the primate-socialists thinking?

But Bill beautifully sold this "re-training/launch your second career" bill of goods to everyone. And it worked: the voters elected him twice.

Building from NAFTA, which dealt with Canada and Mexico, Bill next upped the "Troop Primate" ante to become a one-world supporter of the World Trade Organization (WTO), and in particular he championed the inclusion of China into the WTO, thus becoming Nixon's historical twin.

What a mess of unintended consequences by Bill, the one-people idealist who miscalculated the cunning of the whole human race. Today China uses American profits to own America's supply chain, able to threaten world peace, able to infect the world with Covid, able to take Hong Kong and possibly Taiwan, while controlling key medical supplies and a whole lot more. Bill, the genius primate sticking up for the whole troop – forgetting that primates fight each other.

And after eight years of Clinton, eight further years of Bush and eight additional years of Obama (overall, my whole adult life time), our manufacturing jobs appear gone forever, and many people will live in desolation until they die.

Trump from 2016 onward tried to re-establish U.S. manufacturing, returning some ballast to the manufacturing ship, but then he was "keel hauled" by China via the Covid pandemic, and subsequently cut to pieces by the Democrat barnacles who exploited the situation.

And as I write this, today in 2023, we have Biden, driving everything into the ground – on purpose. Currently, the primates who foisted Biden on us are now scared stiff of the whole situation, looking for new elites, like Gavin Newsom, to comfort them.

But back to Clinton … things got worse.

## Affordable Housing – Breaking the Economy

Besides NAFTA and the WTO, Clinton started the domestic housing bubble to give out homes to the troop, by sponsoring Socialist legislation.

*The Community Reinvestment Act*, which added pressure on banks to lend in low-income neighborhoods even if it made no business sense at all.

*The Commodity Futures Modernization Act*, which exempted credit-default swaps from regulation – the derivatives that insured the bogus mortgages.

*Repeal of Glass-Steagall* (an FDR-era regulation forbidding banks to do certain types of speculative trading), allowing banks to trade in securities such as Mortgage Back Securities – which bundled the bad mortgages together into pools one traded.

Some people do not blame Clinton for housing "going through the roof" because, technically, the bubble burst under Bush II. But that would require one to cross off this chapter and pretend the 90s never happened. Many "Blame Bush" primate-socialists do this.

One who must hold eternal gratitude to Clinton's miscalculations? Obama, who even in the 2012 elections used this distortion of time to still "blame Bush." And it worked! Enough voters actually blamed Bush.

But Bush would affect us in his own ways.

# 12

## GEORGE BUSH

*" You teach a child to read, and he or her will be able to pass a literacy test. "*

—GEORGE W. BUSH—

*" Everything has its limit – iron ore cannot be educated into gold. "*

—MARK TWAIN—

## 1999 – 2007 Socialism's Slippery Slope II

One of the worst socialist outcomes I have witnessed is the ascendance of Government Schools, with their entitlements and indoctrination formulas, all brought to new heights under **George W Bush** with "No Child Left Behind."

Since then, education budgets tripled, SAT scores deteriorated, teachers unions became emboldened, parents became treated as terrorists, and primate-socialist master minds spewed CRT and gender affirmation.

The Bush II presidency, similar to Clinton's NAFTA, WTO, and Affordable Housing doings, left an ongoing, systemic hole in our society's alien-libertarian fiber.

Today 90 percent of American children go to government schools where other adults pay for most of the upbringing of some other person's children. The subsidies? Outrageous, including busing, teaching, computers, food, nursing, sports facilities, performing arts facilities, private tutors, lifetime pension and health plans, gigantic buildings, and police support.

Two percent attend private schools. Two percent receive home schooling, and six percent attend religious schools.

If you send your three children through the government school program for 12 years each, your family costs taxpayers $750,000 – $1 million. For the most part, parents pay none or a fraction of that expense in local property taxes.

If you the parent take this money, then how can you complain about someone else getting food stamps? You can't, and the Socialists are counting on you to reside quietly in that trap.

In the 1950s, the government school model started out as a locally driven institution that meant well – a good type of Socialism – but now education and union bosses bully the whole system in a top-down manner, and most of the administrators and teachers vote lockstep for the primate-socialist Democrats.

> Master **Karl Marx's** vision became reality: *"The education of all children, from the moment that they can get along without a mother's care, shall be in state institutions."*

Many consider government schools America's stepping-stone into socialism. And Bush II, a Republican, added fuel to the fire, turning teachers into government regulators spewing CRT and LBGQ propaganda to children!

Not too long ago, a citizen-led education system existed where parents arranged for their children's education. Just 100 years prior in my hometown, no government schools existed whatsoever. Instead, 17 schoolhouses stood scattered amongst the neighborhoods. The parents paid the schoolmasters, and the parents, therefore, held responsibility for both sides of the coin – the educator and the educated.

Obviously, this quaint system remains impractical today, but the full government school model -- that leaves 90 percent of the children with no other choice, and one that uses open-ended property taxation on everyone to pay for it all -- did not solve the puzzle of growing populations. It just funneled the population into the government's primate-socialist hands.

If free education is something primate society wants, then the obvious alternative to Government-only schools is the much dismissed "voucher" approach. Give every kid a $24,000 annual voucher, funded via state-level sales and income taxes (not our homes), to spend on the school of choice.

Because this would break up the socialist monopoly, the voucher program is not likely to happen anytime soon. In the meantime, pro-public school Republicans won't realize they are being had by buying into socialism's first step.

And this leaves us with "unfunded education mandates", "core curriculums" and "CRT Narratives" funded by local property taxes raised (originated) *without legislative representation.* That's a victory for the primates!

## The Invasion Of Privacy – American Terrorists

Of course Bush's worst mistake was the Patriot Act, which gave the government the authority to spy – via the NSA, the DOJ, the FBI, the CIA, the IRS, etc. – on anyone they cite as a threat to America.

President Bush said this did not mean we the American Citizens, yet the law nevertheless includes we the citizens, not just foreign terrorists. Even if Bush stayed clear of abusing this authority, it does not mean that subsequent Presidents would not use it for political suppression purposes.

And it is not just the NSA. All of the big Federal Agencies with their vast buildings, their badge-toting employees and contractors, their benefits for life inducements ... they are all loyal to their boss, the government, and will do whatever they are told to do.

What will Presidents do with unchecked permissions to spy on U.S. Citizens? Spy! The expression: "power corrupts, and absolute power corrupts absolutely" is a maxim of human behavior that has been forgotten.

Today, Bush's "No Child Left Behind" and his "Patriot Act" legislative legacies have come home to roost, the source of many unintended consequences.

To sum up ... on-going socialist shifts in America happened in little more than 100 years. These historical markers affected self-reliance, wealth building and liberty. But the onslaught by primate-socialists against their alien-libertarian cousins was only getting started. Next, Saul Alinsky, architect of today's socialist war plan.

# 13

## SAUL ALINSKY

*" Any revolutionary change must be proceeded by an
attitude toward change amongst the mass of our people.
They must feel so frustrated, so defeated, so lost, so futureless
in the prevailing system that they are willing to let go of the
past and change the future. To bring on this reformation
requires the organizer work inside the system. "*

—SAUL ALINSKY—

As just described in the Pre-and-post World War II chapters, the
drift away from America's alien-libertarian way of life towards primate-socialism was mainly inadvertent. American presidents were
simply dealing with situations, instituting cures that would then
stick around forever, just as Hegel explained. Predictably, historical
conflict moved society left, as citizens never give up free gifts once
introduced.

As such, the socialist transformation which took place starting
under Teddy Roosevelt (Republican) leading right up to George W

Bush (Republican) was the by-product of human crises managed across disparate historical episodes.

This haphazard pattern would soon be replaced by purposeful, well thought out socialist strategies invented by Saul Alinsky. Alinsky, coming out of Chicago, would publish the book "Rules For Radicles" in 1971, a blue print designed to eliminate America's alien-libertarian institutions, replacing them with a primate-operated pyramid of control apparatus. He died in 1972.

Because the likes of Hillary Clinton and Barrack Obama were brought up under Saul's methods, it behooves the reader to understand the pivotal impact Alinsky has had on escalating the alien/primate conflict.

Let's start by understanding who this socialist visionary was.

The short of it … he was a mobster raised in Chicago by Al Capone and Frank Nitti, Capone's wingman. For a school project, Alinsky wanted to interview the mob, and upon doing so, they adopted him for his keen instinct in suggesting operating tactics that improved one's criminal results while lowering the risk of getting caught.

The kid had a gift.

He saw how to defraud main stream establishments while always staying beneath the radar. At some point he turned from straight crime to politics, which for Alinsky, represented the major league levels of crime. By adopting the mafia's pyramid of control structure within politics, one could own all of the moving parts of society.

In nature, out in the jungle, the primate troop has a top ape, a few lieutenants and then everyone else. In modern times, this organic approach required a new pyramid of control structure that allowed billions of members to be managed. The pyramid of control system needed an upgrade, and Alinsky would handle it.

Here are a few of his directives; you have experienced all of them.

Alinsky Principle #1 – Do not advertise or ever mention the big revolutionary vision. Instead communicate with the tone and promises each interest group wants to hear and refer to yourself positively using the term "progressive."

Alinsky Principle #2 – Patiently move the agenda forward taking any compromise they give you, then ignore the deal and create pressure using public ignorance of the storyline to set up the next compromise.

Alinsky Principle #3 – Prevent individuals from using business to gain personal independence. Instead make business people dependent upon satisfying your goals using government contracts as carrots, and government agents (EPA, FDA, IRS, etc.) as sticks.

Alinsky Principle #4 – Ridicule and silence those who do not embrace you.

Alinsky Principle #5 – Don't be afraid of spending any amount of money necessary to attain the revolution's goals. Once you get into billions and trillions, the people tune out and won't realize what is happening to them.

Alinsky Principle #6 – Blazingly accuse your political opponents of the very crimes you are committing.

Actually there are many pages of numbered directives in the Alinsky manual. It is tedious, but I urge you to read it. The main theme teaches how to penetrate the key institutions of America in league with other hidden, like-minded extremist, who collectively operate the pyramid.

This meant moving primate-socialists into positions of power within academia, law, politics, media, big tech, the deep state and into commercial corporations. In his younger day, Alinsky took great pride into getting "guilt" money out of companies, turning the company's focus away from "share" holders to "stake" holders, where anyone affected by a company ought to be accommodated.

He also urged that a central propaganda office produce daily talking points to deliver a focused socialist narrative to the masses each day. Today, the DNC central propaganda team draws up the points, the New York Times publishes them, and the downstream news organizations ape them – using the same words.

Another tactic … while moving the revolution's agenda along, keep everyone distracted in faux debate over things like race, abortion and transgender bathrooms.

And so today, we have CRT infiltrating the schools, WOKE corporations giving millions to the communist organization BLM, big tech shuttering dialogue, and even financing the socialist operation – for example Zuckerberg paying $400 million in 2020 to finance "street mules" that harvest inner city ballots stuffed into drop boxes.

The disciples of Alinsky became many, but Hillary and Barack proved the top players, coming up next.

For now consider this: Hillary Clinton wrote her 92-page paper at Wellesley on Alinsky, thus garnering an invitation to join his movement, but she instead went to Yale … and the rest is history.

And, In 2008, Alinsky's son David wrote the following to Obama:

*"I am proud to see that my father's model for organizing is being applied successfully beyond local community organizing to affect the Democratic campaign in 2008. It is a fine tribute to Saul Alinsky as we approach his 100th birthday."*

# 14

## DOUBLETHINK

> " *Doublethink" means the power of holding*
> *two contradictory beliefs in one's mind*
> *simultaneously, and accepting both of them* "

—GEORGE ORWELL—

**Vladimir Lenin** set the stage by proclaiming, *"A lie, told often enough, becomes the truth."*, referring to "small, whispered lies". Alinsky went on to teach that "big lies" work just as well – such as spending so much money that everyone loses perspective. Both Barack Obama and Hillary Clinton took this to heart, so much so, that they improved upon Alinsky's tactic. No need for just "big or small lies", as "any lie" can be made to work, the people bamboozled using "Doublethink" with almost every topic out there.

And so Doublethink became the modern primate-socialist tool used to obscure reality, replacing reality with socialist talking points. Examples:

**Speaker of the House Nancy Pelosi** dished out massive quantities of Doublethink when she muttered the famous nonsense: *We need to pass the law to find out what's in it,*

Or how about this for Doublethink, **Hillary's**: *It takes a village,* when we all know it takes parents.

Subtler versions of Doublethink include the trafficking of "confident" sounding nonsense, such as **Hillary's** reaction to Libya, berating the Congress for questioning her, saying: *What difference at this point does it make.*

Or the "Russian Collusion" lie, where in the end **Hillary** the accuser, was actually the "Steel Dossier" conspirator.

**Obama** used Doublethink for psychological erosion, saying things such as, *"This is the end of do it yourself economics",* as surviving in an unfair America proved too overwhelming. Rather than encourage people to get gritty, Obama basically told them they deserved compensation as victims.

This line of thought stems from the old 1875 Marxist slogan: *From each according to his ability, to each according to his need.* This Karl Marx brainchild stands as the open first attack on individuality and human spirit, gnawing away ever since at people's self-confidence, independence, and potential.

**Obama** updated the original Marxist slogan by dropping the words "ability" and "needs," simply citing *The Have's and Have Not's,* and further refined it by inventing *The One Percent,* which makes the same point, but now quantifies the magnitude of unfairness by placing only one percent of America into the fortunate column and 99 percent into the victim column.

**Obama** also employed straight lying, as in *"The affordable care act will reduce your health premiums by $2,400".* Affordable

Care tripled premiums! And let's not forget his infrastructure bill, where rather than roads, Federal money went into state general funds, used to fund state worker unions.

**Obama's** other famous Doublethink transgressions include:

Weaponizing the IRS against Tea Party groups,

Arming drug cartels on the Mexican border during the "Fast & Furious" debacle,

Lying about the Benghazi, Libya incident by citing a video,

Allowing Hillary to destroy her in-home server, eliminating criminal evidence,

Allowing Bill Clinton to meet in plain view of America with Attorney General Lorretta Lynch, on the tarmac in Arizona, to ensure no action would be taken against Hillary,

And allowing his top lieutenants Brennan, Clapper, Comey, et al, to fabricate the Russian Hoax to decoy the public from Democrat dirty tricks designed to thwart in-coming president Trump.

People in the Primate-socialist camp ignore these types of self-evident evils, feeling them necessary to craft some form of kind socialism. Damn the torpedoes – full steam ahead towards the envisioned socialist utopia! All of this illusion Doublethink.

The worst example of Doublethink is, of course, the simultaneous views on the death penalty and abortion. Primates oppose the death penalty in part because it can lead to the death of innocent people, but they support abortion, even though every fetus killed is innocent.

Flagrant Doublethink underpinned Covid 19. It was not China's fault … **Doctor Fouche** did not finance the Chinese lab … the vaccines shielded you, bringing about herd immunity … masks worked … mandates and lockdowns were essential.

And don't forget … according to **Biden**, buying Russian, Iranian and Venezuelan oil is good; buying American oil is bad.

Russian, Iranian Chinese and North Korean aggression under Biden is also Trumps fault as a result of Trump's "America first" policy, which insulted the others.

The top Doublethink dodge … Democrats denying their role in the sufferings of Black Americans. Recall:

That slaves were primarily owned by Democrats, that Democrats fought a war to keep their slaves, that Democrats held down emancipated Blacks using the Jim Crow laws, that Democrats ran the KKK, that Democrats fought the Civil Rights Amendment, that Democrats re-enslaved Blacks into urban plantations, and that LBJ's Great Society dependency programs would break 70 percent of Black American family units down to nothing … yet claiming to be in their corner.

But there is more Doublethink happening.

## National Socialism Doublethink

In addition to unleashing open-ended, Putin-like propaganda on a daily basis, the American primate-socialists have also taken a page out the National Socialist playbook, the one written by Mussolini, Hitler and Putin.

Have you ever wondered why Fascism (essentially Socialism) and Nazism (again, essentially Socialism) are considered to be

Rightwing political philosophies? It's because the socialists have gone to great lengths to recast them as Right-wing philosophies, a classic Doublethink tactic.

*National Socialism* still seeks a version of socialist equality, but not wealth equality. Once Mussolini (in 1922) and later Hitler (in 1933) realized that they needed the big financiers and industrialists to fuel their societies, a new kind of equality became an equality of pure dedication to *national* interests as defined by the leader – hence the label *National Socialism.*

National Socialism means that you are a loyal primate-socialist, a bonified member of the pyramid of control. If you put the team first, then you can get as rich as you want on the side. Mussolini and Hitler followed this tract, but so has Putin with his oligarchs and the Democrats with their big tech agents getting rich while doing insidious jobs for the pyramid – like censorship and vote harvesting.

What can be done amidst this Alinsky/Obama/Clinton/Biden culture of lies?

Out of it all, inner-circle Socialists anticipate lower living conditions, but believe that a low standard of living remains a small price to pay for getting all of those pyramid-membership privileges, such as assured survival where you simply need to show up and obey your superiors. And, they remain confident that once you settle in, and learn to "be kind", that you will love the whole program. And if you don't settle in nicely, well ...

Aliens not born of the pyramid, all spread out here and there amongst the Apes, cannot even consider counter-revolution, where geographic separation, an asset of the human past, no longer plays. We cannot all move to Texas. So slowly, they will get the Alien-libertarians culturally isolated, impoverished by taxes, and manipulated within the justice system.

With the finish line in sight, today's Socialists stand organized to attack anyone at any level of importance who interrupts their seductive narrative. Instinctively, genetically, they yearn to *eliminate (cancel)* those with whom they disagree.

*Now* I get it. It is called genocide: elimination of a genetic foe.

## Global Doublethink

One more thing – The annual Economic Forum in Davos Switzerland. Here the top primates meet and plot – Bill Gates, Blackrock's Larry Fink, the Clintons, Justin Trudeau, etc… They envision something called "The Great Reset". Like Rousseau, they want to end individual selfishness, and transfer personal liberty over to globally-managed societies. After the Great Reset, the Elite will have the inside track and use fear – Covid in the winter, Global Warming in the summer – to cause obedience amongst the Homo Sapient billions – the deplorables … restoring the traditional subjugation of humankind.

They even discuss genetic re-programming and putting computer chips in people. So far Russia and China won't join – already enjoying their own pyramids.

But still, the pyramid of control is on the march, wanting to become a one-world, one-people pyramid, no room for separate national Laws of the Land, and certainly no room for individual liberty.

These Davos jet setters can't help it, they are extreme genetic primate-socialists doing their thing.

And though Doublethink is devised to confuse people, occasionally an Elite messes up and spews out the truth. Here's a reminder:

> *We're going to take things away from you*
> *on behalf of the common good.*

–HILLARY CLINTON–

# 15

## TRUMP

*" Remember two things. Number one, I said, we're going to be saying Christmas again. And, number two, I said I was going to give you a Christmas present. "*

—DONALD TRUMP—

No wonder the deplorables voted for Trump. Hillary, the ice-cold Saul Alinsky disciple, proved much more radical and ruthless than cerebral Obama, who is also an Alinsky-educated disciple. We would have been toast, slowly roasted.

Certainly, Bill Clinton and Obama are the true masters at sweet talking the uninformed, always sounding so smart and comprehensive. And so, when Trump arrived sounding like a single-dimension brute … many cringed. But this blight on decency was exactly what the doctor ordered after the endless polite punches landed on Americans by Clinton, Bush, and Obama across 24 long years.

Actually, the one-dimensional brute was indeed one-dimensional, in the form of "Make America Great Again." With Trump, any policy standing in the way of that common-sense goal was out.

Trump ran his real estate business this way, living the ideology of practical thinking: "What can I fix? What can I improve? What makes sense?"

And as America's living conditions rose during his first three years, with millions off of food stamps, critics claim that Trump's economic gains a) only serve the "already comfortable", despite ALL Americans enjoying the best employment environment ever, or b) that, somehow, these achievements result from, yes, Obama!

Though recognized for fixing unemployment, raising GDP and wages, while holding inflation at bay, Trump's hidden achievement proves restoring national defense, using growing GDP to re-provision the military.

The Trump economic results were mind bending. Most never thought these even remotely possible. "The Donald" remains a grinder, practiced in getting complicated physical and commercial things done. And just as he once worked his way out of corporate bankruptcy, he applied his "digging out" grit to restart the country itself.

What a break getting this guy working for us, and without pay.

Plus, he would rather eliminate bad guy leaders rather than let our boys be used for target practice in middle eastern deserts.

And for sure, he knows the planet as anything but a one-world place. Every one of them … China, Mexico, Canada & Europe … need vigilant push backs, as do Russia, North Korea and Iran. Who doesn't get this!

His distrust of global organizations like the World Health Organization is founded in fact. These are political institutions that feather agendas like promoting China.

And notice that climate change is not Trump's mission. He clearly understands that America at 350 million pales in comparison to the five billion Asians who are running roughshod over the planet – not to mention the actions of those in South America and Africa.

Contrasted with America where we systematically retire inefficient coal-fired power plants, China knows no bounds in pollution, as India builds hundreds of new coal units in a desperate attempt to keep up with its out-of-control population of 1.5 billion.

And then we have France, with its tidy 58 nuclear power plants. France does not burn coal. Neither would America, if nuclear had been embraced. But it wasn't, and so Trump plays with the cards dealt, and against the other players sitting across the table. Don't expect the Chinese, the Indians, or anyone else to clean up their respective environments anytime soon.

Yes, global warming descends, *rapidly*, but we simply do not have leverage over it, so why weaken ourselves for no reason? Perhaps technology will come through. Electric cars come to mind, powered by a nuclear-sourced grid. But nuclear remains a pipe dream, even in America, never mind the concept of spreading cleaner energy across Asia, Africa, Central and South America.

As Trump's opponents yearn for more unsightly windmills popping up here and there, they remain oblivious of the dimensions of the problem. We should not turn the Presidency over to such thinking.

Too bad that years ago Obama didn't fix the 100-most-congested roads in America when allocated money to do so. Since then, day-upon-day, millions upon millions of commuters would have avoided travel delay and wasteful emissions, while providing time for new technology to catch up.

If Trump made a mistake, it could be that he could not fix enough of the entrenched problems quickly enough to avoid the negative PR constantly concocted against him. And in short-sided desperation, people will embrace socialist utopian futuristic promises to cure current "red meat" problems. These include racial strife, student debt, healthcare expense, global warming, income inequity, criminal and mental illness violence and the fallout from the corona virus.

Don't let inept politicians promise you anything. Obama couldn't even fix the roads, let alone these socio-economic behemoths! You will simply become poorer.

With good results filing in, it is no wonder that Nancy Pelosi tore up Trumps 2020 State of the Union speech. What else could she do, as the speech reflected upon the past, her past, Obama's past, not to mention "W" and "Bubba".

The Democrats ignored the virus all through the February Super Tuesday debates, after demonizing Trump in January for shutting air travel down from China and then used the re-start of the economy against him.

Given the plight of the world, more than ever, we need practical ideology. No more experimenting with low-income housing and bad international trade deals à la Clinton, no more fluffy education escapades or foreign invasions à la Bush, and no more of anything concocted by Obama. We certainly do not want a senile Biden, a dismissive Schumer and hidden ex-Obama people at the helm.

People need to work. The country needs a strong defense against a dysfunctional world. This is the Trump ideology.

## The China Virus

Right when everything was on the upswing, the virus hit. I wonder why?

Donald Trump proves the first and only impediment to the expansion of China's wealth and power in recent times. Nixon opened the door, Reagan and H.W. Bush cultivated the relationship, Clinton invited China into the WTO, and both Bush and Obama sat and watched as China lured major flows of the global economy into its sphere. Trump and his trade policy presented the first cease and desist marker ever posted on the Chinese Communist freeway.

China, the long rang strategist controlling its socialized 1.4 billion people, would fight back. Consider this "conspiracy theory".

1   Because of China's one-child policy, today its population is skewed to older people, hundreds of millions that do not work.

2   The Corona virus would *likely* kill older people, in case the Chinese government wanted to cull its population.

3   In late 2019, the virus was *intentionally* released into Chinese society.

4   The release purpose did not just focus on the killing of a few hundred thousand older Chinese, as it was designed for.

5   Instead the spread was sequenced as best as possible inside of China by *curtailing intra-China travel*, yet it was allowed to leak out to the world by maintaining *international travel*.

6   New York, L.A. and London – the international gateways – would get the brunt of it.

7   Communist China could rely upon the Ethiopian Communist Doctor Tedros, head of the WHO, to provide cover and help spread confusion throughout the world.

8   Because Doctor Fauche used American monies to finance gain of function experiments at the lab in Wuhan, he would also provide cover by obfuscating the facts of the disease.

9   Global fear of the virus would cover up China's brutality then taking place in Hong Kong.

10  Fear of the virus would stymie Western economies.

11  Fear of the virus would be used by America's press to craft Trump's "Katrina Moment", right when Trump was reining in China's exploitation of the U.S. economy and U.S. intellectual property.

12  Trump would lose the election, allowing a Democrat to revert to prior pro-China patterns.

13  China had also corrupted the Biden family, so a Biden win would be to their great advantage.

14  China would resume its quest for world domination, using its slave society to entrap Western economies via cheap labor.

*Regarding Doctor Tedros, the Epoch Times – 2020 spring edition, dug into his backstory. "Tedros is a former politburo member of the Tigray People's Liberation Front, an Ethiopian Maoist group that had waged a guerrilla war in the 1980s. Tedros scored the WHO's top post in 2017 with strong backing of Communist China's lobby."*

Then there are our guys – Doctor Fouche, et. al, who first reinforced Tedros' report that the virus was not dangerous and that China had done a top shelf job in containing it. Next, the virus, Fouche assured us, was transmitted via physical contact, not through the air, and that masks were superfluous. Then came the flattening the curve episode, which in a bait-and-switch manner, led to an open-ended shut down of everything, even after the curve was flattened and after medical capacity was well provisioned for by Trump.

But suddenly masks were deemed the key. And next we looked like Chernobyl victims waiting around to die. Something is amiss for sure.

The claim by the likes of the NIH, the CDC and the WHO that *they* represent true science is wanting. First, they only promote the aspects of true science they are interested in – "civilization is doomed until a vaccine comes along". And, to keep us on our heels, they use infection/death models to spread fear throughout the globe – making citizens heed every decree.

Their infection models are not real science, they are academic equations with variables – mere "what if" speculations. Neither the equations themselves nor the variables selected are proven through scientific methods and empirical data. They are dimensioning tools, apparently left in the wrong hands.

Data from Italy showed that 99.1 percent of deaths involved pre-existing conditions -age, lung, diabetes, weight, and still Fouche and the Democrats want to keep everything shuttered no matter who you are. Fouche, never showed us science, only fearmongering.

I cannot prove the degree of this China/American-Left axis, but the dots connect. As Rahm Emanuel – Obama's Chief of Staff – once said "Never let a good crisis go to waste". Again, read up on Saul Alinsky to see what's up.

No matter, the Democrats, clear enemies of America's economic resurgence and connoisseurs of fear and rioting, hope to win the day, and another era of Clinton/Bush/Obama decline will commence, orchestrated by those controlling an aged Biden. The plan: as American's descend into poverty, they will surrender to the primate socialists.

## Rioting & Black Lives Matter

But, just in time, another shoe dropped – the murder of five-time felon George Floyd by a dirty and disturbed veteran cop, who worked in some capacity with Floyd at a night club.

Just as Trump needed to be stopped by China, the Democrats needed to stop Trump from making further inroads into black America's voting preferences. So, this was their big opportunity.

Trump was gaining traction with Black voters through prison reform, inner-city "tax free" enterprise zones, funding for Black colleges and mainly, *the lowest Black unemployment rate ever*. Over time, as victim politics would slowly wane, Black support for Democrats would likely evaporate. Four more years of Trump could even fuel a permanent re-alignment, a death spiral for the left.

The murder of Floyd was the worst thing seen by me in my lifetime, comparable to that Vietnamese man having his head shot apart in the 60's.

The Floyd murder could have united America, but instead the Democrat machine had no choice – race mongering needed to be played for all it was worth.

And using the "blame your enemy" tactic Obama honed so well, blame Trump for dividing the country.

Funded by George Soros and by corporations paying what amounts to be protection monies, BLM raised hundreds of millions. It infiltrated peaceful local protestors, instigated rioting, proclaimed vast levels of black men being murdered by the police, and got anyone opposed to the BLM orthodoxy fired.

More, like Stalin eliminating all photos of his competitor Leon Trotsky, BLM tears down all mementos of America's past, even the noble ones, bulldozing the old-world order, installing new law and a promising a new fear-led utopia punishing the past. This propaganda is the mission of the funded Black Lives Matter organization.

The other Democrat army, the media, will be counted on to dictate this politically correct thinking and to infuse dread throughout the land, just as they did when the China virus fear-mongering opportunity took shape.

At some point, the theory goes, the people will beg for a savior – Joe Biden.

# 16

## JOE BIDEN

*" If the prosecutor is not fired, you're not getting the money "*

—V. P. BIDEN—

Since when do we go into countries and tell them who to fire? Never, until Hunter's $1 million a year job at Burisma was threatened.

Somehow, even now, in 2023, 40% of Americans still back Biden. These are the opposites of Hillary's deplorables, these are the primate troop loyalists – the obedient socialist apes – its generic, and it requires a doublethink mind to stay this loyal.

I have spoken to Biden supporters about his performance. This is their doublethink response.

**Afghanistan** – Biden was boxed in by the deal Trump cut. He had no choice.

**The Border** – Trump held back the desperate asylum seekers for four years, and now, in Biden's time, they are finally surging through.

**Sanctuary Cities** – The immigrants need to live somewhere. The Federal government needs to help the mayors.

**Energy** – How could Biden have caused a jump in world-wide energy prices? All he did was to stop the pipeline which wasn't even in operation yet.

**Inflation** – Covid did this, by interfering with the supply chain.

**Vote Harvesting** – There is no proof that the $400 million contributed by Facebook founder Zuckerberg was used for illegal vote harvesting. This is Trump mis-information.

**Bribery** – There is no proof whatsoever that Joe ever took a dime from Hunter. The bribery narrative is mis-information.

**Crime** – These people are desperate to feed their families. Income inequality and racism are to blame. Do you want to send everyone to prison just to preserve "white supremacy"?

**The DOJ** – Merritt Garland is doing his job! Your theories on "slow walking" politically-sensitive cases to protect Biden is just more dis-information.

**Education** – It's true, once a child enters a classroom, they belong to the teacher. America is a nation built upon slavery, and the children need to hear about it.

**Global Warming** – Those resisting government intervention to stem global warming are a threat to the whole planet.

Thank goodness all that has been cleared up. Ok, where does this lead to?

# 17

# AMERICA'S LAW OF THE LAND

*This land is my land. This land is your land.*
*This land belongs to you and me.*

—AN AMERICAN FOLK SONG—
BY SOCIALIST WOODY GUTHRIE

Not true ... every parcel of American land is owned by individuals, corporations, or federal, state, and local governments. "The people" have no collective legal claim to any of it. When rangers close Yellowstone park, you must leave: it's not yours.

*The Law of the Land is the collection of traditions,*
*customs, statutes, usages, and laws of a country that*
*apply to everyone, including the government.*

—BLACK'S LAW—

This chapter recalls America's Law of the Land, the core principle which elevates Life, Liberty, and Property as natural rights above government, an alien-sourced Libertarian construct.

Overall, by ignoring our Constitutional protections, Socialists endeavor to create a new Law of the Land, to "flip the script". Yet the American *Law of the Land* still retains its Life, Liberty, and Property roots, and does so with *formal constitutional protections.*

American natural rights exist as the very antithesis of Socialism, and hence, in court, we need to use these legal swords against the primate-socialist, to stop them without compromise. Compromise, as seen in the Hegel/Marx section, only works for the socialist agenda, for with each compromise, one moves slowly away from America's Law of the Land and closer to government/mob authority and the pyramid of control way of life.

Yet even with law clearly on one's side, bringing our massive, agenda-laden government to heel simply through citizen claims of natural rights will pose a momentous challenge. Individuals have neither the money nor legal training to go up against an army of infinitely funded government attorneys.

It will require organized, provisioned task forces bringing land-mark cases up to the Supreme Court. I will shortly outline the property tax case I have in mind, but first, a deeper understanding of the Law of the Land.

## There are Many "Laws of the Land" World-wide

On the first page of this book, I described that Homo Sapiens have divergent views of reality, leading to different operating mores.

The following insights came to me during another research project investigating the Mongol 12th century conquests. The Mongols prove an excellent example of how people thrive while living harmoniously within their particular Law of the Land.

*Mongolia* – Before their 100-year domination of half the civilized world, Mongol culture already comprised warring, stealing, revenge, rape, and enslavement amongst themselves—a brutal way of life to which we cannot relate. Hence, once Genghis Khan consolidated the tribes, turning them outward to run over entire peoples, Mongol soldiers had no psychological objections to killing every man, woman, and child they encountered, chopping off the heads to make giant piles of skulls. This did not conflict them.

Probably almost none of these proud Mongols suffered from *post-traumatic-stress syndrome* as a result of their experiences. For good or for bad, conquest and annihilation made up part of their Law of the Land, and so they thrived in a setting that would destabilize the psychological solidity of, say, an American soldier, who believes in the natural rights of everyone.

*China* – Likewise, the Chinese, who forever lived subserviently under the emperors, came out of that ancient Law of the Land only to enter the modern Communist system, a new Law of the Land, but one that still treats individuals as drones of the hive. But being *their* Law of the Land, I am sure that most of the Chinese who for 4,000 years lived under these conditions thrive, living happy lives. Any alien-libertarian not happy was killed off centuries ago. Conforming to a *pyramid of control* remains the Chinese Law of the Land, not ours.

*Russia* – The same can be said of Russia, with its brutal czars, its heartless Communists, and now Putin, Russia's latest totalitarian dictator wanting to restore the USSR. Not a single Russian commoner living in Russia has ever experienced what Americans call liberty. Stalin himself killed 24 million Russians who "looked cross-eyed" at his troop. Life, Liberty, and Property is not Russia's Law of the Land... it's ours.

*India* – And how about India? One billion + people living according to their caste as determined at birth... racism on steroids. That is their Law of the Land, not ours.

*Latin America* – In 1991, on my honeymoon in Chile, when I thanked a local boy for lending me his guitar, the estate owners—who owned a hacienda the size of Rhode Island granted to them by Pizarro in the 1500's—pulled me aside and "educated" me that the boy cannot be treated as my equal. This is their Law of the Land, not ours. But all are happy.

*The Islamic Theocracies* – And consider the world of Islam with its theocracies, Sharia Law, and mutilation of woman ... those are not our Laws of the Land, but theirs. And it all proves that if one's political genes align with one's governmental apparatus, then happiness abounds.

In America's case, our unique Law of the Land—Life, Liberty and Property—sits central to our happiness, more so than we realize. This remains the keystone of who we are.

But due to our softness over the past 100 years in equating liberalism (protecting individuals) with socialism (handouts to individuals), socialist forces have incrementally compromised our traditions, erecting a new, *shadow* Law of the Land, where under the auspices of helping people, government authority gradually trumps natural rights ... the people's properties subordinated. And Socialists achieve this without changing written law, quietly end-running our legal footings by not enforcing laws they dislike ... *illegal immigration*, a case in point.

American immigrants in earlier times were given nothing, and this weeded out those seeking a free ride from those genetically seeking liberty at all costs. Earlier forms of immigration buttressed our alien-sourced Libertarian gene pool. Today's handout system feeds the primate-sourced Socialist camp. No wonder Nancy Pelosi, et. al wouldn't fund the wall...

Yes, our American ship lists "hard to port," and our demise sickens many traditional "alien" Americans, while primate-socialists live in ecstasy, hoping to reinvent a new Law of the Land subjugating what they see as "arrogant" individualism—no uppity apes allowed outside of the pyramid.

But the technical facets of the law still exist to stop things like illegal home taxation levied by municipalities. Constitutionally, only legislatures can levy taxes, and only then based upon commercial activity – e.g. sales tax, income tax, capital gains tax. Because dormant homes make no money, a Supreme Court case needs to be brought – the people versus those state governors allowing municipalities to by-pass the state's House of Representatives to directly tax the people's private homes and vehicles.

This is why the Supreme Court – with a technical focus on the law – is a better bet for sustaining our natural rights, our law of the land, then is retail politics, controlled by the media.

For more on this, visit my property tax web site Hoodwinked.net, which presents a full Constitutionally-based legal brief on the topic.

I will finish Volume III with a "checklist", suggested to me by my mother right before she passed in 2019.

# EPILOGUE

## The Checklist

*" The Bill of Rights is not a Chinese Menu "*

−JOHN F. KENNEDY−

The *Libertarianism* (pro-property, pro-individual) versus *Socialism* (anti-property, anti-individual) checklist follows. If you are a Socialist you are probably not reading the manuscript, as Socialists do not consider arguments justifying traditional American law. Just as alien-libertarians seek laws that protect America's "open-highway" lifestyle, primate-socialists solely want a new *dictated* law centered around obedience.

To protect the pyramid, Socialists dismiss facts, saying "I don't know about that..." or "That can't be true!" or "I've never read that", or they appear dismissive ... simply pining for what they want: a managed society where we cede our inalienable, natural rights to government authority. Using "fair share" slogans, they harness some to open-ended tax obligations, and others to a life of dependency, controlling both halves of society. This done, they herd desperate immigrants into the pyramid.

For this, Socialist use talking points like: "Immigrants are hard-working people, doing the work we won't do; they fuel America's success, pay taxes, and their children are innocent", and spin like, "America is both a land of laws and a land of immigrants" ... as if this false equivalency provides *carte blanch* to open the floodgates for all the earth's billions of impoverished peoples.

387

America is not fueled by immigrants. Prior to welfare, immigrants were motivated by *liberty and wealth, the true fuels.* Today we attract different orientations. At 350 million, America has sufficient talent.

More, one is not to call them "Socialists"; instead they condition us to use the softer "Progressive", "Independent" and "Liberal" monikers—wolves in sheep's clothing. They bristle at the Socialist label, yet increment Socialism every chance they get. Doublethink! Doublethink! Doublethink!

Here is the Libertarianism versus Socialism checklist:

| TOPIC | LIBERTARINISM | SOCIALISM |
|---|---|---|
| Goal | Liberty | Obedience |
| *Power* | *The Individual* | *The State* |
| Decisions | By the Individual | By Pyramids of Control |
| *Economy* | *Run by the Citizens* | *Run by the Government* |
| Property | Strictly Private | Tax, Confiscate |
| *Rights* | *Allodial/Absolute* | *Feudal/Conditional* |
| Wealth | Personally Earned | Owed to Society |
| *Taxes* | *A Standard Contribution* | *Assed Value Multiplier* |
| Finance | Savings | Debt |
| *Wellbeing* | *Each Family's Priority* | *Government Handouts* |
| | | |
| Government | Liberty's Protector | Wealth Distributor |
| *Military* | *Liberty's Protector* | *National Police* |
| Congress | Our Representatives | Elite Masters |
| *Voters* | *Able/The Ship's Ballast* | *Deplorable/Need Masters* |
| Speech | Unfettered | Muzzled |
| *Debate* | *Encouraged* | *Distract People with It* |
| Education | Knowledge/Thinking | Crafted Indoctrination |
| *Teachers* | *Encyclopedias* | *A Union Voting Block* |
| Electorate | Expect Honesty | Stupid, Lied To, Duped |
| *Press* | *Independent/The Facts* | *An Ally Spin Department* |
| | | |
| Immigration | A Trickle/Vetted | A Flood/Invited |
| *Religion* | *Accepted* | *Shunned* |
| Environment | Preserve It | An Obedience Stick |
| *Guns* | *Right to Protect* | *A Disarmed Citizenry* |
| Race | Irrelevant | Victims/A Divider |
| *Sexuality* | *Irrelevant* | *Victims/A Divider* |
| Opportunity | Educate, Train, Intern | Spread Dependency |
| *America* | *Blessed/Extraordinary* | *Socialize It/End It* |

This is not a "Chinese menu" letting you pick from each side. Your root choice between the two stands pre-determined by your genetic pull. Don't fight it!

# APPENDIX –
# ARTIFICIAL INTELLIGENCE

"Live Free or Die"
The New Hampshire State Motto

Which reminds me of the song I wrote about John Brown, the 1850's slavery abolitionist.

*In bleeding Kansas he opened the door, set the stage for civil war, like this. Like this! And he did it with his fists.*

"Old Brown" (mentioned in the Transcendentalist chapter of VOLUME III), was quite the alien/libertarian, wanting to free 4 million slaves controlled primarily by Democrats. He was promptly hung by the Virginia governor, ready to die once convicted of defying the "unnatural" dehumanizing slavery laws of 1859.

Liberty, as "Soviet" *Vladimir Lenin* pointed out, is so precious that it needs to be dolled out carefully. History proves *liberty* not for everyone, and although it has never been perfected, liberty none-theless reached a high water mark in the United States, by, say, the 1980's, providing a meaningful range of self-determination enjoyed by millions.

But today we have primate/socialists like Mark Zuckerberg, keenly wanting to control the national narrative, passionately working in stealth with his "creepy" government allies, up against the likes of an Elon Musk, a true "last ditch" alien/libertarian counter-puncher asserting free speech. I wonder … with Zuckerberg holding the inside authoritarian track, how AI will be used to end this remaining American standoff?

How? Just as the NAFTA/WTO policies of Bill Clinton triggered the siphoning off of U.S. manufacturing jobs to China … leaving millions of Americans without earned income, AI will next absorb many of the service-oriented duties that currently prop up society – like fast food jobs, office administrators, cab and truck drivers. Conceivably, one computer able to monitor AI-operated equipment could farm all of Iowa. Ironically, this trend which would feed many, would further squeeze out one's potential to even feed oneself, leaving many with no place to turn.

As a result, an ever-expanding "survival of the fittest" vortex will herd the un-competitive, worried masses into government safe zones that feed, shelter, transport and medically-care for whole swarths of society. And AI itself provides the productivity that pays for all of this, so don't fret. No one starves.

More, by being poor yet well fed, there is no need to come into the office; actually, no need to do anything at all, all day long. Embracing poverty while voting primate/socialist grants you *freedom from* survival's brutal threats. But in accepting safety, you inherently embrace a lifetime of no *economic freedom to do* … anything … anything involving liberty, adventure, or achievement. You only survive.

Even now, in 2023, at the advent of AI, 41 million Americans live off food stamps, with little *freedom to do*. Many see themselves as victims, not responsible for their predicament. Newcomers who stumble into the vortex will come to the same conclusion. The troop owes them for their loyalty, plus their voting plurality backed by regular street rampages ought to ensure that "fair share" payouts are extracted from the fortunate members of society.

As explained (in the *Genetics* chapter of SUBJUGATED VOLUME I – the Scopes Monkey Trial addendum), for the average person, socialism stands the only solution to evolution's "survival of the fittest" ruthlessness. As populations spillover and the opportunities for economic self-determination dry up, socialism becomes the sole choice. Think China today at 1.4 billion souls; how else can China operate? Then project America; how can it operate as more and more cannot feed themselves?

Finally, this *AI economic herding* of Homo Sapiens will be sealed shut by *AI speech & behavior processors*. Orwell's "big brother is watching you" environment … just recently implemented by the DOJ, the FBI, Facebook and Twitter (pre-Musk) … already "finger" political resistors of the primate/socialist lifestyle. There will be no hiding, no safe harbor for those opposed to pyramid mores. Severity, the proven result of every one-party, primate/socialist society, will prove no different under Democrat one-party rule.

Undoubtedly, AI's coming technological *gifts* will exceed our imaginations, as did mobile phones, PCs, the Internet and GPS, but as the *Wooden Horse* Trojans learned: "Beware of Greeks bearing gifts".

And so, though Homo Sapiens possess vast "alien" intellectual powers that should lead to liberty, the population/AI vortex will overwhelm these, and in desperation, most will scurry to find a "primate" survival perch within the troop's Pyramid of Control. The highest perches, of course, will still provide bits of liberty to the elite apes, but for others, a life of obedience will be in order. To tolerate this tedious existence, all will be instructed to *Be Quiet and Be Kind*.

So much for the 6,000-year Homo Sapient experiment. AI will leverage our *primate* roots against our overall potential for *alien* liberty, reinstating our historical subjugated way of life. No "uppity" apes allowed.

*We are stardust*
*We are golden*
*And we've got to get ourselves*
*Back to the garden*

Joni Mitchel, Woodstock, 1969 – Then, still hopeful.

## Pyramid of Control – AI Automation

_AI_ Conditions Used to Measure Behavioral Violations

BE KIND

BE SILENT – BE OBEDIENT

BE TAXED – BE MEAGER – BE DISRESPECTED

BE IGNORANT – BE DIVERTED –
BE GASLIT – BE MANEUVERED

BE TREATENED – BE GUILTY –
BE COMPLIANT – BE GRATEFULL

BE CENSORED – BE MUZZELED –
BE AFRAID – BE MEEK – BE SUBJUGATED

BE REWARDED – BE LOYAL – BE HUMAN –
BE GLOBAL – BE ASSIMILATED .

_The more society drifts from truth the more
it will hate those that speak it._

–GEORGE ORWELL–


_The real division is not between conservatives and
revolutionaries but between authoritarians and libertarians._

–GEORGE ORWELL–

www.ingramcontent.com/pod-product-compliance
Lightning Source LLC
Chambersburg PA
CBHW020430130626
46549CB00001B/60